PETER HOPKIRK

Peter Hopkirk (1930–2014) travelled widely over many years in the regions where his six books are set – Russia, Central Asia, the Caucasus, China, India and Pakistan, Iran and Eastern Turkey. Before turning full-time author, he was an ITN reporter and newscaster for two years, the New York correspondent of the old *Daily Express*, and then worked for nearly twenty years on *The Times* – five as its chief reporter, and latterly as a Middle and Far East specialist. In the 1950s he edited the West African news magazine *Drum*, sister paper to its legendary South African namesake. Before entering Fleet Street he served as a subaltern in the King's African Rifles – in the same battalion as Lance Corporal Idi Amin, later to emerge as the Ugandan tyrant. No stranger to misadventure, Hopkirk was twice held in secret-police cells – in Cuba and the Middle East – and also hijacked by Arab terrorists. His words have been translated into many languages. In 1999 he was awarded the Sir Percy Sykes Memorial Medal for his writing and travels by the Royal Society for Asian Affairs.

Also by Peter Hopkirk

Foreign Devils on the Silk Road

Trespassers on the Roof of the World

The Great Game

On Secret Service East of Constantinople

Quest for Kim

SETTING THE EAST ABLAZE

Lenin's Dream of an Empire in Asia

PETER HOPKIRK

JOHN MURRAY

First published in Great Britain in 1984 by John Murray (Publishers)
An Hachette UK Company

This paperback edition first published in 2006
Reissued in 2016

9

A CIP catalogue record for this title is
available from the British Library

ISBN 978-0-7195-6450-5
Ebook ISBN 978-1-84854-725-4

Printed and bound by Clays Ltd, St Ives plc

John Murray policy is to use papers that are natural,
renewable and recyclable products and made from wood
grown in sustainable forests. The logging and manufacturing
processes are expected to conform to the environmental
regulations of the country of origin.

John Murray (Publishers)
Carmelite House
50 Victoria Embankment
London EC4Y 0DZ

www.johnmurray.co.uk

'Our mission is to set the East ablaze'

inscription over the Bolshevik First Army H.Q. at Ashkabaa

CONTENTS

ACKNOWLEDGEMENTS

My principal debt must be to those, now all dead, who took part in these events and left written accounts of them. Without these, this book could not have been written. They include Colonels Bailey and Etherton, Captain Brun, Paul Nazaroff, Dmitri Alioshin, M.N. Roy, Ferdinand Ossendowski, Georg Vasel and Sven Hedin. Their adventures and misadventures provide much of the drama of this book, and their narratives, now long out of print, are listed in my bibliography.

Two other works I found particularly valuable were *India and Anglo-Soviet Relations (1917–1947)* by the Indian scholar Dr Chatter Singh Samra, and Lars-Eric Nyman's *Great Britain and Chinese, Russian and Japanese Interests in Sinkiang, 1918–1934*. All my other principal sources, to whose authors I am indebted, are to be found in the bibliography.

The individual to whom I owe most, however, is my wife Kath, who has contributed so much to the narrative in the way of suggestions and improvements, and on whom I tried it out as it unfolded. She is also responsible, as with my two earlier works, for the index.

I am indebted, too, to William Drew, perhaps the only western survivor of that period, whose memories of troubled Sinkiang between the wars were a valuable source of insight to me. I am grateful also to Dr Shirin Akiner, the Central Asian scholar and linguist, for translating material on Enver Pasha for me from the Turkish.

Others who have kindly let me pick their brains include my colleague Denis Taylor of *The Times*, a Soviet affairs specialist, and Dr Craig Clunas of the Victoria and Albert Museum, a Mongolian scholar. I must also thank the staff of the India Office Library, where I did much of my research, for producing an endless succession of files and for photocopying numerous once-secret papers and intelligence reports.

Finally I am indebted to my editor and publisher, John R. Murray, whose enthusiasm has been a constant spur – and to Gustav Mahler, whose heady symphonies were my companions during long hours of writing, and which seemed to synchronise so well with this stormy tale.

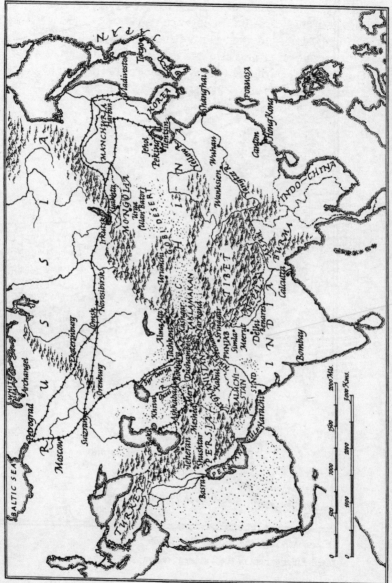

Russia, India, China and adjacent areas

Central Asia after the Russian Revolution

Inset: Enlargement of the Tashkent region

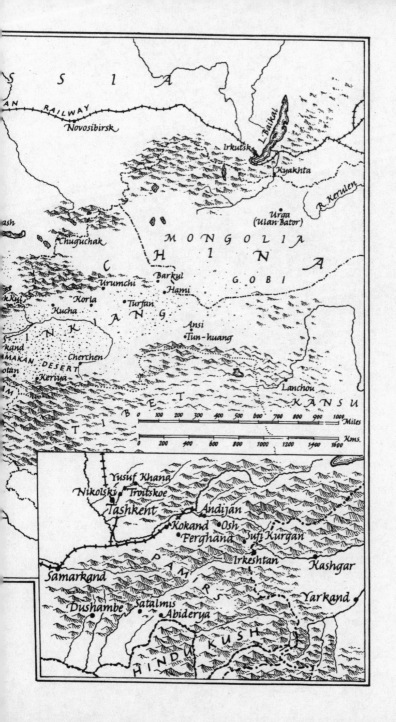

Prologue

'There is a dry wind blowing through the East, and the parched grasses wait the spark. And the wind is blowing towards the Indian frontier . . . I have reports from agents everywhere.' So Sir Walter Bullivant, head of British Intelligence, tells Richard Hannay, the hero of *Greenmantle*, before sending him off to try to prevent the coming conflagration.

But truth, once again, was to prove stranger than fiction. Within three years of John Buchan writing that in 1916, the missionaries of Bolshevism had sworn to set the East ablaze, using the heady new gospel of Marxism as their torch. Their aim was to liberate the whole of Asia. But their starting point was British India, richest of all imperial possessions. For Britain, then still the foremost imperial power, was seen by Lenin as the principal obstacle to his dream of world revolution. 'England', he declared in 1920, 'is our greatest enemy. It is in India that we must strike them hardest.'

If India could be torn by insurrection from Britain's grasp, then no longer would she be able to buy off her workers – unwitting shareholders in imperialism – with the sweated labour and cheap raw materials of the East. Economic collapse, and revolution, would follow at home. If similar uprisings could be fomented throughout the colonial world, then the long-awaited revolution would blaze its way across Europe. 'The East', Lenin proclaimed, 'will help us to conquer the West.'

But the British, although exhausted by war, were not a people to take such a challenge lying down. Their secret service was still the world's most formidable, with its tentacles everywhere. A clandestine struggle for India and the East followed, the story of which is told here. It is set largely in Central Asia, where three great empires – those of Britain, Russia and China –

met. It is a tale of intrigue and treachery, barbarism and fear, and occasionally pure farce.

Wherever possible I have told it through the adventures and misadventures of those, on either side, who took part in this undeclared war. From remote listening-posts far beyond India's frontiers, British Indian intelligence officers monitored every Bolshevik move against India and reported these back to their chiefs in Delhi and London. Their names are now long forgotten, buried deep in the secret archives of the day, but it is from their reports and memoirs that I have pieced together much of this tale. Often their stories read like vintage Buchan – and none more so than the amazing adventures behind Bolshevik lines of Colonel F.M. Bailey.

For sixteen months this deceptively mild-looking officer played a lonely and dangerous game of hide-and-seek against the 'Bolos' (as the British called the Bolsheviks), even being hired at one stage by the dreaded Cheka, the Soviet secret police, to track himself down. He is still remembered there, some sixty years later, with a mixture of awe and animosity, as I found when retracing his footsteps across Soviet Central Asia. Lucky to escape with his life (thanks to a remarkable skill at disguise), he died only in 1967, at the age of eighty-five, in quiet retirement in Norfolk.

Another formidable player in this shadowy war was the veteran intelligence officer Sir Wilfrid Malleson. Not a lovable man, this early master of dirty tricks ran a vast network of spies and secret agents from Meshed, in north-eastern Persia. His greatest satisfaction was to set Bolshevik and Afghan at one another's throats by judicious leaking of the other's double-dealing (invented, if necessary).

A third British officer whom the Soviets had no reason to love was Colonel Percy Etherton. He fought a ruthless, almost personal war against them from his lonely outpost at Kashgar, in Chinese Turkestan, close to the Russian frontier. So effective were his anti-Bolshevik operations that a price was put on his head by the Soviet authorities in Tashkent, the ancient caravan town which they used as the principal base for their clandestine operations against British India.

The Bolsheviks, too, had their heroes in this secret war. They included the professional Indian revolutionary and Marxist theoretician M.N. Roy, who was high on the British security service's list of wanted men, and the extremely able (and likeable) Mikhail Borodin. Both were dedicated to the liberation of 'the toilers of the East' by violent insurrection.

This new struggle for ascendancy in Asia had its roots in that earlier contest between the British and the Russians, the Great Game. So christened by one of its players, and immortalised by Kipling in *Kim*, this had officially ended only ten years before, with the signing of a treaty apportioning out the spheres of influence of these two great powers. It had begun in the middle of the nineteenth century when Britain and Russia found themselves confronting one another across the great deserts and mountain ranges lying between their expanding empires.

As the Russians had advanced ever closer to India's thinly guarded northern frontiers, war had seemed inevitable. For it was no secret that some of the Tsar's most brilliant strategists had drawn up plans for an invasion of India. Central Asia was rarely out of the headlines, and each week brought news of the hard-riding Cossacks getting nearer. The vast political no-man's-land, stretching from Persia in the west to Tibet in the east, became for young officers and explorers of either side an adventure playground. Ostensibly they were on shooting trips or (as the Russians preferred to call theirs) scientific expeditions. Some chose to travel in disguise as native traders, though one wonders how convincingly. Ever in danger from murderous tribesmen, both British and Russians sought out and mapped the secret passes and strategic approaches to northern India.

Then, as the century drew to a close, the threat – if there ever really was one – began to recede. In their headlong race eastwards towards the Pacific coast the Russians had unexpectedly met their match. For in 1905 they suffered a devastating defeat at the hands of a rising new power in Asia, the Japanese. Within two years a chastened Russia and a relieved Britain had signed the Anglo-Russian Convention, a treaty which officially brought the Great Game to an end. The Russian bogy, and with it the threat to India, was over at last, or so it seemed. Any remaining doubts appeared to vanish when the two great rival powers found themselves fighting side by side in 1914 against the Central Powers.

All such hopes, however, were swiftly dashed when, in October 1917 (November by our calendar), the Bolsheviks seized power in Russia. One of their first moves was to tear up all treaties signed by their predecessors. Overnight the Anglo-Russian Convention became a worthless scrap of paper. Far from being over, the Great Game was about to begin again with a vengeance. Once more, as the war dragged on in Europe, the storm clouds began to gather over Central Asia. Only this time they were a distinct shade of red.

But before Russia's new masters could carry the banner of Marxism across Asia they had first to reconquer the Tsar's former territories there. It was to be a time of appalling bloodshed and famine, an unending nightmare for everyone living there. Barbaric deeds were performed by both sides. Some of those carried out in the name of Bolshevism would have dismayed Lenin. But he himself was fighting desperately for survival against a fanatical White Russian resistance and the Allied intervention of 1918–20.

Only when he was at last in control, and Russian Central Asia firmly in the Bolshevik grip, was Lenin able to turn his thoughts to the liberation of the East. The revolutionary he chose to lead his ideological crusade into British India was Roy, the Indian 'Greenmantle'. Just how successful he was (and other Comintern agents were elsewhere in Asia) we shall see.

Lenin, however, was not the only one then dreaming of an empire in the East. During those turbulent years which followed the Revolution, three other would-be Genghis Khans were to arise in Central Asia, the battlefield of the new Great Game. The most notorious by far was a psychopathic White

Russian general named Ungern-Sternberg, 'the Mad Baron', whose dreadful atrocities are still remembered with a shudder in Mongolia.

The next to try his luck was Enver Pasha, Turkey's flamboyant but defeated wartime leader, then in exile in Central Asia. After double-crossing his host Lenin, he tried to foment a holy war against the godless Bolsheviks by rallying the Muslim masses of Soviet Asia. But outgunned and outnumbered by the Red Army, the handsome Turk was to meet his end with ferocious courage in the Pamir foothills. There, it is said, pilgrims from his homeland still secretly visit their hero's lonely grave.

The last of these dreamers of empire was a young but charismatic warlord called Ma Chung-yin, known sometimes as 'Big Horse'. A Chinese Muslim visionary barely out of his teens, he was to leave a trail of blood across the Gobi desert before fleeing westwards along the Silk Road in a stolen lorry, pursued by Soviet bombers.

It is from all these strands that I have pieced together the little-known story of what happened in Central Asia during that violent era. Its echoes are being heard today in Afghanistan and elsewhere. For there the Great Game still goes on. Only the players are different.

Like my two earlier books, this is primarily a story about people. Of the powerful forces at work at that time I have merely sketched in the essentials for an understanding of the narrative. It is thus neither a history of the Civil War, nor of Anglo-Soviet relations – nor for that matter of India's struggle for independence. These are vast subjects in themselves, and anyone wishing to pursue them further – as I hope this narrative will encourage some to do – must turn to the heavily-laden shelves of the specialist libraries.

But now we must return to the beginning, to the middle of 1918, some nine months after the Bolsheviks' seizure of power in Russia. The European nations were still at war – a war whose outcome was then very far from certain. For Russia's sudden withdrawal from the battlefield had tilted the balance momentarily in favour of the Central Powers. In British India, moreover, it raised the alarming spectre of a combined German-Turkish attack through Central Asia. Such then is the setting for the story which follows.

1 'An Absolutely
First-Class Man . . .'

In the summer of 1918, a small party on ponies could be observed winding its way upwards through the silent passes of the T'ien Shan mountains, in Chinese Central Asia, heading for the Russian frontier. The travellers, who were armed, advanced cautiously, as if expecting trouble. Four of them were Europeans, including one woman, and the other twelve Asiatics. They had left Kashgar a week earlier and hoped to reach the Russian frontier-post at Irkeshtan the following day. It was a curious direction for anyone to be travelling in. Most people, in those troubled times, were getting out of Russia. But then this was a very unusual party.

Its leader was a British officer – Lieut-Colonel Frederick Bailey of the Indian Political and Secret Department – who before the war had earned himself a considerable reputation as a Central Asian explorer. In 1904, as a Tibetan-speaking subaltern, he had ridden into the holy city of Lhasa with Sir Francis Younghusband. Later, his hazardous journeys through lawless regions of Tibet and China had won him the coveted gold medal of the Royal Geographical Society. From one of these pre-war expeditions he had brought back the tall blue Himalayan poppy which today bears his name.

Twice wounded in the war – a German bullet in the arm in Flanders, and a Turkish one through both legs at Gallipoli – he had been posted, after coming out of hospital, to Persia for intelligence duties. There, enemy agents led by Wassmuss, the German 'T.E. Lawrence', were enjoying considerable success stirring up the tribes against the hard-pressed British. But the adventure which he was now about to be pitched into would prove to be more bizarre and dangerous than anything he had hitherto experienced.

Besides himself, the party included a second British officer –
a monacled major named Stewart Blacker, seconded from the
Indian Army's élite Corps of Guides. Like Bailey, he was an
experienced Central Asian traveller, and before the war he had
visited Tashkent, the Bolshevik stronghold they were now
hoping to reach. He too had been wounded in France. Subsequently he had enrolled in the newly formed Royal Flying
Corps, but a near-fatal nose-dive had brought his career as a
pilot to an abrupt end.

The two other Europeans in this oddly-assorted group were
both Russians, a Mr and Mrs Stephanovich from the Consulate-
General in Kashgar, of which he was temporarily in charge. The
remaining dozen members of the party were hand-picked
NCOs from the Indian Army, pony-men and servants, most of
whom would return to Kashgar on reaching the frontier. For
the rest it would be a step into the unknown.

The Bolshevik Revolution was now some nine months old.
But with civil war raging from one end of Russia to the other,
little reliable intelligence was reaching London or Delhi. As to
what was going on in the Tsar's former Central Asian territories,
even Lenin himself had only the haziest idea. Particularly
anxious to discover who was gaining the upper hand in Central
Asia were those responsible for the defence of India. At one
remote spot, only a narrow corridor of Afghanistan just a few
miles wide separated British and Russian territory. After endless exchanges of secret telegrams between London and Delhi,
it was decided that there was only one thing to do. And that was
to send someone to Tashkent to find out. So it was that two
British officers now found themselves approaching the Russian
frontier, uncertain of what lay in store for them.

The idea of sending officers into Central Asia to find out what
was happening there was nothing new. In the days of the Great
Game, a succession of Indian Army officers – 'Bokhara' Burnes,
Henry Pottinger and Francis Younghusband, to name only
three – had done just that. But in December 1917, on the
assumption that the Russian Empire was about to break up, a

bold plan had been put forward for reviving the idea. It had come, surprisingly perhaps, from a Liberal Member of Parliament, although hardly a typical one. Commander Josiah Wedgwood had served with distinction in both the Boer War and the one now in progress. He had won a DSO at Gallipoli and twice been mentioned in despatches.

Wedgwood put his proposal to John Shuckburgh, then Secretary to the Political Department of the India Office in London, who summarised it thus for his chiefs: 'His idea is to send a number of energetic and determined officers (not necessarily military officers) from India, and to give them a kind of roving commission to work for British interests in Central Asia. They would travel under whatever "cover" might be thought best. They would, of course, have no official status, and must be prepared to be disowned by the British Government if things went wrong.'

Wedgwood still saw the Germans, not the Bolsheviks, as the threat, and his plan was intended to keep them out of Central Asia, from where they could menace India. The officers would have orders to spoil the Germans' game by every possible means ('They mustn't hesitate to shoot, if necessary'), and to organise resistance among the local population by appealing to their patriotism. They would also gather intelligence. Shuckburgh's summary continued: 'By this means, Commander Wedgwood thinks that an effective pro-British buffer could be established along the whole of the northern frontier of Persia, Afghanistan, etc., and enemy expansion to the East might definitely be held in check.'

Shuckburgh passed the idea to his immediate superior, Sir Arthur Hirtzel, commenting: 'the suggestion is somewhat of a counsel of desperation, but there are times that call for desperate expedients.' He recommended that at least Delhi should be consulted, though it might be wise to try it 'privately' on the Foreign Office first. Hirtzel took it personally round to the Foreign Office, pencilling on it afterwards: 'This appeared to me preposterous, and I took it into the F.O. who thought the same.' To this another hand, less identifiable, had added: 'I don't see why this office should be called upon to promote the views of private Members of Parliament as to the policy to be pursued by HMG in different parts of the Russian Empire.' (Commander Wedgwood had already put forward a similar idea for Siberia.)

So much for the civil servants' views. The document, complete with annotations, was next passed to the Parliamentary Under-Secretary for India, Lord Islington, a former Guards subaltern and Boer War DSO. While (in a two-page memorandum) condemning the idea as 'irresponsible', he conceded that 'the conception that underlies it' was not in fact so preposterous, adding: 'We are now receiving information that Russian Central Asia is becoming affected, and if the process is left to develop undisturbed we may anticipate a dangerous fomentation all along the border of Afghanistan and India. As to what can be done to stem this tide it is difficult to suggest. A few officers sent in an irresponsible way into this vast country, as proposed by Commander Wedgwood, would undoubtedly be of but slender avail, and would be exposed to dangers beyond any results they could hope to achieve.'

All this, it should be said, was before the unorthodox activities of T.E. Lawrence and other British officers behind Turkish lines had become generally known, and a quarter of a century before the founding of the SAS in World War II. Needless to say, Wedgwood's plan was officially rejected. But it is clear from the secret correspondence of the time that he had set people thinking. Indeed, very shortly afterwards he was given the rank of colonel and, thinly disguised as a newspaper correspondent, despatched to Siberia to try to stiffen anti-German resistance. At the same time, the India Office archives reveal a sudden flurry of secret inter-departmental telegrams and minutes on what should be done about the growing crisis in Central Asia, following the collapse of the Eastern Front. Within a matter of weeks, a number of officers of 'initiative and enterprise' found themselves short-listed for special duty there (though quite what would be expected of them remained extremely vague).

On February 4, Shuckburgh signalled the British Political Resident in the Persian Gulf urgently requesting the services of Bailey, and another officer named Marshall, for a mission 'which HMG have decided to send to Turkestan'. The reply came next day: 'If Bailey is medically fit I can spare him.' Marshall, however, could not be spared. He was at Nejef, on the Euphrates, 'where situation urgently needs an officer on whom I can rely'. The refusal to part with him cost Marshall his life. On the file copy of the telegram, against the name Nejef, a neat hand has pencilled in the words '. . . where he has unfortunately been assassinated'. A number of Arabs were later hanged publicly by the British for his murder after a German-inspired plot to liquidate him and all his colleagues, including Bailey, was uncovered.

Bailey's superiors seem to have been in no hurry to let him go, despite London's plea for urgency. For a full month passed before the proposition was put to him by wire at Shushtar, where he was the sole European living. Had he recovered sufficiently from his wounds, he was asked, to undertake a long and arduous journey? Just where to, the telegram did not specify. Bailey at once signalled his readiness to go, and by return was ordered to proceed to the Indian hill-station of Simla. There he would receive further instructions regarding a secret mission to Kashgar, in Chinese Turkestan.

He had no regrets about leaving Shushtar. Indeed, it was with some relief that he did so. Only a few days before the telegram's arrival he had been warned that three assassins had entered town with orders to dispose of him. 'The narrow streets', he observed afterwards, 'made murder very easy.' The sudden prospect, moreover, of leading a secret mission to Kashgar, where he had never been, was an alluring one to a man born with a strong sense of adventure. Also it meant immediate promotion to Lieutenant-Colonel. 'An absolutely first-class man,' the Viceroy, Lord Chelmsford, noted on Bailey's file.

Bailey, Blacker and another Indian Army officer, Major Percy Etherton, reached Kashgar on June 7 after a six-week trek over the Pamir from northern India. Etherton was being sent to take over from Sir George Macartney, due to retire as British Consul-General there after twenty-eight years. There now arose the question of the mission's next move. London and Delhi were still locked in telegraphic debate over whether or not Bailey and Blacker should try to reach Tashkent and make contact with the Bolsheviks, whose blood-stained authority the British Government did not recognise.

On April 22, the day the mission had left India, Shuckburgh had advised Lord Chelmsford: 'The situation in Central Asia is exceedingly obscure . . . I do not know what the general policy of HMG is towards the Bolshevists.' He added anxiously: 'I do venture to urge that, before furnishing our officers with instructions, we should make up our minds quite clearly what our policy really is.' The Viceroy himself had already signalled London with his own reservations about the mission. Its object, he feared, seemed 'hopelessly vague', while its chances of success were 'extremely problematical'. Now, as Bailey and Blacker tapped their heels impatiently in Kashgar, both London and Delhi appeared as much in the dark as ever about what was happening in Russian Central Asia.

What little intelligence was reaching them emanated either from Kashgar, which had now resumed its role of Great Game days as a British listening-post, or from Meshed, which lay close to the Russian frontier in north-eastern Persia. From the former, Sir George Macartney had maintained a steady flow of intelligence obtained from travellers and refugees coming out of Russia and from other contacts built up over many years. In this, Bailey, Blacker and Etherton were able to give him a hand while London kept them waiting. But for all Macartney's experience of Central Asian politics, Bolshevism was an entirely new game, in which none of the old rules applied. The situation, moreover, was constantly changing and information fragmentary and more often than not conflicting.

From Meshed, nearly a thousand miles to the west, a similar flow of intelligence had been emanating since the arrival there of Lieut-Colonel Ernest Redl, an old hand at the game, who spoke fluent Russian and knew the region intimately. He also, unlike Macartney, had a powerful radio transmitter. Not only did this enable him to signal his chiefs directly (messages from Kashgar took at least three weeks to reach India by runner), but he was able to use it to eavesdrop secret communications between Tashkent and Moscow, the Bolsheviks' newly proclaimed capital.

In addition to gathering intelligence, Redl was entrusted with a further task – for which he had been liberally supplied with high-explosives. The collapse of Russian resistance left India wide open to an unexpected new threat, that of a combined German-Turkish invasion from Central Asia. It was Redl's job to cross the frontier into Russia and destroy the strategically crucial Transcaspian Railway in the event of its falling into German or Turkish hands. Were they to get control of it, they could use it to transport troops and munitions eastwards across the great Central Asian deserts to bases from which they could menace northern India. In the words of one senior British intelligence officer: 'It needed the appearance of but a detachment of German or Turkish troops on the northern frontiers of Afghanistan to precipitate a *jihad* against us.'

Although the Russian collapse had caught the British badly by surprise, Redl had not been left entirely single-handedly to hold back the enemy from the approaches to India. Ever since 1915, a joint British-Russian force – known as the East Persian Cordon – had been positioned along the Afghan-Persian frontier to deny German and Turkish agents access to Afghanistan. On Russia's withdrawal from the war, its sector of the cordon had been taken over by British troops under the command of Major-General Sir Wilfrid Malleson who set up his new headquarters in Meshed, from where Redl had already been operating for two months.

Fears of a joint German-Turkish assault on India had been intensified by the presence in Russian Central Asia of forty thousand former prisoners of war who had originally been transported there by the Tsarist government after capture on the Eastern Front. About three thousand of them were Germans, and the rest Austrians and Hungarians. In theory now free, they were mostly living in their old camps, often in appalling conditions, while they hopefully awaited repatriation. Others had found lodgings, and even jobs, in the surrounding towns and villages. A number had set up small cottage industries, including a shoe factory which was said to employ a hundred men. Some, in exchange for food and warm clothing, had gone over to the Bolsheviks who, without their support, would probably never have held on to Tashkent.

Reports reaching Delhi warned that German agents, as well as their own officers, were actively at work among the prisoners trying to organise them into fighting units. It was a prospect which caused India's defence chiefs to lose much sleep. With so many of their own units serving away from home, they were only too aware how ill-guarded their vast frontiers were. Here was an army of forty thousand trained men which might, if properly organised and armed, join forces with a combined German-Turkish assault on northern India. The only good news from Tashkent was that the Bolsheviks were equally anxious to woo more of these troops into the Red Army to help them maintain their own precarious position there.

But this was not the only Allied worry to emanate from Russian Central Asia in the summer of 1918. Stockpiled there were some 200,000 tons of raw cotton, desperately needed by both sides for the manufacture of explosives. British hopes of acquiring it had been abandoned when it was worked out that to shift it all to India would require around seven hundred and fifty thousand pack-animals and cost several million pounds on top of the purchase price. But that did not lessen the War Cabinet's fears of its falling into German hands, for it was no secret that their agents had orders to buy the entire stock and export it by camel caravan, the rail link with Europe having been cut.

These, however, were short-term fears which would end with the war. More far-sighted minds were already beginning to ponder the question of what the Bolsheviks' own long-term intentions might be towards British India and the rest of Asia. They had, in fact, received a clue, although in the turmoil of more momentous and pressing events this had passed almost unnoticed. On December 7, 1917, exactly a month after his overthrow of the Provisional Government, Lenin had issued a clarion call to Asia's millions to follow the triumphant example of the Bolsheviks and overthrow their own oppressors.

To Sir George Buchanan, the British ambassador to Petrograd, Lenin's revolutionary call had seemed to be aimed directly at British India. The following day he had called a press conference (for the British Government did not recognise the new government) and vigorously denounced the Bolshevik leader for inciting Indians to rebellion. Describing Lenin's exhortation as 'scurrilous', he had added: 'Mr Lenin spoke of us as rapacious extortioners and plunderers, while he incited our Indian subjects to rebellion . . . It is an unheard-of thing for a man who claims to direct Russian policy to use such language to a friendly and allied country.'

Eighteen days later had come another warning which should have removed any remaining doubts about Bolshevik intentions. The Council of People's Commissars had unanimously agreed to set aside two million gold roubles to be spent on fomenting revolution 'in all countries, regardless of whether they are at war with Russia, in alliance with Russia, or neutral'. This, too, seems to have passed largely unnoticed at the time, which was not entirely surprising. In the winter of 1917, when Allied fortunes were at a low ebb, there was a great deal more for the British and Indian Governments to worry about than the revolutionary rhetoric of a few hotheads in Petrograd whose own future looked anything but promising.

Back in Kashgar, Bailey and Blacker now received the long-awaited go-ahead to proceed to Tashkent to try to find answers to these various questions and, if possible, to influence events in

Britain's and her allies' favour. On July 12, 1918, under strong pressure from London, the Viceroy had finally signalled his agreement. There was only one slight change of plan. Sir George Macartney, due to leave Kashgar for London, had decided to try to reach home via Tashkent, a route he had used more than once in pre-Revolutionary days. He was to follow in the footsteps of Bailey and Blacker after he had formally handed over as Consul-General to Etherton.

Also to accompany the mission were Mr Stephanovich, the Acting Russian Consul-General in Kashgar, and his wife, who were as anxious as anyone to discover at first hand what was going on in their troubled country. Courageously, if perhaps naïvely, they had offered their services to Bailey and Blacker. Officially anyway, Stephanovich was still his country's diplomatic representative, and he hoped to be able to smooth the way of the mission both at the frontier and in its dealings with his fellow-countrymen in Tashkent. Indeed, such was the general state of ignorance about the Bolsheviks, that Bailey had gratefully fallen in with the idea, although he was aware that Stephanovich had done little to endear himself to the new regime. When ordered by Moscow to place himself under the authority of the Commissar for Foreign Affairs at Tashkent, he had refused, just as he had when instructed to haul down the old Imperial Russian flag on the consulate building and run up the new, blood-red one of the Revolution.

So it was that against this confused and turbulent backcloth, and not without foreboding, the four Europeans cautiously approached the frontier-post at Irkeshtan. For Colonel Bailey it was to be the last he would see of friendly soil for well over a year.

2 The Strange Adventures of a Butterfly Collector

In the three months which had passed since Bailey and Blacker left India, relations between the Bolsheviks and Russia's former allies had deteriorated rapidly. Even after Russia's withdrawal from the war, which many regarded as an act of treachery at a time when a German victory still seemed on the cards, some felt that it was too early to judge the new regime. It was far from certain anyway that it would remain in power for very much longer. No other country had so far followed the Bolsheviks' revolutionary example, and at home they were locked in a desperate struggle against forces more powerful and more numerous than themselves. At that time their rule scarcely extended beyond Petrograd and a few other cities.

But on July 16, 1918, just as Bailey and his party were preparing to leave Kashgar, something momentous had happened in the small mining town of Ekaterinburg which was to cause worldwide revulsion against the Bolsheviks. Originally it had been planned to put the Tsar and Tsarina on public trial in Moscow, with Trotsky as prosecutor. In the meantime, together with their children, they were being held prisoner at Ekaterinburg, in Siberia. A sudden thrust by anti-Bolshevik forces, however, brought them within three days' march of the town, and a dramatic rescue of the Russian royal family seemed more than likely.

At midnight, therefore, on July 16, Tsar Nicholas and the Empress Alexandra, their four daughters and invalid son, were taken down into the cellar of the house where they were being held and executed in cold blood. To prevent their bones from being used as holy relics by White Russian troops or superstitious peasants, their bodies were taken by lorry to a nearby mine and burnt. The remains were then tossed down a disused mineshaft, to be found later by White Russian soldiers.

As Bailey and his party approached the frontier, they knew none of this, nor of the sudden worsening of relations between Britain and the new Bolshevik regime. With hindsight it is easy to see that they should never have been allowed to leave Kashgar. Already theirs was a lost cause, and worse was to follow. But there was no way now they could be recalled.

Despite this, they encountered no difficulties at the frontier. Bolshevism, it appeared, had not yet reached the remote border post, and the handful of officials and soldiers manning it showed little sympathy for their new masters in Tashkent. They took the word of Stephanovich that this was an important British Government mission, and made their unexpected guests welcome for the night. The travellers spent the evening playing cards with their hosts and dancing to the clarinet of a young cadet. But despite the party atmosphere, it was obvious to them that the Russians were deeply anxious about their future. Fearing an attack, they had fortified the post, which stood at 10,000 feet, with a stockade built from heavy bales of cotton. While they waited they passed the days growing roses in their tiny garden and shooting game in the surrounding mountains. Bailey, who himself had served on the frontier, warmed to these friendly and hospitable men with their uncomplicated lifestyle. 'Many a British subaltern', he wrote in his memoirs, 'would have enjoyed this isolated but sporting post.' Later Bailey heard that these men had themselves joined the forlorn stream of refugees fleeing into China.

Next day Bailey and his party rode on towards Tashkent, still ten days' march away. As they travelled Bailey, an ardent and skilled naturalist, sometimes stopped to catch rare butterfly specimens, including *Parnassius* and *Coleas*. During their long journey from northern India he managed to collect no fewer than thirty-nine different varieties, some of them at 14,000 feet. Today, besides the blue poppy, there are at least four species of butterfly and two mammals named after him. Even when, much later, he was on the run for his life, Bailey still found time to pursue butterflies.

Not long after they had crossed the frontier they learned of an embarrassing rumour which appeared to be preceding them. They were, it was whispered, the advance guard of a twelve-thousand-strong (sixty thousand, some said) British invasion force being sent from India to deliver Russian Central Asia from Bolshevism. It was a rumour, Blacker recalled afterwards, 'which was to cause some unease to our adversaries'. But it was also one which was likely to prove highly dangerous to themselves, and wherever they encountered it Stephanovich did his best to scotch it.

It was at the village of Sufi Kurgan, some thirty miles inside the frontier, that they encountered their first Bolsheviks, a small detachment of the newly formed Red Army. Only two of the soldiers were actually Russians, the rest being former prisoners of war. But they were too busy taking over the military post there to bother with Bailey's party which continued on its way towards Osh, the first town of any size. It was here that they decided to make official contact with the Bolshevik authorities. To attempt to bypass them and press on towards Tashkent would have been to invite trouble, particularly in view of the wild rumours circulating about them. These, it transpired, had already reached the ears of the local Soviet. Fortunately Stephanovich was known and well respected in Osh, and his denials of the rumours and explanation of the mission's peaceful purpose were finally accepted, after he had been closely questioned by the local Commissar for War. It was agreed that, provided clearance could be obtained by telegraph from the authorities in Tashkent, Bailey and his party would be allowed to proceed.

All seemed well, for two days later they were permitted to continue by horse-drawn *tarantas* to the railhead at Andijan, thirty miles further on, where they could board a train for Tashkent. But on arrival there they discovered that because of fuel shortages, and heavy fighting further down the line, all civilian traffic had been halted for the past fortnight. Three days later, however, the trains began running again. Seats were found for the small party (their pony-men and others having now left for home) on the first one to leave for Tashkent.

So far, much to their surprise, they had encountered no serious problems. The local Bolsheviks had more urgent matters to contend with, including their own survival. But by now it was becoming clear that it was no longer safe for Stephanovich to come with them. At any moment it would dawn on the Soviet authorities where his sympathies really lay, with unpleasant consequences for both himself and the two British officers. For very likely they would conclude that Bailey and Blacker were also sympathetic to the counter-revolutionaries, who were still a considerable threat, and that they were perhaps actively hand-in-glove with them. And at that very moment men, and even women, were being shot for less.

Beyond knowing that the Bolsheviks were in control of Tashkent, however precariously, the two officers had little idea what was really going on there, or what kind of a reception they could expect. Not that they were particularly worried. Both were extremely resourceful men, which was why they had been chosen, and anyway these were the very things they had been sent to find out.

A great deal had, in fact, happened in Tashkent in the ten months between the Bolsheviks' seizure of power there and the arrival of the British mission. For a vivid account of these momentous events we have the valuable, if unexpected, testimony of a Danish officer. Early in December 1917, when the Revolution was still only a month old, Captain A.H. Brun had been sent by his government, officially neutral, to try to ease the sufferings of the thousands of Austrian and Hungarian ex-prisoners trapped in Central Asia by the Revolution. Although Brun's humanitarian mission had been sanctioned at highest level by the revolutionary leaders in Petrograd, he quickly learned that, when it was inconvenient, their authority counted for very little in Tashkent. His experiences in the course of the next fifteen months were often to prove harrowing, and at times hair-raising. But at least he was to escape with his life, which was more than could be said for his Swedish opposite number, sent to look after the interests of the German prisoners.

The violent events leading to the Bolshevik seizure of power in Tashkent, including four days of bloody and bitter fighting, are to this day extremely confused. No two accounts appear to agree, and everything depends upon whose version one chooses to accept. Fortunately we are only concerned with what happened after the Bolsheviks came to power, and here we have Brun as an eye-witness, for after his escape from his nightmarish adventure he published an account of it, *Troublous Times*, now long out of print and difficult to find.

The train which brought him to Tashkent from Petrograd was among the last to get through before the line was cut by White Russian forces, and took ten days to reach its destination. A Russian on the train to whom he showed the letters of introduction he had been given warned him that every one of those to whom they were addressed had been arrested by the local Cheka, or secret police. Brun was strongly advised by his fellow-passenger to destroy the letters. Even his neutral status, he was told, would not protect him from the unpleasant consequences of being found with them in his possession. It was hardly an auspicious beginning to his peaceful mission.

Yet Brun's first impressions as he drove into town from the station were not unfavourable. Everything appeared orderly enough in the still dawn of Central Asia. Turtle-doves fluttered over the low roof-tops. Neat rows of silver-limbed poplars lined the wide streets of the model, colonial-built capital. There was little sign here of the revolutionary turmoil and destruction which Brun had witnessed in Petrograd. But it was still very early, and in their respective quarters both natives and Europeans slumbered uneasily.

Through a contact made on the train, Brun managed to find lodgings at the home of a former judge who, although he had been dismissed by the Bolsheviks, still enjoyed his freedom. In this he was more fortunate than many of his colleagues who had either been executed or killed in the fighting. The Governor, a retired Tsarist general, had been murdered in his official residence by the revolutionary mob and his corpse thrown from an upstairs window onto the pavement. It had lain there for several days before his widow had been allowed to remove it for burial. Many other former officers and officials, Brun learned from his landlord, were languishing in the city's jail while their fate was being decided.

Tashkent's new rulers made a poor impression on the Dane during the first of his many meetings with them. To be fair, the commissars were mostly ordinary working men who lacked the organisational genius of Lenin and Trotsky or the other Petrograd revolutionaries. They were ill-educated, without experience of government or administration. Before the Revolution many had been drivers or oilers on the railway. Now they suddenly found themselves trying to run a city with a population of nearly half a million people, many of them extremely hostile towards Bolshevism or actively plotting against their new rulers. Nor did they even enjoy the support of those whose interests they professed to represent, the huge Muslim population, who outnumbered Russians of European origin by more than ten to one. The very reverse, in fact.

The trouble stemmed largely from the neo-colonial attitude of the Tashkent Bolsheviks, Europeans to a man, towards the native populace. On seizing power, Lenin had led the different ethnic communities making up the former Tsarist empire to believe that they would be granted self-determination. But it soon became clear that whatever Petrograd might be promising, the Tashkent Bolsheviks were little different from their predecessors. The Revolution, one of the Tashkent commissars had argued, had been carried out in Central Asia by Russians of European origin. 'It is only fair', he added, 'that its direction should be theirs.' This was not a view shared by fifteen million disillusioned Muslims.

An uprising by the native population was expected at any

time, Brun had been warned on his arrival. It took place on Boxing Day, 1917. Early that morning huge crowds of Muslims – Brun estimated some two hundred thousand in all – had begun to gather on the streets, in their white turbans, long multi-coloured silk coats and high leather boots. Many had ridden in from the surrounding countryside and were still on horseback, while others bore aloft religious banners. Although the demonstration began in an orderly way, the heavily out-numbered Europeans, both Bolsheviks and those opposed to them, had good reason for fear. What they most dreaded was a *jihad*, or Holy War, declared against the infidel minority. As Brun wrote afterwards: 'All knew what a revolt amongst the Mahommedans of the country would signify. It would mean the . . . death of every European on whom they could lay hands. . . . If religious fanaticism got the better of reason, it would be mere child's play for 15,000,000 natives to root out 1,500,000 Russians.'

The crowds, still peaceful, began to converge on the enormous square in front of the former Governor-General's palace, now the Bolshevik headquarters. A deputation of Muslim elders was allowed to enter the building and present its demands. The Bolsheviks, who had no intention of conceding anything, deliberately dragged out the negotiations, hoping to weary both the emissaries and the waiting crowds. But the strategy backfired, for the demonstrators lost patience and marched angrily on the jail where the Bolsheviks held their political prisoners, many of whom were awaiting execution.

The mob – for that is what it had now turned into – broke down the heavy gates and freed all the prisoners, some of whom they carried shoulder-high through the streets. Determined to arm themselves, they next marched on the citadel containing the arsenal. But here they were met by canon and machine-gun fire which broke up the ill-organised attack, leaving many dead.

During the night, however, they were reinforced by sixty thousand Kirghiz tribesmen from the surrounding hills, and the following day they again pressed home their attack on the

Bolshevik positions. But the Turkic peoples of Central Asia are no longer a warrior race, and they were beaten off, leaving them with no further stomach for the fight. The uprising, without leaders and modern weapons, had been easily crushed. The blood-letting was not yet over though. Convinced that the prisoners liberated by the mob were really behind the insurrection, the Bolsheviks ruthlessly executed many of those unfortunate enough to be recaptured.

Relations between the native population and the local European-born Russians, never good even in Tsarist times, now began to deteriorate rapidly throughout Central Asia. Promises of self-determination, the Muslims soon realised, only referred to India and other colonial possessions of the imperialist powers. They did not apply to the Tsar's former territories in Asia and elsewhere. There now occurred an incident which was to poison relations between the two communities for years to come, and drive many Muslims into the counter-revolutionary camp.

It happened at the ancient mud-walled caravan town of Kokand, one hundred miles to the south-east of Tashkent. Here disillusioned Muslim nationalists had set up a rival government to that of Tashkent. Calling itself the Muslim Provisional Government of Autonomous Turkestan, it claimed to speak for the great mass of the native population. At first its demands were fairly moderate, for its leaders believed that the Tashkent Bolsheviks were acting without the authority of Lenin. But after receiving an unsatisfactory reply to an appeal to Petrograd, on January 23, 1918 they telegraphed the Tashkent Bolsheviks saying they intended to elect a parliament in which one-third of the seats would be apportioned to non-Muslims.

Realising that this was a serious challenge to their own claim to authority in the former Tsarist territories, the Tashkent Bolsheviks immediately denounced the Kokand government as counter-revolutionary and declared war on it. They then assembled the strongest force they could muster, including many ex-POWs, and surrounded the old town, which was defended only by a hastily raised and ill-armed militia. The great wall was breached and a general massacre ensued. The number of Muslims slain is put by historians at anything between five thousand and fourteen thousand. Rape and plunder took place on a horrifying scale against a people unable to defend themselves. Homes, mosques and caravanserais were burned down or desecrated in this once-prosperous cotton town. Clearly the whole thing had got out of hand, and news of it was hurriedly suppressed lest it unleash a full-scale *jihad* against the Russian minority throughout Central Asia.

But in Tashkent Brun was quick to hear of it, and later wrote with distaste of the prisoners' part in this massacre of the innocents: 'I was told that every one of the members of the Kokand expedition had become a rich man, 10,000 to 20,000 roubles being an average share, and 200,000 a man nothing surprising. I regret to say that these marauding expeditions were a strong temptation to some of the lower natures among my charges who let themselves be drafted into the army of the Reds.'

That some of the ex-prisoners had chosen to work for the Bolsheviks (if not actually to espouse their cause) was not really surprising in the light of their wretched circumstances. Many had been captured in the early days of the war, and had therefore been in camps in Central Asia for several years. They had been sent there in the first place because food had still been plentiful, while escape was extremely difficult. But as Russia's situation gradually deteriorated, so did the conditions in the prison camps. By the time of the Revolution, the prisoners were desperately short of clothing, food and medicines. Many died – particularly from spotted-fever, which only the very young or strong seemed to survive. The cemetery of one camp outside Tashkent contained more than eight thousand graves. In winter the camps were ankle-deep in mud and melted snow, and in summer unbearably hot. On top of that there was the problem of boredom. It is surprising perhaps that many more of the prisoners did not succumb to Bolshevik blandishments.

Brun's task of trying to improve the conditions in the camps had proved a fairly thankless one from the beginning. The local Bolsheviks looked upon this highly polished Danish officer, in his immaculate uniform, with a mixture of suspicion and hostility. That he was a neutral meant little to these rough working men to whom all foreign governments were the sworn enemies of the socialist revolution. Nor did the official credentials he brought from the revolutionary leaders in Petrograd impress them. For, once they had consolidated their authority over Russian Central Asia, they had dreams of setting up their own autonomous Bolshevik state there, free from all interference by Petrograd or Moscow, or anyone else. Yet, with the rail link between Tashkent and Petrograd cut by White counter-revolutionaries, Brun depended for all his needs on the co-operation and goodwill of the local Soviet.

During his stay in Tashkent, Brun tells us, he had to deal with no fewer than ten successive Commissars for War. The more intelligent and reasonable an official was, the more quickly he was likely to be purged and, eventually, liquidated. Every kind of obstacle was put in his way by officials who showed no interest in the fate or welfare of prisoners unless they were willing to join the revolutionary cause. When Brun reminded the head of the Tashkent Soviet that Lenin and Trotsky had signed an order expressly outlawing the recruitment of prisoners into the Red Army, the commissar dismissed this as 'merely a scrap of paper'. Asked whether this meant that Tashkent was now independent of the authorities in Moscow and Petrograd, he told Brun that, with them so far away, 'we do what seems right to us'.

During those early months of Bolshevik rule in Tashkent, life was hazardous for everyone, particularly after dark. Shooting was to be heard almost every night, Brun recalls, as rampaging soldiers broke into houses and looted them. His own orderly had questioned one fellow prisoner who had joined the Red Army, and the Dane was horrified to discover 'the amount of money one could get by means of a revolver'. Criminal elements naturally took advantage of the prevailing anarchy, either by joining the Bolsheviks and misusing their authority, or simply by posing as such when raiding homes or robbing terrified citizens.

This blood-letting and anarchy was not confined to Tashkent. In the towns and villages of the ancient Silk Road, Bolsheviks and White counter-revolutionaries fought it out in a civil war that engulfed vast areas of the country, ebbing and flowing as first one side triumphed and then the other. The Bolsheviks had managed to seize Samarkand, Tamerlane's former capital, early on and virtually without resistance, but without the help of Austrian prisoners of war they would undoubtedly have lost it again. For one night four train-loads of mutinous Bolshevik soldiers – 'seduced by Tsarist promises', the local commissars claimed – managed to capture the railway station. Such was their shortage of troops that the Bolsheviks had left the town itself virtually undefended. There was only one way to save it from falling into the hands of the mutineers, and that was to arm the ex-POWs.

In exchange for a promise that one of the trains would be theirs to take them home, the Austrians agreed to capture the railway station. This they did with the loss of eleven of their number. The two thousand mutineers were disarmed and handed over to the Bolsheviks – as were the arms with which they had been issued for the attack. But the promise of one of the trains was conveniently forgotten, and the NCO who led the Austrians – one Gustav Krist – found himself sentenced to death, although this was commuted at the very last minute to three months' imprisonment.

At the ancient caravan town of Bokhara, further along the Silk Road, the Bolsheviks were less fortunate. Under the Tsars this great stronghold of Islam had never been fully absorbed into the Russian Empire, but had been allowed to remain a protectorate under a hereditary Emir. The Bolsheviks were determined to liberate this backward, mediaeval society from its harsh and autocratic ruler.

In March 1918, the President of the Tashkent-based government himself arrived unannounced at Bokhara to seek what he described as the Emir's 'co-operation'. Just in case this was not forthcoming, he had with him some six hundred Red Army troops. A whiff of Russian grapeshot, the ex-railway oiler believed, was all that would be needed to make the Emir comply. A twenty-four-hour ultimatum was delivered to the Emir demanding that he dismiss his ministers, disarm his troops and hand over authority to young Bokharan leftists inside the walled city. If he failed to accept these terms, then he would be overthrown by force.

Playing for time, the Emir quickly began to mobilise his army, while the mullahs stirred up the populace against the godless Russians and the young revolutionaries in their midst. The Russians were told meanwhile that it would take the Emir three days to persuade his fanatical troops to disarm. All this time the Bokharans were bringing up reinforcements from outlying stations. To prevent the Bolsheviks from doing the same, the rail link with Tashkent was severed. Although the Bokharans had no love for their Emir, they had even less for the Bolsheviks, and they now rallied to his defence. Accounts of the fighting differ greatly, but it began when a mob fell upon the Bolshevik delegates and their armed escort and slaughtered them almost to a man. Two managed to escape, however, and make their way back to the main Bolshevik force.

Meanwhile in the town rioting had spread and several hundred Russians who had been living peacefully in Bokhara were brutally slaughtered by the rampaging crowds. Many of them had their throats cut – the town's traditional method of execution. Finding themselves now cut off from all assistance, the Red Army began to shell the town, but they scored few if any hits and very soon their ammunition ran out. This was put down by the mullahs to divine intervention, for Bokhara is regarded by Muslims as a holy city. On March 17, after two days of fighting, President Kolesov and his troops were forced to beat a humiliating retreat back along the railway line towards

Tashkent. In some places this involved taking up the rails over which they had just passed and then laying them down again ahead of the locomotive.

More than two years were to pass before the Bolsheviks felt confident enough to challenge the Emir again, this time with very different results. But elsewhere their excesses against the Muslim population continued. Farmers were forced to surrender their stocks of cotton – often their only source of income – while in the name of 'war communism' their precious stores of food were seized by armed requisitioning squads. Altogether, in the great famine which swept through Russian Central Asia at this time, at least nine hundred thousand people (the figure is from *Pravda*) are believed to have died. Some authorities put the figure considerably higher. And if that were not enough, there was the added nightmare of the Cheka, the Bolshevik secret police, who in the name of the new faith terrorised the populace.

Years later, in the official Soviet *History of the Civil War in the USSR*, it was admitted that in the early months of the Revolution in Central Asia 'many of the local Bolsheviks distorted the policy of the Party on the national question and committed gross mistakes in their dealings with the native population'. But in the meantime these excesses continued, driving more and more Muslims into the ranks of the fanatical *basmachi*, the local freedom-fighters.

Such then was the scene in the Tsar's former Central Asian territories when, on August 14, 1918, Colonel Bailey and Major Blacker stepped off the train in Tashkent and drove to the Regina Hotel.

3 Bailey Vanishes

The two officers were extremely fortunate, as it turned out, not to have been arrested, and even shot, on their arrival in Tashkent. Unknown to them, just hours before, troops of General Malleson's East Persian Cordon had clashed with Bolshevik forces near Ashkabad, and routed them. They had been ordered across the frontier to assist anti-German (and also anti-Bolshevik) White Russian forces holding the vital Transcaspian rail link. For the first time in the history of Anglo-Russian rivalry in Asia, British and Russian troops had fired on one another in anger. Even more awkward, it had happened on Russian territory. For Bailey and Blacker this was an acutely embarrassing – not to say dangerous – new development. And it was by no means the last such shock they would encounter.

When they reached Tashkent at 3 a.m. on the day following the clash, they were totally unaware that anything was amiss. They had been out of touch with India and the rest of the world now for some weeks. The news therefore caught them totally by surprise when the Commissar for Foreign Affairs confronted them with it at their first meeting. He coldly invited Bailey to explain what, he insisted, amounted to a declaration of war by Britain on the new Soviet republic.

Even before this dumbfounding question, the meeting had got off to an uncomfortable start when, intending to be courteous, Bailey had referred to the 'Bolshevik Government'. The commissar, a man named Damagatsky, had interrupted him, pointing out sharply that it was not a Bolshevik government at all, but an alliance between the Bolsheviks and the Left Social Revolutionaries, the party to which he himself belonged. To Bailey this seemed like hair-splitting, for there appeared to be little to choose between these two groups of extremists.

As head of a supposedly friendly and peaceful diplomatic mission to the new government, Bailey found himself hard-pressed to explain away the news of the armed clash. The reports, he insisted to Damagatsky, must be false. What evidence, he demanded to know, was there to show that British troops had been involved in the incident?

The Russian's reply, to quote Bailey, was both 'simple and flattering'. The artillery fire, he told the Englishman, had been far too accurate to be Russian. Furthermore, English lettering had been found on some of the shell fragments picked up afterwards. But that, Bailey countered, meant nothing. In the course of the war, Britain had supplied her Russian allies with enormous quantities of ammunition. Very likely some of this was being used by the White Russians against the Red troops advancing on Ashkabad. Neither this nor the uncomfortable accuracy of the artillery fire, Bailey insisted, amounted to evidence that any British troops were involved. 'In that case,' retorted Damagatsky, 'I will try to produce a prisoner for you.'

Although they had managed to gain a breathing-space, the two officers realised only too well how perilous their situation was. But they had little choice except to remain there in the Bolshevik stronghold and try to bluff their way through. To attempt to leave now would be seen by the Bolsheviks as evidence of their guilt. Escape was obviously impossible. And anyway, following a few days behind them, and due to join them in Tashkent on his way through to London, was Sir George Macartney.

In the light of what had happened, they realised they were lucky not to have been arrested, although it might be merely a matter of time until they were. The Bolsheviks, they had to admit, would have been perfectly justified in interning them. And Tashkent's prisons, they knew, had an evil reputation. As Bailey recounts in his book *Mission To Tashkent*, the narrative of his Central Asian adventures:

'There was nowhere to keep us except in the gaol, and unauthorised executions of people in gaol were of very frequent occurrence. A party of drunken soldiers would go to the gaol, take people out and shoot them. Once as we were walking down the street we heard cries and shots from a house. One of these murders was being perpetrated. In excuse it was said that the victims had been so roughly handled by the men who had escorted them that they were shot to put them out of their misery.'

Other executions, Bailey adds, took place simply 'when the gaol was full and it was necessary to make room'. Their own situation was not improved by the local Bolshevik press which clamoured repeatedly for them to be shot. When the first train-load of wounded, including Austrian ex-POWs, arrived in Tashkent from the Ashkabad front, it became embarrassingly clear that British Indian troops were indeed involved. Blacker, less scrupulous than Bailey, decided to disown them. These troops, he told the Bolsheviks, were nothing whatever to do with the British Government (in fact they were three companies of the 19th Punjab Infantry). They were, he declared, *former* Indian Army troops – Afghan Hazara tribesmen to be precise – who had hired themselves out to the anti-Bolsheviks as mercenaries. Astonishingly, the Bolsheviks appeared to swallow this, for miraculously the two British officers continued to enjoy their freedom.

Despite everything, much of life in Tashkent appeared to carry on fairly normally. At first, as veterans of France, Bailey and Blacker had found it difficult to adjust to the sight of field-grey uniforms everywhere – those of the ex-POWs. Almost every restaurant had its orchestra of Austro-Hungarians, though it was a mystery where they obtained their instruments. They showed no hostility whatsoever towards the two 'enemy' officers in their midst, and whenever Bailey or Blacker entered Tashkent's once-fashionable *Chashka Chai* – or 'Cup of Tea' – restaurant, they would good-humouredly strike up with *It's a Long Way to Tipperary*. Some prisoners, less fortunate, were to be seen on occasion begging in the streets. Others had married local girls, often the widows of men killed in the war, or of those who had disappeared in the Revolution. Mostly they intended to stay on in Turkestan after the war, hoping for more settled times. One such ceremony in the Catholic cathedral had to be halted when a fellow-prisoner stood up and revealed that the bridegroom already had a wife in Austria.

The almost Ruritanian atmosphere created by the *thé dansant* orchestras, and the film *The Prisoner of Zenda* showing in the cinema, was heightened by the arrival of an Englishman with a troupe of performing elephants on their way across the passes to Kashgar, and eventually to India. Just who he was and what he was doing in wartime in the middle of Central Asia remains a mystery. Bailey and Blacker were evidently too busy keeping out of prison to try to discover. It is curious, however, that they did not make use of their fellow-countryman to convey news of their situation to Etherton in Kashgar. Perhaps, in view of his bulky travelling companions, they considered him too slow. Yet none of the other couriers they hired during those early days to carry concealed messages – written in invisible ink and in code – to Etherton ever succeeded in reaching Kashgar.

Apart from the Bolshevik spies who trailed them everywhere, one man they did keep a keen eye on was a young German officer named Zimmerman whom they suspected of being part of a plan to organise the German ex-prisoners into a small but potentially troublesome fighting force for use against northern India. Lieutenant Zimmerman had incurred Bolshevik displeasure – and the admiration of the two British officers – by his determined efforts to prevent German prisoners from joining the Red Army, warning that anyone who did would face a court-martial on his return home. At the same time, in face of the most daunting obstacles, the young lieutenant did everything he could for his men. In keeping them from joining the Bolshevik ranks, however, he was not wholly successful. Bailey recalls seeing a squad of them, dressed entirely in black, marching through Tashkent under a fierce-looking sergeant-major and singing the *Internationale*. In his memoirs, *On Secret Patrol in High Asia*, Blacker describes Zimmerman's eventual fate – at the hands of a British firing squad, a year or so later near Merv. He tells us that 'the young lad, who was a gallant officer' went to his death 'like a man', but does not say why he was shot. Blacker, who saw him shortly beforehand, describes him as wearing 'ragged civilian clothes', which suggests he might have been spying. Brun, writing nine years later, confirms this, but says that he escaped death 'in some miraculous way' after the firing-squad had been ordered to shoot. If this is true, then perhaps the troops deliberately missed, and Blacker was covering up. But our concern here is with Zimmerman's activities in Tashkent.

In his meetings with Damagatsky, which went on despite the worsening relations between the two governments, Bailey pressed the commissar to keep a tighter rein on Zimmerman. Damagatsky insisted that there was no danger of his obtaining weapons or of combining in any way which might threaten the British. He added, moreover, that it was the Bolsheviks' aim to recruit as many of the prisoners as possible into the Red Army. On the question of their huge cotton stocks, and the danger of these reaching the German munitions factories (one caravan had already got through), Damagatsky said that this war between the imperialist powers was not their concern. The cotton would be sold to the highest bidders, provided they would come and take it away.

By now Sir George Macartney had arrived in Tashkent, and on September 1, 1918, he and Bailey were summoned to the White House, residence of the former Governor-General, to see the President of the new republic. This was Kolesov, the ex-railway oiler who had been vanquished at Bokhara by the Emir's troops, and had ordered the Kokand massacre. Bailey left it to Macartney, a diplomat of many years' experience, to explain the purpose of the mission. Kolesov waited until Macartney had finished before dropping his bombshell.

Why, he asked, if this was a peaceful mission as it claimed to be, had seven thousand British troops with tanks and guns just landed at Archangel, in northern Russia? This disconcerting piece of news, like that of General Malleson's clash with the Bolsheviks only two weeks earlier, caught them totally by surprise. All they could do was suggest that the landing must be directed against the Germans, whose troops were already in Finland. Kolesov looked unimpressed. 'I had visions of the interior of a Bolshevik gaol,' Macartney said afterwards. But their luck held. Kolesov's mood unexpectedly changed, and he told them he would have to seek instructions by telegraph from Moscow.

There seemed little point in Macartney staying on in Tashkent. To return home across a Russia torn apart by civil war was now clearly too perilous, so he decided to travel back to Kashgar by the route he had come, and thence make his way home via India. At least he would be able to report at first hand to the British Government on the situation in Central Asia. Blacker had for some weeks been suffering from a mysterious illness, so it was agreed that he would return to India with Macartney. Their departure was unaccountably held up at the last moment – possibly by news reaching Tashkent of the attempt, on August 30, on Lenin's life in which, momentarily anyway, a British agent was thought to have played a part. In the circumstances, Macartney and Blacker got away just in time. The assassination attempt was to unleash a wave of indiscriminate terror and repression by the dreaded Cheka in all Bolshevik-controlled areas. It was directed against anyone even remotely suspected of having counter-revolutionary connections or sympathies. Anti-British phobia was running especially high. For Moscow, not entirely without reason, blamed many of its misfortunes on Britain's intelligence services.

But worse was to follow. Only six days after Macartney's departure, an incident took place at a remote spot to the east of the Caspian which was to bring Anglo-Bolshevik relations to a new low. Early on the morning of September 20, twenty-six prominent commissars and leading Bolsheviks who had the misfortune to fall into the hands of White Russian troops during the fighting for Baku were taken out into the desert and summarily executed. General Malleson, aware that they were being held, had tried to obtain their custody so that they could be transported to India. There, if necessary, they could be held as hostages in exchange for British and other Allied nationals in Cheka custody. Before this could be arranged, however, the executions were carried out, though on whose orders will probably never be known. Ever since then, Moscow has accused Britain of responsibility for their martyrdom. One official artist's reconstruction of the scene shows two British officers in uniform standing behind the firing squad. In fact, no British officers were present or even aware of what was about to happen, although it has been suggested that Malleson and his officers should have foreseen the inevitable outcome of their being held by White Russians, and acted more promptly.

Fortunately for Macartney and Blacker, who could easily have been stopped at the frontier, and even more so for Bailey, news of the massacre, which has now become part of the great revolutionary epic, did not reach Moscow or Tashkent until the new year. Otherwise, in the anger of the moment, all three Britons would more than likely have been shot out of hand. One reason for the surprising forbearance which had so far been shown to the mission was very likely the Bolsheviks' desire for recognition by Britain, then still the world's leading power. When Bailey had first called on Damagatsky, the latter had immediately asked to examine his official credentials. 'It was hoped', Bailey wrote afterwards, 'that I would produce papers which would indicate recognition of the Soviet Government . . '

But there was possibly another, much more personal reason why they had not shot Bailey and his colleagues, like so many of their other victims, long before. It is to be found in an intelligence report from General Malleson after the debriefing of one of his spies just back from Tashkent. According to the agent, the only reason they had not been shot was that 'the Bolshevik leaders intend bolting to Kashgar in case of disaster, and do not wish to go to extremes with us for this reason'. This has the ring of truth to it. Defeat was then a real possibility for the hard-pressed Bolsheviks, particularly since the British had begun to step up their support for the anti-Bolshevik forces, the only Russian troops still fighting the Germans. The unfortunate fate of the twenty-six commissars from Baku, when word of it finally leaked out, was an unpleasant reminder to the beleaguered revolutionaries in Tashkent of their own likely nemesis if the other side triumphed. In his anxiety to discover the true situation, Damagatsky asked Bailey one day whether it would be possible for him to obtain any 'reliable' foreign newspapers. Bailey, who himself had had no news for weeks, was unable to oblige.

Besides the thousands of ex-prisoners living in or around Tashkent at that time, there were several other foreigners in the town. By now Bailey and Brun had made contact with one another and become firm friends. But another foreigner – somewhat incredibly – was Roger Tredwell, the American consul. He had arrived in Tashkent shortly before Bailey, sent by his government (ostensibly, anyway) to try to develop commerce with the region once the war was over. He was lodging with a Russian family who with the incongruity of those bizarre times still employed an Irish governess, a Miss Rosanna Houston. As the situation deteriorated, every day becoming more dangerous for them, the foreigners kept a close watch over one another's interests. Without this, it is unlikely that the men, anyway, would have survived the coming weeks.

By now Brun's humanitarian mission on behalf of the prisoners was being made more and more difficult by the authorities as well as by circumstances. When he had first arrived, the death toll in the POW camps was running at about seventy a month. By May 1918, this had soared to a horrifying five hundred, many of them killed by malaria. Through strenuous efforts, Brun managed to reduce this to some fifty a month by buying rice and grain in bulk for his camps wherever he could find it. The Bolsheviks were supplying only about 1,000 of the 2,500 calories needed daily by each prisoner to fight off illness, and even this they were beginning to cut back on. To relieve the desperate shortage of medicines in his twenty-five camps, the resourceful Dane managed to purchase, for 70,000 roubles, the entire stock of a chemist's shop which the authorities were about to requisition.

The nomadic Kirghiz, whose flocks had been taken by the food-requisitioning squads, were also undergoing great hardship. Two cases of cannibalism were discovered in Tashkent, both of them traced to Kirghiz encampments. In one of these, a healthy young man had been seized and eaten. The desperate nomads, Brun tells us, were driven to abandoning children they were unable to feed – 'a ghastly thing to do, since large packs of wolves were constantly following the trail of the Kirghiz'.

With his movements becoming increasingly restricted, his premises raided for arms, his funds frozen and couriers arrested, and with *agents provocateurs* trying to lure him into every sort of trap, Brun's relief work finally ground to a halt. The end came when a group of prisoners who had gone over to the Bolsheviks visited his house one night and informed him at the point of a revolver that they were taking over his job. Their leader, who produced a document authorising this signed by Kolesov himself, demanded that Brun hand over to them all his cash – the property of the Danish Government – and his records. 'Your house', he was told, 'is surrounded by soldiers. All resistance is useless.' Brun had no choice but to submit, for it was clear that they meant business. But this, as it turned out, was merely the beginning.

The net was closing on Bailey too. He had an extraordinary facility for making friends in improbable places, and from a contact in the Bolshevik-controlled wireless station he learned that the Government of India had telegraphed him with instructions to close down the mission and return home. But word of this had been deliberately withheld from him by the authorities, and he was unable to act on it lest he endanger the life of his informant. The following day he learned that he, Tredwell and others were to be arrested. Having warned them, he immediately set about hiding or destroying certain papers – and planting others which were deliberately intended to mislead the authorities.

On the evening of October 15, he was arrested by the secret police who searched his room, taking away every scrap of paper as well as his revolver (he had another hidden away which they failed to discover). They told him that Tredwell had also been arrested. Word of what had happened spread quickly through the town, including a rumour that both men had been shot, and friends began turning up at the house shortly afterwards to try to discover the truth. One woman, a friend of his landlady, walked boldly from the garden into the ground-floor room where he was being held. Before the startled sentry could prevent her, she shook hands with Bailey as though unaware that anything was amiss. Without anyone noticing, she managed to slip a tiny rolled-up scrap of paper into his hand. It was a scribbled message from Tredwell saying that he had been able to secure his own release, and was now doing everything in his power to get Bailey freed.

Another visitor was Brun, who managed to see him briefly after slipping past the sentry and before being ejected at bayonet point. As he left, Brun realised that he was being followed by a soldier. When he turned to ask the man what he was doing, the soldier said they were going together to the Cheka headquarters. '*You* may be, for all I know,' Brun told him, 'but I am *not*. I am going home.' Eventually though, he was forced to accompany the soldier to the secret police headquarters where he was subjected to a lengthy grilling on why he had been to see Bailey. He was finally allowed to leave, aware that his own position was now becoming increasingly insecure.

Bailey, meanwhile, was himself being interrogated by senior Cheka officials. He had warned them, grimly, that when news of his arrest reached the British Parliament, 'I would not care to be the people who ordered it.' The Bolsheviks, he knew, misled by its name, believed the House of Commons to be some kind of revolutionary body, whose approval and recognition they were anxious to obtain. He demanded, furthermore, to be told the reason for his arrest, and to be permitted to telegraph this immediately to his government. The latter request was refused, but his principal interrogator – a youth called Siderov – told him that he was suspected of passing two million Tsarist roubles, at that time still worth more than their Bolshevik equivalent, to Irgash Bey, leader of some twenty thousand *basmachi*, or anti-Soviet Muslim guerrillas, hiding out in the mountains around Kokand.

Laughing at this suggestion, Bailey told Siderov: 'But I know who did.' Everyone in town, he said, except themselves knew that it was the German agent Hermann. For extra plausibility, he added a date, time and a precise location where the money had been handed to the counter-revolutionaries. While awaiting arrest Bailey had carefully written this into a letter addressed to the Indian Government and sealed up the envelope. He now allowed himself to be persuaded to unseal this and show it to his interrogators. Its effect on them was visible. Once more Bailey's bluff had succeeded, for shortly afterwards he was freed. But the authorities kept his passport, although both he and they were aware that escape to India was impossible, the passes now being closed by snow.

When Bailey sought official authorisation to return to India, Kolesov told him: 'I cannot let you leave. My Government have grave suspicions of you.' He added that he personally had none. But Bailey knew that this was simply to protect his own skin if ever he had to answer to the British. Bailey also knew that Kolesov was awaiting further instructions by telegraph from Moscow before deciding his and Tredwell's fate. Tredwell was in a rather stronger position than himself, being the accredited representative of the United States, a country towards which the Bolsheviks, as yet, felt no particular hostility. His own standing on this score could hardly be worse. At any moment, he knew, his hitherto charmed life would desert him. He immediately began to make preparations for his escape. Nor was he any too soon. The following day – October 20, 1918 – he was lunching with Tredwell when a message was delivered to the house. It warned: 'You are both to be arrested at once and the situation is particularly dangerous for Bailey. Shooting is not out of the question.'

Bailey finished his lunch and made his way home, closely followed by half a dozen Cheka agents. Safely inside, and out of sight, he set about making the final arrangements for his disappearance. That evening he was seen to leave his lodgings and make his way to Tredwell's, where he had supper. After supper he left, and strolled along the tree-lined streets to a row of houses not far away. He entered one of these, and the spies took up their usual positions in doorways and on street corners while waiting for him to emerge. It was the last they were ever to see of him. Had they been more observant, however, they might have seen the front door of a house at the other end of the row open, and a man in the uniform of an Austrian prisoner walk away into the dusk.

*   *   *

At about the same time that Bailey was giving the Bolsheviks the slip, in another part of town armed Cheka officers were preparing to raid the house of an important suspected counter-revolutionary. But their quarry, a well-to-do mining engineer – and shadowy acquaintance of Bailey's – called Paul Nazaroff, was too quick for them. By a lucky chance he saw their car draw up outside his house and the six black-uniformed occupants leap out. In a flash he was out of his chair, through the house, across the garden and over the wall. He then vanished into the night.

Nazaroff knew very well why they had come for him. For he was the ringleader of a White Russian plot to overthrow the Tashkent Soviet and link up with the British to the west. Someone had betrayed him – but who? Nazaroff hid for two days (Tashkent was full of such fugitives at that time) before venturing out in search of a safer and more permanent sanctuary. But as he crossed a square in the native quarter of town he saw, to his dismay, two Cheka agents, both of whom he knew.

One had been a clown in the local circus before the Revolution, the other a Tashkent shop assistant. At the very moment Nazaroff spotted them, they saw and recognised him. He was unarmed. Within seconds he was staring down the barrels of their revolvers.

In triumph they marched him back to Cheka headquarters, a place of vile reputation, where he was subjected to the first of many interrogations. During one of these he learned how they had smashed the plot – or so they believed – and discovered his own involvement in it. A White Russian colonel whom Nazaroff had sent off to the Kokand region to make contact with anti-Bolshevik forces there, had – despite warnings that nothing must ever be put in writing – prepared a report of his visit and a breakdown of his spending. The Cheka had intercepted this, and immediately raided the homes of everyone mentioned in it, thus rounding up most of the leaders, including Nazaroff.

During one of his interrogations, at which he faced the entire Cheka hierarchy, Nazaroff was handed a sheet of paper on which were written a series of questions. He was told that if he gave detailed answers to them all he would be pardoned. If he refused, or gave false answers, he would be shot. Nazaroff studied the questions. They wanted to know the names of all those in the plot, where they got their money from, where their arms were hidden, and what their links were with the British. Nazaroff knew very well that they would shoot him anyway, whether he answered the questions or not. 'Shoot away,' he told them. 'I cannot answer a single question, because this is all rubbish.' There was no plot, he insisted.

'Think carefully,' the head of the Cheka told him. 'Tell the truth, and we will give you money and a passport, and send you secretly over the frontier.' Nazaroff repeated that there was no such plot. But in order to avoid Bolshevik persecution, a number of former Tsarist officers had fled Tashkent for the Kokand region. He admitted that he had given them money for the journey from his own bank account. That was all.

It soon became obvious to his interrogators that they were

going to get nothing out of Nazaroff. It is surprising perhaps that they did not attempt to torture this key suspect. According to Nazaroff, prisoners were regularly tortured by the Cheka, who brought in Chinese and Lettish experts to undertake this. Possibly they feared reprisals if the British did seize Tashkent, as it was strongly believed they might. Nazaroff was instead transferred from the Cheka basement to a prison cell, where he was to spend the next month in solitary confinement. At night he would listen wistfully to the migrating birds passing overhead on their way to India. He could recognise the trumpeting of the cranes, the 'honk honk' of the geese and the whistling of the waders. Nazaroff envied them their freedom, for he expected every night to be his last.

He became aware that relations between the Cheka and the more conservative prison guards were somewhat strained. To get their wishes carried out, the Cheka needed the co-operation of the guards, and they had to tread warily. The removal of a prisoner from his cell for interrogation by the Cheka made everyone nervous, including even the guards. 'Sometimes', Nazaroff recalls, 'the poor devils simply disappeared, and sometimes they came back in deplorable condition.' When a man was executed, the guards had an expression for it. So-and-so, they would say, 'does not want any more dinners'.

After his removal to a prison cell, Nazaroff's interrogations continued. One of these took an entire day, and he returned to his cell at ten o'clock that night. The guard, whom he had known as a cab driver in the town before the Revolution, looked surprised but glad to see him. 'God be praised,' he said. 'You have come back safe and sound. We were very anxious. Even in the criminal section no one went to bed, they were so worried about you.' For Paul Nazaroff was a well-known and well-liked figure in Tashkent. Educated in Moscow, where he studied zoology, and at the Petrograd Mining Institute, he had devoted much of his life to searching for minerals in the Tashkent area, often making important finds where government geologists had found nothing. He was also an authority on the flora and fauna and native peoples of Central Asia. All this was to prove invaluable to him in the months ahead.

Because the prison authorities were having difficulty in feeding so many prisoners, relatives were allowed to send in food from outside. It was always an anxious moment for them, for this was when some would be told that their husband or son would not be needing any more dinners. One day, when Nazaroff was being escorted across the prison yard for a Cheka interrogation, he saw his wife waiting at the gates with their fox terrier. 'This was the first time I had seen my wife since my arrest, so that our agitation can well be imagined,' he recalled afterwards. The dog, too, became frantic, and on subsequent visits would try to dig beneath the prison gates to get to her master. So torn did her paws become that she had to be left at home, howling with misery.

Finally, when Nazaroff's interrogation was complete, he was called before the Cheka and told the result. His story must have been convincing, for he was informed that 'no definite charges' were to be brought against him. But he was to be shot nonetheless, 'as a known enemy of the proletariat'. He was now moved from solitary confinement to cell number 22 – the death cell – where he found a number of his fellow plotters awaiting a similar fate. They had already managed, however, to organise an ingenious means of obtaining news from outside. Although all meals sent in by families were searched thoroughly by the guards, they hardly bothered to look at the rolls of native bread which arrived from the bazaar for the Muslim prisoners. Baked into some of them were secret messages. The name of the prisoner to whom one of these was addressed – only discernible to someone knowing what to look for – was pricked into the surface in Arabic letters. By this means the condemned men had learned that, following their own arrest, others had taken over the organisation of the coup.

It was extremely cheering news. But the question now in everyone's mind was whether the uprising would come in time to save them. It was clearly going to be touch and go. Preparations were not yet complete, and a date for the coup had not finally been fixed. For Nazaroff the wait was particularly harrowing, since he – according to prison gossip – would be the first to be shot. Only later did he discover the reason for the Cheka's delay in carrying this out. The advancing White Russians, it was rumoured, had by now reached a point on the Oxus only two days' march from Tashkent. At the same time the British were believed to be working their way along the railway from the west, also with Tashkent as their objective. Some of the commissars were said to be in favour of surrendering to the British, who might be expected to treat them more mercifully than the Whites, who were thirsting for their blood.

At last news was smuggled in to the anxious prisoners that the date for the uprising had been set. It would take place three days from then, on January 6, 1919, the Feast of the Epiphany. That morning the prison was to be stormed and everyone set free. Early on the day of the coup a second message reached the condemned cell to say that the prison was already secretly surrounded by White troops. The assault would take place on the stroke of ten. To pass the time, Nazaroff retired to his bed with a copy of Jules Verne's *A Voyage to the Moon* and tried to read. The tension in the cell now became unbearable as, with only minutes to go, the hands of his watch crept towards zero hour.

But at ten o'clock nothing happened. The prisoners looked in dismay at one another. Five minutes passed. Then another five. Nazaroff's spirits began to sink. At twenty past ten they all began to fear the worst. Something had gone badly wrong. Then, all of a sudden, came the sound of heavy firing. It was followed, moments later, by a loud explosion. The prison gates, Nazaroff knew in a flash, had been blown open.

4 The Executioner

The man who overthrew the Tashkent Government was himself – or so he had lulled his fellow commissars into believing – a fanatical Bolshevik. His name was Osipov, and before the Revolution he had been a junior officer in the Tsarist army. At the time of the Tashkent uprising, although still only twenty-three, he was Commissar for War.

His is hardly a name to bring up in Tashkent today, more than sixty years later, and my enquiries there revealed little else about him. But for reasons which appear to have had more to do with personal ambition than any devotion to the White Russian cause, he determined to replace the Tashkent Soviet with a regime headed by himself. To achieve this, he hit upon a plan which combined the utmost simplicity with base treachery.

From the barracks of the Second Turkestan Regiment, Osipov telephoned his fellow commissars and, with a convincing note of alarm in his voice, warned them that he had a mutiny on his hands. The only way to save the situation, not to say their own skins, was for them to come immediately to the barracks and talk to the men while there was still time.

Having no reason to suspect Osipov of treachery, eight of them hastened to the barracks where, one by one, they were shot down in cold blood as they arrived. Osipov next issued a proclamation declaring Bolshevik rule in Central Asia to be at an end. Meanwhile his supporters, who appear to have included some prominent Bolsheviks as well as White Russians, were seizing the key points of the town. The prison gates were blown open, and the prisoners, including Nazaroff, freed. In some parts of Tashkent troops and others remaining loyal to the Bolsheviks continued to resist, and fighting was to go on for at least two days. But in the meantime, in anticipation of an anti-Bolshevik victory, many people began to celebrate openly in the streets – and Osipov, according to Colonel Bailey, to get gloriously drunk.

Captain Brun describes seeing the former head of the Cheka, who had joined the counter-revolutionary cause, reading aloud Osipov's proclamation to the rejoicing crowds as he rode through Tashkent with a Cossack escort. He promised them that the tyranny of the Bolsheviks had been broken for ever (coming from him this must have struck many of his audience as ironic), and that the new government would end the bloodshed and restore stability to everyday life. But anyone attempting to oppose the government, he warned, would be shot out of hand.

Brun learned that casualties had already been heavy, and shooting could still be heard in the distance. Many positions held by the Bolsheviks had to be shelled before they could be rushed and their defenders killed. During that day, however, news continued to come in of victory after victory as Bolshevik strongholds on the outskirts of town fell one after the other.

The new government, it was said, had already established itself in the former Bolshevik stronghold, and was busy issuing decrees. Just what role Osipov was playing in this is not clear, although the official line today is that he was continuing to drink heavily. A large oil-painting depicting Osipov's treachery, which hangs in Tashkent's Museum of Art, underlines this point. It shows him slouched drunkenly in a chair while one of his henchmen armed with a revolver is disposing of the commissars as, one by one, they enter the room. On the table beside Osipov is a half-empty bottle, while lying at his feet is a second bottle, empty.

But whatever the truth, Osipov's overthrow of the Tashkent Soviet saved Nazaroff and his cell-mates from the firing squad. Only moments after hearing the prison gates being dynamited, the door of their cell burst open to reveal an officer in the uniform of the Imperial Russian Army, complete with spurs and epaulettes. It was an old friend of Nazaroff's. Saluting, he declared: 'Welcome, gentlemen. The town is in our hands. All the commissars except one were shot this morning.' The Cheka headquarters, he added with satisfaction, had been burned to the ground, together with all its files.

From the prison yard outside came the sound of cheering and rejoicing as the liberated prisoners embraced and thanked their rescuers. There Nazaroff saw a huge ape-like man being held at rifle-point against the wall, pleading for his life. He was one of the most feared and hated of the Bolsheviks, a former sailor in the Black Sea fleet called Pashko. Before coming to Tashkent, he had won notoriety as one of the leaders of the Odessa mutiny in which the sailors had tortured their officers before feeding them to the sharks. According to Nazaroff in his memoir *Hunted through Central Asia*: 'On his soul were thousands done to death, some butchered with his own hands, hundreds handed over to be tortured . . . Pashko was the real type of degenerate, half-man, half-brute, to whom the people had so light-heartedly entrusted the government at the time of the revolution.'

Nazaroff was asked whether Pashko should be shot there and then, but suggested that he be interrogated first. Making his way through the crowds and into the street, Nazaroff found himself surrounded by friends and well-wishers who congratulated him, embraced him, and kissed him. In the town, as he hurried home to his wife, he could hear the church bells ringing wildly.

But the celebrations were to prove all too premature. On the second day of the uprising, Captain Brun's orderly warned him that, far from being defeated, the Bolsheviks were fighting back strongly. They had, moreover, managed to regain the support of the railway navvies, who had briefly espoused the anti-Bolshevik cause. Armed and trained to protect the remoter stretches of the railway network from lawless tribesmen, they represented a formidable paramilitary force. They had joined the counter-revolutionaries hoping for a less extreme form of socialist rule. But when it became clear that the new government was royalist and reactionary, they quickly changed their minds. Their defection, Brun tells us, was to prove catastrophic to the counter-revolutionaries. That night the Bolsheviks managed to recapture the former Government House, and by the following morning, in the words of Paul Nazaroff, the town 'was again in the hands of the mob'. Darkness now descended over Tashkent once more as the victors unleashed a reign of terror infinitely worse than anything that had gone before.

Osipov, in the meantime, had fled. The moment he saw that the tables were being turned on him, he drove straight to the central bank and helped himself to several million roubles, much of it in gold bullion. (The unfortunate clerk who was forced at gunpoint to hand it over to him was later shot by the outraged Bolsheviks.) He then vanished in the direction of Bokhara with a handful of his followers, never to be seen or heard of again. According to one account, he is said to have escaped into Persia. But a Soviet official in Tashkent told me in 1982 that he was believed to have been killed while fighting with the *basmachi*, though nobody knew for certain.

Paul Nazaroff, having no horse or other means of transport, was unable to join those now fleeing town to escape the Bolsheviks' wrath. All he could do was go into hiding until the blood-bath was over, and then slip away. Meanwhile, the Bolsheviks were appointing new commissars to replace Osipov's victims, and setting up revolutionary tribunals to punish anyone suspected of having helped the counter-revolutionaries. Captain Brun describes what followed: 'The result was organised, wholesale murder, since these tribunals naturally recognised no other form of punishment than death, frequently without any preceding inquiry into the case. There was, as a rule, one Robespierre among the members of such a tribunal, and the rest of the members bowed to his decisions.'

Brun was writing from first-hand experience of revolutionary justice, for very shortly his own nightmare was to begin. He, like everyone else, had been warned not to leave home under any circumstances, as anyone seen on the streets would immediately be assumed to be a fugitive or counter-revolutionary. But after a few days he felt that it would be safe again to venture out and try to contact his two Swedish Red Cross colleagues. He reached the home of one of them safely, and together they set out to walk to where the other lived. This, unfortunately, took them past a police station, outside which was standing one of the new commissars, a man named Uspenski.

Spotting them, he called out: 'Comrades, who are you and what are you doing here?' Brun answered that they were two neutrals sent to look after the interests of the ex-POWs. Ignoring this, Uspenski ordered his men to detain them. When Brun protested that they were in Tashkent on the authority of the government in Moscow, and that both held diplomatic status, the commissar snapped: 'Never mind that.' Then, turning to his men, he ordered: 'Arrest them!'

Brun and his colleague – a man named Hall – were taken under armed escort to a building which had been turned into a makeshift prison and were locked in a cell already containing twenty-five other suspects. These included Johannes Kleberg, the Swede they had been on their way to visit when arrested, and a number of women. The cell was already badly overcrowded, but every now and again another Cheka victim would be added. The cell door was guarded by two soldiers with loaded rifles and fixed bayonets.

Around midnight, on their first night in captivity, Brun and Hall were awoken by Kleberg who told them that he was being released. This was very good news, since he might be able to negotiate their own release once he was out. Shaking hands with him, they wished him luck as he left with his escort. But it was the last they were ever to see of him. For instead of being freed, the unfortunate Swede was shot that night. Brun only learned of this some days later, when he also learned that such promises of freedom invariably meant an immediate appointment with the firing squad. The Bolsheviks had found that prisoners made less fuss if it was done that way.

The following day, escorted by a detachment of Red Guards,

Brun and Hall and fifteen other prisoners were marched through the snow to the barracks of the railway navvies near the station. As they entered the yard they saw several large pools of fresh blood. It required little imagination to guess its source. Brun and his fellow prisoners were now herded into a bleak, unheated barrack room with barred windows. In an ante-room, they were told, a revolutionary tribunal was sitting. Before this each of them would appear in turn.

Their cases were taken alphabetically, and Brun's was among the first to be heard. He found himself facing three revolutionary judges, one of whom spoke German. He was accused of taking part in the counter-revolution, having been seen out in the streets during Osipov's brief period of rule. Brun pointed out that there had been thousands of people out in the street. 'But you had no papers on you permitting you to walk in the streets,' the German-speaking judge told him. Brun replied that he had never heard of any such document. 'In my country', he told the court, 'everything is permitted which has not been prohibited. Here it seems to be exactly the reverse.'

Brun was told that he had committed a serious offence, even if it was done through ignorance. The tribunal would now consider its verdict. He was ordered back to the barrack room. That night was bitterly cold, for they had no blankets, only the clothes they stood up in. In the middle of the night they were awoken by the arrival of four armed Kirghiz guards and a young man wearing a blood-stained linen smock which once had been white. From this, and what now followed, it was obvious what he had come for. He called out the names of two prisoners who were promptly removed by the guards. Moments later several shots were heard from the wash-room downstairs, and later, through the barred window, Brun and Hall discerned the four Kirghiz digging graves beside the barrack wall. This same grisly ritual took place every night. Brun describes the horror of it: 'Now and again the poor victims protested most desperately, begging and beseeching their torturers to let them go. This was really the worst punishment of all – to have to witness the conduct of one's fellow-beings in their moment of abject fear, without any trace of human dignity . . . Nerves already strung up to the highest pitch suffered agonies at the sight of their craven, yet understood, fear of death.'

He and Hall were transferred from one nightmare to another when they were moved from the barrack room to a make-shift prison containing two hundred Kirghiz, all awaiting execution for bearing arms. As the Kirghiz would shortly be 'going', they were told, there would soon be plenty of room. Fully aware of their coming fate, the condemned men knew they had nothing to lose. 'Every now and again', Brun recounts, 'they made an attempt at forcing back the guard.' The soldiers broke up these attempts to escape with heavy blows from their rifle butts. It was, Brun writes, 'a ghastly scene'.

When Brun and Hall first moved into the cell, two of the Kirghiz prisoners were ill. The following day this had risen to nine, and Brun persuaded the guards to bring a doctor. One arrived, himself a prisoner, and diagnosed both cholera and typhoid among the Kirghiz. As a result Brun and Hall were moved back to the barrack room where once again they had to suffer the nightly horror of the executioner's visit, and the pathetic pleas of his victims. Finally, after ten horrifying days and nights, the tribunal delivered its verdict. Both men were to be freed. The next day, however, Brun was rearrested, this time on the orders of the young executioner, whose name was Kolgatjof. He was only saved by the prompt intervention of the Chief of Police, a man called Serul, with whom he had been on reasonably good terms since arriving in Tashkent.

Brun nonetheless had a very close shave. He had only been in his cell for an hour when the door was flung open by an anxious-looking Serul, who told him: 'I'm glad to find you still alive. You would have been dead within an hour had I not interfered.' When Brun called on him in his office the following morning to thank him, Serul told the Dane that Kolgatjof was in the habit of arresting people, and then taking them from their cells the same night and executing them. The unfortunate

Kleberg, it appears, had been one of his victims. Some years later Brun heard that the psychopathic Kolgatjof finally went mad and died a lunatic, but not before he had accounted for many more victims. Bailey credits him with more than seven hundred executions, adding that the Bolsheviks, grateful to him for doing their dirty work, gave him a special ration of wine to help him with his macabre task.

Just how many people died during the Bolsheviks' orgy of revenge following Osipov's abortive coup will never be known. No figures were ever published and it is doubtful whether any were kept. Brun put it at two thousand eight hundred, while Bailey believed it to be nearer four thousand. One woman he knew lost her husband and three sons to the executioners (for there were others besides Kolgatjof who enjoyed killing, including a number of Hungarian ex-POWs). The victims, Bailey tells us, were first taken to a large barrack room where they were stripped naked, before being shot 'in circumstances of the greatest brutality' which he declines to go into. Nor was the blood-letting confined to Tashkent. At one small town nearby, nearly one and a half thousand actual or suspected counter-revolutionaries were liquidated by the local garrison commander, according to Brun.

But the atrocities of the Bolsheviks, it must be said, were no worse than those being perpetrated by White Russian troops in areas they controlled, especially by the much-feared Cossacks. When three sealed railway wagons labelled 'fresh meat' reached Petrograd from the south, they were found to contain, in the words of a French diplomat, 'the stiffened corpses of Red Guards, covered with frozen blood . . . placed in obscene positions'.

*   *   *

For months now those Russians opposed to Bolshevik rule in Central Asia had been looking in desperation to the British for deliverance. The conspiracy originally planned by Paul Nazaroff, but ill-fatedly taken over by Osipov, aimed to link hands with General Malleson's forces advancing (or so it was generally assumed) from the west. Some Russian families were even learning English so they could welcome the liberators when they arrived.

In February 1919, however, something happened which was destined to shatter any such hopes. General Malleson received orders from India to withdraw his forces from Russian territory, and pull back to Meshed. For the war with Germany and Turkey was over, and the British army was being demobilised. They were not there to take on the Bolsheviks, however much they might have wished to. Few of Malleson's officers doubted that, given the go-ahead, they could have brushed aside any Bolshevik resistance, and liberated Tashkent in a matter of days.

But Malleson's troops had been sent into Russia to support those White units still fighting the Germans, and thus keep the latter out of Central Asia, from where they could have menaced India. The possibility of the Bolsheviks themselves posing a serious post-war threat to India from their Central Asian stronghold had not yet been fully appreciated. Nonetheless, with the civil war still at a critical stage, it was decided that Malleson could not simply walk out on his former allies, thus leaving them in the lurch. It was obvious that the moment the Bolsheviks discovered that the British were pulling out, their own forces would advance westwards to fill the vacuum. What little White Russian morale remained would collapse, and many of the demoralised soldiers would go over to the Bolsheviks. If this was to be avoided, then the withdrawal would have to be carried out in the utmost secrecy.

General Malleson, a former intelligence officer, set about the task with relish. For a start, his agents began to spread word that the British were preparing to evacuate, as ostentatiously as possible, their troops from the Ashkabad region. But this, it was whispered, was merely to conceal their real purpose – a sudden advance westwards towards the Bolshevik-held positions. Simultaneously, bogus documents which appeared to confirm these rumours were planted on known Bolshevik agents. Some of these were so convincing that they have since found their way into the archives used by Soviet historians of this period.

Intelligence reports reaching Malleson soon began to indicate that the Bolsheviks had been fooled into acting on the 'leaked' information, and were making hasty preparations for a retreat at the first hint of a British attack. The rumours had also begun to reach the ears of those praying for British deliverance, convincing many that this was now imminent. In a lecture which Malleson gave in London on his return, he told his audience: 'These stories, and many others which we put about almost daily, evidently made so great an impression on the Bolsheviks that they never attempted to advance when we did leave the front. Indeed, they had packed their baggage and sent it to the rear, while their main body at Charjui [Malleson's supposed first objective] lived in a state of nervous apprehension for many weeks.'

In Tashkent, meanwhile, the Bolsheviks had at last granted permission for Brun, Hall and Tredwell, the American consul, to leave for Petrograd by the newly reopened rail link. The journey was to take them a month. The American consul had been held under house arrest ever since his friend Bailey had slipped through the fingers of the Cheka, four or five months earlier. But he had not on the whole been molested – except for one very close shave. During the blood-bath following Osipov's abortive uprising, he had been taken forcibly from his house and thrown into prison. His abductors told him that he was to be shot the following morning. Shortly before this was due to take place, he heard the tramp of boots outside his cell, and assumed that his last minute had come. But it had turned out to be Serul, the police chief, on another of his eleventh-hour rescue missions.

What neither Tredwell nor, for that matter, Bailey knew at that time was that General Malleson had seized three senior Bolshevik officials as hostages against their safe return. On being informed of this, the Tashkent commissars had telegraphed an angry protest to the British Indian Government insisting that they were not holding Bailey. 'He has disappeared,' the telegram declared. 'It is not known where.' Nor had Tredwell been arrested. He was merely 'interned in his own rooms', on Moscow's orders. Nonetheless, the Tashkent Soviet was prepared to make an offer. It would trade Tredwell for their own three men. But Delhi was not interested in this three-for-one offer. They wanted Bailey back. They only had the Bolsheviks' word for it that he had disappeared. Nothing had been heard from him for weeks. For all anyone knew, he might have been shot.

Then Malleson signalled news of a development which put paid to any question of a deal. The three hostages had asked for political asylum. None of them, he advised Delhi, 'would return to Bolshevik territory for any consideration whatever'. Indeed, one of them had asked to join the White Russian cause. He was promptly despatched there – only to be unceremoniously shot by his would-be friends. The Bolsheviks nonetheless continued to press for the return of the two surviving hostages in exchange for Tredwell.

What finally induced them to let Tredwell go, without getting anything in return, is not clear, although it is possible that it was ordered by Moscow in the hope that the gesture might help to win American recognition for the new regime. But seven months later, long after Tredwell's safe return home, the Tashkent Bolsheviks were still pressing for the return of the two surviving hostages, this time offering to exchange them for 'two British officers taken prisoner on the Ashkabad front'. Asked about this by Delhi, Malleson signalled back: 'As no British officers of this force taken prisoner, and nothing known of any others, suggest asking Bolsheviks by wireless to state where and when captured and names and units.' Nothing more was heard, and that is where the saga of the hostages ended. Possibly by then Tashkent had learned of the unwillingness of their own two officials to return.

Having survived their various nightmares, Tredwell, Brun

and Hall were now safely out of danger. This left only Bailey unaccounted for. What had been happening to him all this time? By now he had become the subject of growing concern in Delhi and London. 'We can only hope', observed one senior official of the Political Department in a secret minute, 'that he is making his way through the mountains towards Kashgar or India.' To this John Shuckburgh, Bailey's immediate chief, added anxiously: 'I am very uneasy as to the fate of this valuable and intrepid officer.'

He could have spared himself the worry. For Bailey, a Great Game player to his fingertips, was in his very element.

5 Hunted

When Colonel Bailey, in the field-grey uniform of the enemy, walked away from his unsuspecting Cheka shadows on the evening of October 20, 1918, he embarked on a series of adventures whose bizarre climax even John Buchan might have thought far-fetched. Bailey himself, with characteristic modesty, has told the story of those fourteen months on the run in *Mission to Tashkent*. But even today, so many years later, we do not know the entire truth about his activities behind Bolshevik lines. And with himself, Nazaroff and other witnesses now dead, it is unlikely that we ever shall. However Soviet historians, as will be seen, have no such doubts.

The last glimpse the Bolsheviks got of Bailey on the night of his disappearance was of him entering one of a row of houses in a quiet residential street, in front of which his shadows took up their positions while awaiting his emergence. Once inside and out of sight, Bailey moved fast, his lightning change of clothes and nationality taking only moments. 'I tore off my overcoat, pulled on the Austrian tunic and kepi which were lying ready on the hall table, tucked the trousers into the boots, wrapped my overcoat around the civilian hat, and taking these with me dashed out into the garden.'

From the garden of the first house he ran into the next, and so on. One of the connecting doors between two of the gardens was locked, but 'a couple of good kicks' saw to that. A minute or so later, in the first of the many disguises he was to adopt in the coming months, Bailey emerged from a house at the far end of the row and, unrecognised by his Cheka shadows, sauntered off into the darkness.

Shortly afterwards, growing bored, the Cheka men decided to repair briefly to the nearest *chai-khana*, or tea-house, for refreshment. When on their return to their posts Bailey failed to emerge, they assumed that he must have left and gone home during their absence. They decided to do likewise, and thus it was not until the following morning that his disappearance became known.

It is not recorded what became of his shadows, but the Bolsheviks immediately began to turn the town upside down in their frantic hunt for him. A night's start would have given their quarry time to get well clear of Tashkent, and to encourage this belief Bailey had arranged for it to be leaked in the appropriate quarter that he was making a dash for the frontier, hoping to reach Kashgar. Nevertheless, the Cheka painstakingly searched every house he had ever visited – or at least the ones they knew about – and questioned everyone known to have had contact with him. A price was put on his head, and shortly afterwards one local newspaper reported that he had been arrested in Samarkand and was being brought back to Tashkent under escort.

But after a while the hue and cry began to die down. The Cheka, Bailey learned later, had come to the conclusion that he must either have got clean away or been disposed of by the Germans who – with the war still on at that time – had good reason for wishing him out of the way. The evidence for the latter, it seems, rested on the fact that he had disappeared without his toothbrush. This, the Bolsheviks felt, no Englishman would ever do. In fact, he happened to have two.

Bailey, all this time, was still in Tashkent, hiding under his pursuers' very noses. The town just then was full of wanted men and women, and those who hid them took a dire risk. Bailey, still in his guise as an Austrian prisoner, was being sheltered by a family called Lebideff – in his book he calls them Mateveev, to protect them from possible reprisals, even though twenty-eight years were to pass before it was published. Although omitted from the book for the same reason, a snapshot of their house taken by Bailey, together with one of a later sanctuary, is to be found in an album of his now in the India Office Library.

It shows a yellow-washed, single-storey building of Russian colonial style, fronted by poplars. Since those times street names have been changed, and much of Tashkent razed by an earthquake, thus thwarting any attempt to locate the house today.

In case of a sudden raid, the Lebideffs had prepared a secret hide-out for Bailey under the floorboards, with food and water always there, but this was never required. His face was by now well known in Tashkent, so to reduce the risk of recognition he shaved off his Indian Army moustache and ran hair-clippers over his head. Then, to simulate the appearance of the average Austrian ex-POW, he let his beard, moustache and hair grow again from scratch. His 'borrowed' Austrian passport named him as Andre Kekeshi, a professional cook.

Recalling the advice of Peter Pienaar, the veteran Boer tracker in one of Buchan's early novels, he set about adopting Austrian habits and forgetting his own. He hoped thus, when he emerged from hiding, to be able to melt anonymously into the mass of uniformed ex-POWs who formed so large a part of Tashkent's white population. He learned to click his heels, and to don his trench-coat, if not the Austrian way, at least the way he had noticed the Russians do it. He could not quite remember how the Austrians got into theirs, but thought he would be less conspicuous if he adopted the local way.

'It was a comparatively simple matter to pretend to be an Austrian prisoner,' he declared nonchalantly afterwards. With such a variety of nationalities and languages represented among the prisoners, if one did run into an Austrian 'one could always pretend to belong to one of the other nationalities.' Both Rumania and Albania were thus, at different times, to acquire him as a son, while to explain his knowledge of English he invented a year he had spent working in America before the war. It was while he was being sheltered by the Lebideffs that he was visited, at great personal risk, by Miss Houston, the Irish governess to the Russian family with whom the American consul was lodging. She brought with her a badly needed extra pair of boots and spare clothing which she had managed to remove from his house without detection.

Concern for Bailey's safety was now acute among his chiefs in Delhi and Whitehall, as still nothing was heard from him. Telegrams passed frequently between them seeking word of him, but none was forthcoming from any source. They were certainly not alone in their anxiety. On November 21, a month after his disappearance, and ten days after the signing of the Armistice bringing World War I to an end, Bailey's widowed mother wrote to John Shuckburgh enquiring about her son's safety. 'I know he has been sent on a special mission by the Government of India,' she wrote. 'I do not ask where he is, nor the nature of his mission, but . . . I am naturally very anxious about him, and fear that he is too remote for news of the cessation of the war to reach him.' She had heard nothing from him for more than three months, she added.

Shuckburgh was in no position to help her, but two weeks later, still without news, she tried once more. 'I feel almost ashamed to trouble you again, but I am so very anxious about him,' she wrote diffidently, adding: 'He has been in many a tight hole and extricated himself, but I fear circumstances must be beyond him now.' The last message from her son, she said, had been more worrying than reassuring. Unsigned, and three weeks old, it simply stated: 'Nothing I can write, but things are pretty interesting here for us.' Mrs Bailey added apprehensively: 'When we know what that word implies these days, you will scarcely wonder at my great anxiety.'

Meanwhile, just six days before the signing of the Armistice, Bailey had left Tashkent driving a hay-cart, feeling somewhat self-conscious in his alien grey uniform. His immediate purpose was to try to discover how much support Malleson could expect from the anti-Bolshevik forces in the area. Little did he know that the general had been ordered to pull back into Persia. He himself had no illusions about the Bolsheviks. He had already seen enough of them to perceive the threat they would pose to British India. Yet to topple them in Central Asia, he knew, would have taken very little. It seemed to him inconceivable that Malleson's force was not preparing to do just that.

But without news or instructions from Delhi or London, Bailey could merely guess what British Government policy was towards the Bolsheviks – a task made no easier by the fact that there *was* no policy. Malleson's defeat of Bolshevik forces near Ashkabad, and the landing of British troops at Archangel, appeared to confirm Britain's interventionist intent. Added to this were the rumours, put about by Malleson's own agents, of his coming advance on Tashkent. So convincing were these that even Damagatsky, the Commissar for Foreign Affairs, had begun to put out discreet feelers about obtaining political asylum.

In a secret report to his chiefs on his return, many months later, Bailey wrote: 'I could, I believed, give a good deal of useful information to the force in Transcaspia which I believed to be advancing on Tashkent.' This, it appears, had been his intention from the moment he learned from an angry Damagatsky that Malleson's troops had crossed into Russia and engaged Bolshevik forces. In other words he would gather intelligence while continuing his negotiations with the Tashkent Soviet, only going underground when Malleson began his thrust. He would then make his way through Bolshevik lines to join up with him, armed with the intelligence he had gathered. In readiness, he says, he had made 'the necessary preparations' to disappear, including obtaining the uniform and papers of Andre Kekeshi, the Austrian POW, and concealing these.

He had been equally prepared, however, to jump the other way. Were relations with the Bolsheviks to improve, then he hoped that he might be accepted, like Tredwell, as the diplomatic representative of his government. He had done his best therefore to maintain polite and formal relations with Kolesov and Damagatsky. But all this had been overtaken by orders from Moscow for his arrest.

Nor was this all that he revealed to his chiefs in his seventeen-page secret report. 'Soon after my arrival,' he wrote, 'I got in touch with what I judged to be the chief of several anti-Bolshevik organisations.' While a White Russian general was its nominal head, Paul Nazaroff was its 'real organiser'. In his report, which he never expected the Bolsheviks to see, he discloses that he supplied Nazaroff with funds. Verification of this can be found in the India Office archives, where I came across a secret message from Bailey, smuggled out to Kashgar, requesting Colonel Etherton to pass 200,000 rupees (£15,000) to Nazaroff's agent there.

None of this is so much as hinted at in Bailey's published narrative. This omission was deliberate – to deny the Soviets, ever on the look-out for the hand of the British secret service in their affairs, evidence of just that. Bailey, nonetheless, has always been denounced by Soviet historians as a British master-spy sent, under cover of a bogus diplomatic mission, to try to topple Bolshevik rule in Central Asia. His accomplices, they claim, were Tredwell, who was really an American agent, and counter-revolutionaries and others like Nazaroff and Osipov. However, they had no real evidence for such claims.

But then, in 1970, a Soviet researcher working on the Indian National Archives in Delhi stumbled on a copy of Bailey's long-forgotten, top-secret report, which had been declassified under the fifty-year rule. Here at last, Soviet historians proclaimed in triumph, were the mission leader's own confessions of what he had really been up to. This was true, although all those years later it hardly seemed to matter. But to the Soviets it did. His report proved, they claimed, that after going into hiding Bailey had 'actively continued his anti-Soviet activity and prepared the Turkestan counter-revolution for revolt'. By that they meant something which they had always maintained – that Bailey was the mastermind behind the Osipov uprising. It is hardly surprising if Bailey's name is not one to use lightly in Tashkent today – even though, for reasons which will shortly become apparent, he was in no position to play any part in Osipov's abortive *coup*.

But to return to Bailey himself as, at the reins of his hay-cart, he rode undetected out of town and up into the hills some sixty miles away. Here it had been arranged that he would hide in an isolated bee-farm owned by counter-revolutionary contacts of his. His intention was to try to make contact from here with the *basmachi*, the fanatically anti-Bolshevik Muslim guerrillas headed by Kurbashi Irgash, a local chieftain. Some 20,000 of them were said to be massed in the Ferghana Valley region, to the south-east, eagerly awaiting the opportunity to wreak violent revenge on the Bolsheviks for their brutal sacking of Kokand. If Bailey could reach Irgash, he would be able to gauge the strength of his forces, and size up his worth as an ally, were Malleson to advance on Tashkent.

At the bee-farm, which was soon to be further isolated by heavy snowfalls, Bailey found other counter-revolutionaries in hiding, including General Kondratovich, the nominal head of Nazaroff's anti-Bolshevik conspiracy. He, it appears, had managed to escape when the Cheka stumbled on the plot and rounded up most of the conspirators, including Nazaroff himself (who at that moment was still awaiting execution in Tashkent, for this was before the Osipov uprising). From his fellow fugitives Bailey learned that the Bolsheviks had sealed all the approaches to the *basmachi*-held Ferghana region to prevent any contact between Irgash and the counter-revolutionaries who had escaped arrest. To attempt to reach Irgash alone, over unfamiliar terrain, would have been dangerous, even for a veteran Asiatic explorer like Bailey, so he arranged for a courier to take a message from him through the mountains to Irgash, hoping that a *basmachi* guide might be sent to escort him past the Bolshevik patrols. But some twelve days later the courier returned with bad news. All approaches to Ferghana were impassable, with Bolshevik patrols and look-outs everywhere. Any attempt to run the gauntlet would clearly be madness.

It was while Bailey was at the bee-farm that he received a message from Tredwell, by then under house arrest in Tashkent, to say that the war was over, and had been for over a month. It was strongly rumoured, moreover, that under the peace settlement Russia's Central Asian territories were to be ceded to Britain for twenty-five years, together with the Caucasus. Bailey decided to return at once to Tashkent where at least he could discover what was happening. Stuck up there in the hills, although safe from the Bolsheviks, he would be of little use to anyone. Snow had now begun to fall heavily and there was a serious risk of being trapped there until the spring. But first it was necessary, by means of a courier, to arrange for somewhere to hide in Tashkent. It was while he was awaiting word of this that misfortune struck him.

He was out hunting wild boar for the communal larder when he slipped badly in the snow and glissaded nearly one hundred yards down a mountainside, dislocating one leg and injuring the other. There was now no question of his travelling to Tashkent until he was able to walk again, or at least ride. This, a Turki doctor told him, would not be for several weeks, during which time he must remain immobile.

But then, barely two weeks later, a warning reached the bee-farm that the Bolsheviks had somehow got wind of their presence there. Despite his injuries, Bailey had no choice but to get away as quickly as possible before the Bolsheviks raided the farm. His fellow-fugitives managed to carry him for two miles through four feet of snow to the nearest point which could be reached by pony. But when they got there they found no ponies, and the small party had to struggle slowly on to a tiny meteorological station run by an Austrian ex-POW at the hamlet of Yusuf Khana. A sledge should have been there to take Bailey to Tashkent, but for some reason the driver had not waited.

It was as a result of this series of accidents that Bailey was not in Tashkent at the time of the Osipov uprising, when proper professional leadership might have tipped the balance in favour of the counter-revolutionaries. But with his injured legs, Bailey's effectiveness would obviously have been greatly restricted. As he wrote years later: 'I might have been able to influence the issue in some way, or I might equally have been shot along with Kleberg and the other four thousand in the reprisal which followed Osipov's failure.'

So much then for Soviet claims that Bailey played a major role in the uprising, today officially referred to as 'the January events'. In fact, it was not until he reached the village of Troitskoe, some fifteen miles out of Tashkent, that he first got wind of it. (At least in Tashkent they now have Bailey's version, even if it suits them to disbelieve it, for recently I presented the Historical Museum there with a copy of his book which they knew of but had never seen.) That some kind of trouble was brewing became evident when a detachment of Red Army troops arrived in the village and began a house-to-house search for illegal arms. Hurriedly, Bailey snatched up his few possessions, including his camera and notebooks, and hid them by the river bank. He then busied himself watering the pony belonging to his host. A few moments later he noticed that several of the soldiers were pointing to him. They were clearly asking who he was. His host explained that he was an ex-POW who worked for him. This appeared to satisfy them, for the soldiers moved on to the next house.

When the soldiers had left the village, Bailey and his host set off by sledge for Tashkent, unaware that heavy fighting was going on there. But before they had gone very far they met people who had been turned back, as well as others fleeing the town. Bailey, being anxious to know what was happening in Tashkent, pressed hurriedly on. As he and his companion, an anti-Bolshevik, got closer to the outskirts of the town they heard the rumble of artillery and angry sound of small-arms fire. Finally they were warned by people they met on the road that it was impossible to enter town. Red troops were checking everyone's papers, and either arresting them or turning them back. Still hampered by his injured legs, Bailey realised that it would be madness to try to elude the checkpoint. He decided reluctantly to return to Troitskoe for the night and await developments there.

The next day the sound of gunfire could be heard getting

closer. The fighting was evidently spreading. But then the following day it suddenly ceased, as the counter-revolution collapsed, although Bailey only discovered this after Osipov had fled and it was all over. The campaign of revenge and terror which ensued made it impossible for him to leave Troitskoe. During the next few days truck-loads of Bolshevik troops passed through the village in pursuit of Osipov and other fugitives. Fighting seemed to be going on to the east still, and Bailey saw lorries carrying Red Army wounded returning to Tashkent.

One night a commissar from another town stayed the night in the house where he was sheltering. His boasts about what he did to counter-revolutionaries he caught, and how he could always spot them, made Bailey feel somewhat uncomfortable as they shared a bowl of soup together, and later slept on the floor under the same quilt. He asked Bailey for the number of his regiment and what nationality he was. Bailey explained that he was a Rumanian serving in a Hungarian unit – the 32nd regiment – which he knew had Rumanians in it. Luckily the questioning went no further, but it was merely one of many close shaves he was to experience during his months on the run.

While sheltering at Troitskoe he learned that very shortly after he and his companions had left the bee-farm it had been raided by Red Army troops, and their host, its owner, killed in the ensuing shoot-out. By the middle of February the blood-letting and other reprisals appeared to be over, and Bailey felt that it would be safe for him to travel to Tashkent. To have attempted this any earlier would have been too risky and would have exposed the Lebideffs, who had agreed to shelter him again, to unnecessary danger. Hitching a lift on a cart for part of the way, he walked the rest on legs which had still not fully recovered. He was relieved to find that the bridge leading into town was now guarded only at night.

The Lebideffs were delighted to see him again. Having heard nothing from him for many weeks, they had feared that he must be dead. They told him that at the time of the uprising, General Kondratovich, with whom he had shared the bee-farm for a while, had been sheltering under their roof. Osipov's supporters had come to him and begged him to direct the counter-revolution. But he had refused, and the Lebideffs had turned him out of the house. Bailey later heard that he had made his peace with the Bolsheviks.

Meanwhile the White Russian forces, having missed their opportunity of overturning the Tashkent Soviet, were regrouping in the hills a hundred miles or so to the east, preparing for what would turn out to be their last stand. Paul Nazaroff, Bailey's principal contact among the anti-Bolsheviks, with whom he had now lost touch, had been unable to escape with the fleeing Whites it will be recalled, and had been forced into hiding once more. The Cheka had been quick to discover that this most dangerous and wanted man was still in Tashkent. During his six days there, no fewer than seventeen checks were made on the house in which he was being hidden. From his own description it sounds as though it was the courageous Lebideffs who were harbouring him, although, like Bailey, he is careful not to identify them. Not only does he mention that a British officer had been in hiding there, but also that a bolt-hole had been prepared beneath the floorboards, its entrance concealed by a chest of drawers.

But Nazaroff knew that it was only a matter of time before they found him. He decided therefore to take his life in his hands, and walk boldly out of town. One evening, armed with false papers and in disguise, he strolled casually past the Red Army checkpoint. To his relief he was not stopped, and he walked on, unrecognised, to the home of a friend living just outside the town. His aim now was to try to reach the White Russian forces to the east. He wrote long afterwards: 'I little thought that I was setting forth on a long and distant odyssey which would take me right across Central Asia, to the mysterious land of Tibet, and over the Himalayas to the plains of Hindustan.' He still believed that, with the aid of the British, the Bolsheviks could be dislodged from Russian Central Asia, and that he had a major organisational role to play in the crusade.

Nazaroff remained with his friend for a week, in constant fear of a Cheka raid, while all day long convoys of Red Army troops and cavalry streamed past the house. From there he rode on a borrowed horse across the frozen bogs and snowfields to his next sanctuary, the home of a wealthy Kirghiz friend. During Nazaroff's years of wandering through Central Asia as a geologist, he had won the respect and friendship of the Muslim peoples, whose languages and customs he understood. This was to serve him in good stead now he was on the run.

His Kirghiz host, who had thought him long dead, asked Nazaroff what brought him there. 'I am going shooting in the mountains,' the Russian told him. But later, when they were alone, the Kirghiz insisted: 'Tell me the truth. You are not going shooting . . . you have neither gun nor dog with you.' Nazaroff, knowing that he could trust his friend, confessed that he was fleeing from the Bolsheviks, for whom he knew the Kirghiz had no love. Their rule had brought terror and famine and appalling disruption to everyday life. Nazaroff, as a fugitive from them, had to be helped.

The next morning his host rode off to the bazaar to make enquiries among fellow Kirghiz down from the mountains. He returned late that evening, on foot and greatly distressed. Bolshevik soldiers had robbed him of his horse, his thick fur coat, his hat and even his whip. 'The whole road', he reported, 'is crammed with Red troops advancing against the Whites. They are helping themselves to horses, clothing and anything they want.' Clearly it would be impossible, in these circumstances, for Nazaroff to get through to his friends in the mountains. They had, it appeared, withdrawn to a remote valley whose sole approach was now in Bolshevik hands. Nazaroff would have to stay put until things quietened down, and it was safe for him to continue on his journey. But he could not remain with the nomadic Kirghiz. Their life was too open, and word of a stranger among them would quickly reach the ears of the Cheka, whose spies were everywhere.

'You would be safer with the Sarts,' they told him. The Sarts, like the Kirghiz, were Muslims. But they had long ago abandoned the nomadic life to settle in permanent homes in villages and towns. Their homes and family life were secluded, unlike the Kirghiz. Doors and gates were kept locked and no one would dare to enter their homes uninvited. Like the Kirghiz, however, they had suffered greatly at the hands of the Bolsheviks. To them, even Tsarist rule, for all its shortcomings, was preferable to the anarchy and blood-letting which now reigned.

Before long an enormous Sart named Akbar arrived – 'a fine looking man with a small black beard, piercing clever eyes and an enigmatic expression', Nazaroff observed. He was asked whether he would be willing to shelter the Russian. He nodded. Then, addressing Nazaroff, he said: 'I will hide you in my home. I am accustomed to sheltering those who are being pursued. I detest Bolsheviks – children of Satan! – and am glad to be of service to men of the days of the Tsar. I have heard a lot about you and am glad to help you.'

That night, when everyone was asleep, and led by a Kirghiz, Nazaroff rode through a snowstorm to the primitive smallholding where his new host lived with his son and their various wives and children. Nazaroff was acutely aware of the rare privilege being extended to him, and was profoundly grateful for it. 'It has seldom, if ever,' he wrote afterwards, 'fallen to the lot of a European in Turkestan to live in a purely Mohammedan home and see the intimate life of a Sart family.'

He looked around the humble dwelling with keen interest. There was no glass in the windows and the door fitted only loosely. It was intensely cold, the only heat coming from a glowing charcoal fire. The floor was of mud, the walls plastered with clay and the ceiling made from rushes. The only carpets were a few pieces of dirty felt, while two large wooden boxes represented the sole pieces of furniture. The one source of illumination was a small oil-lamp which gave off a feeble yellow glow. Nazaroff, used as he was to roughing it in the wilds, was aghast at the prospect of living in these conditions, though he managed to conceal his dismay from his host.

The family did their best to make him feel welcome, but were careful not to ask him any questions about himself. 'They knew perfectly well', he wrote afterwards, 'who they had invited into their home, and to what danger they had exposed the whole family by so doing.' Before retiring to bed that night, everyone gave him one of their blankets, while a quilt was taken out of one of the large boxes for this special guest. Lastly Akbar told him to sleep without worrying. If anyone were to come looking for him, he said, 'I would slit his throat.'

During the daylight hours it was too dangerous for Nazaroff to leave the house and walk in the small yard. Because of his height he could be seen easily over the top of the wall. He could thus only stretch his legs at night, for the house faced directly onto the poplar-lined highway, along which passed a continuous stream of military traffic. Not far away, moreover, was a Russian village. As Nazaroff read and re-read the two geological works he had seized before fleeing, he could hear the jingle of cavalry and the oaths and revolutionary songs of the Red troops. Often, too, he listened to the plaintive tolling of the church bell in the village, as yet another victim of the fighting was buried in the frozen earth.

In the evenings the women of the house would ask Nazaroff what he believed was going to happen. When would the British arrive, and when they did, would everything be as before? Would there once again be cotton on sale in the bazaar, and needles and thread? These were questions that Nazaroff would have dearly liked to have been able to answer, but, cut off now from all news, he could not even hazard a guess.

Despite the cold, the women walked about the house barefooted. Their clothes were old and falling to pieces. They wore nothing but a *khalat*, the loose gown of Central Asia, with shirt and baggy trousers and no underclothes. On washing days the children wandered about naked while their only clothes were washed and dried. Even the youngest of the family, still a baby, sat naked in the snow in the yard as his only shirt was washed.

Amazingly none of them became ill.

One day, Akbar was telling Nazaroff about a mysterious lake he knew of, surrounded by mountains and not marked on any map. A hunter's paradise, it teemed with leopards, tigers, bears and ibex, while it was also rich in every kind of mineral, including gold. Sometimes, he told Nazaroff, they had washed a whole pound of gold there in a week, adding: 'No Russians know of it. When they drive the Bolsheviks out, you will ride up there with me and I will show you this beautiful place.' As he spoke, his wife suddenly burst into the room, quickly blowing out the light. Two suspicious-looking men, she warned, were standing by the gate and peering at the house. By the time Akbar had leapt to his feet and gone to look, both men had vanished.

But some days later a native policeman approached Akbar in the bazaar, and told him that they had information that he was hiding a Russian in his house. He hotly denied this, and managed to buy the man off with a hundred roubles. 'I will tell the chief there is nobody at your place,' he promised Akbar. After this close shave, Akbar insisted on moving Nazaroff to another room on the far side of the yard, which had no windows and was partly below ground-level. Reading now became quite impossible. As the days passed in this semi-prison, Nazaroff's spirits began to sink. The Cheka noose seemed to be getting tighter, as scare followed scare, and the prospects of his joining the counter-revolutionaries in the hills grew ever remoter.

Then, shortly before Easter 1919, word reached Akbar that an intensive search of all homes in the Tashkent area was to be carried out by Cheka officers and soldiers. Every village would be sealed off while each house was combed from top to bottom. On the Wednesday Akbar returned with the news that this systematic manhunt would begin the following morning. Already the troops were being moved into position for it. 'The search was clearly meant for me,' wrote Nazaroff afterwards. With troops patrolling every road and guarding every bridge, his chances of getting away this time seemed remote.

Suddenly Akbar had a brainwave. He would wall Nazaroff in. The Russian had little choice but to accept. Akbar explained that he and his son would fill in the door of his tiny cell with bricks, plaster it with mud, rub it over with dust, and finally smoke it with a lamp. 'It will look just like an old wall,' he assured Nazaroff. 'No one will ever guess that there is a room behind it.' Having provided him with food and water, they then proceeded to brick him in. Nazaroff could hear the muffled voices of Akbar and his son as they worked.

The arrival of the Bolsheviks was accompanied by the sound of heavy boots and oaths. Nazaroff waited grimly as the house was turned upside down. The children were asked whether there was a Russian hidden anywhere. But they had been well briefed, and they shook their heads and swore they had seen no one. Satisfied that Nazaroff was not there, the soldiers finally left. Only when Akbar was certain that the last of the soldiers had left the village, and would not be returning, did he demolish the false wall and free Nazaroff, who crawled out into the fresh air, blinking at the daylight but relieved to be alive. It had seemed like an eternity in his claustrophobic cell, but Akbar's quick thinking had undoubtedly saved his life.

That Easter, after dark, Nazaroff climbed alone onto the roof and listened to the distant church bells, remembering with sadness happier years when he and his family had celebrated this great Russian festival together. He knew that his family would be thinking of him that night and praying for him, wondering where he was and whether he was still alive. He was touched to learn later that Sarts living near his home, fearing him to be dead, had held a Muslim requiem to his memory. His wife had been so overcome by their tears that she too had found herself weeping, despite the fact that by then she had received word secretly that he was safe. To have admitted this would have endangered him, although an old Sart fortune-teller, after consulting some pebbles, declared that Nazaroff was still alive and hiding with a Sart family.

But soon the strains of sharing their tiny and already crowded home with a fugitive, let alone the risks this involved, began to tell on Akbar's family. Finally, after a violent quarrel with her husband, one of his daughters-in-law threatened to go to the Cheka and inform on Nazaroff. Fearing that she might carry out her threat, Akbar advised Nazaroff to leave while there was time. So it was that he was driven to embark on what he later described as 'the life of a hunted animal'.

Ever on the move, with the Cheka perpetually on his trail, Nazaroff was to sleep often in the forest, and at other times in the homes of sympathetic Kirghiz families. He was to suffer great hardship as he wandered across Turkestan, totally isolated from his family and friends, and cut off from all news of what was happening elsewhere in Russia during the closing stages of the Civil War. At one time he managed to obtain false papers which described him as one Nikolai Novikoff, an itinerant bee-merchant. These authorised him to travel through the mountains with his strange charges, and Nazaroff was soon to be seen riding at the head of a caravan of six camels laden with humming bee-hives. In one village, two Red Army soldiers incautiously approached him, intending to question him. But Nazaroff warned them sharply: 'Comrades, do not come too close. If the bees escape they will certainly sting you.' The soldiers hastily backed away, and Nazaroff went on his way unmolested.

As the weeks and months passed, and he failed to make contact with the scattered White forces, he came to realise that theirs was a lost cause. The only course open to him now was to try to evade the Soviet border guards and slip through the mountains into China. From there he would try to reach Kashgar, where he had heard that the Russian community still remained loyal to the Tsarist cause, and the Imperial Russian flag still flew proudly over the Consulate-General.

Eventually, in the summer of 1920, after being turned back at his first attempt by the Chinese border guards, Nazaroff succeeded in giving them the slip and making his way to Kashgar, where he was safe from Cheka vengeance after so many months on the run. It was not to last, however, and eventually he was forced to move on once more. But at least he was able to catch up with the news. General Malleson's force, he learned, far from advancing on Tashkent, had crossed back into Persia, allowing the Bolsheviks to consolidate their hold on the Tsar's former Central Asian territories. This process had been expedited by the withdrawal of the Cossacks from Orenburg, enabling the rail link with European Russia to be reopened and Red Army reinforcements to be rushed in, thus tilting the scales in the Bolshevik's favour. On top of that, the ill-conceived and half-hearted Allied intervention in the Civil War had ended ignominiously with the evacuation of all their forces, except for the Japanese in Siberia. By the time Nazaroff reached Kashgar, therefore, the White armies had been smashed, and the Civil War was all but over.

But for one man the drama was anything but finished. Still on the run from the Cheka, and out of touch with his government, Colonel Bailey was now on his own, wondering how on earth he was going to get home.

6 Bailey Joins the Soviet Secret Service

On the night that Paul Nazaroff stood in the darkness on the roof of Akbar's home listening wistfully to the sound of the Easter bells, Bailey had attended midnight mass in Tashkent's packed Orthodox cathedral. For a man wanted by the Cheka, it was an act of extraordinary daring, if not recklessness. To take such a risk under the very noses of his pursuers he must have felt supremely confident about his disguise. So far from home, he must, like Nazaroff, have experienced a pang of sadness on this most family of occasions. If so he does not tell us, for that was not in Bailey's nature, yet something other than bravado must have driven him there that night. Years later, in a rare moment of emotion, he concedes: 'It was a moving ceremony.' It proved, moreover, that 'the shocking and revolting posters condemning religion', which the Bolsheviks had plastered everywhere, had had little effect.

The service was conducted by the Bishop of Tashkent, a man greatly loved and admired, who was shortly afterwards to be executed by the Bolsheviks. As midnight approached, the bishop led the long procession of icon-bearing worshippers into the candle-lit cathedral for the great climax. The congregation, Bailey tells us, was in a state of intense fervour. 'As the clock struck midnight,' he writes, 'everyone in the church kissed those near them, saying *Kristos Voskress*.' It means 'Christ is risen'. To this they answered '*Vo istinu Voskress*', or 'He is indeed risen'.

The bishop, in his jewelled robes, then moved forward to the altar steps where the huge congregation filed past, everyone receiving an embrace and a kiss from him. Because of the risk of someone recognising him as he walked back from the altar, Bailey did not join them. By now he had undergone four changes of identity. On returning to Tashkent from the bee-farm, he had found to his embarrassment that Andre Kekeshi, the Austrian cook whose identity he had assumed, was still very much alive and had been greatly inconvenienced by being without his passport. So, briefly, he became one Vladimir Kuzimovich, a Galician ex-POW. But as such he would have been able to speak fluent Russian, so a day or two later, he managed to acquire another passport, that of a Rumanian officer named Georgi Chuka. It then transpired that Chuka, too, was still alive. For a brief spell, black-market passports being in very short supply, Bailey became a Lett, a civilian named Justus whose papers showed him to have lived in Tash-kent for fourteen years. As such he would not only have spoken Russian, but would be known to many people in town. Worse, his papers showed him to be seventy-five, although this was successfully altered to forty-five while a more suitable identity was found. Finally, he became a Rumanian again, one Joseph Lazar, a coachman in civilian life. 'I could pass for a Rumanian prisoner with a smattering of German', Bailey recounts, 'with-out the likelihood of a Rumanian being at hand to show that I was a fraud.' For there were comparatively few Rumanians among the ex-POW community.

At times the hunt for those on the run became so intense that Bailey was forced to sleep in a different house each night, although, as usual, he makes light of the continual dangers he faced. Once, by ill-chance, he found himself at the barber's shop occupying the next chair to one of the Cheka officers who had arrested him the previous year. By this time, like many of the prisoners, he had discarded his well-worn uniform and taken to wearing Russian civilian clothing. In addition, he now sported a pair of pince-nez.

Most people in such circumstances would have been content simply to survive. But not so Bailey. For some time he had been sending, by an assortment of secret couriers, detailed intelli-gence reports on the situation in Central Asia to Etherton in Kashgar and General Malleson in Meshed. As it happened, none of these messages – written in invisible ink and in code, and sent at great personal risk – had reached its destination. At least one of Bailey's couriers had been caught and shot. The rest had just disappeared. Bailey had no way of knowing whether his messages were getting through or not, having heard nothing from either Etherton or Malleson for months. This was not for want of trying on Etherton's part. Two of his couriers had been shot by the Bolsheviks, while four others had never been heard of again.

At last, on July 6, 1919, one of Bailey's couriers succeeded in reaching Kashgar with a message concealed on him. It had been sent nearly a month previously, but word that her son was apparently alive and well was immediately relayed to Bailey's much relieved mother, as Shuckburgh's neat hand records on his file. Owing to difficulty in making Bailey's invisible message become visible – a schoolboy-like process involving applying ammonia to the paper – there was a slight delay in decoding it, for some sentences were so faint as to be virtually indecipherable. But the report contained intelligence of considerable importance, not to say concern, to Bailey's chiefs in London and Delhi.

A group of Indian revolutionaries, he warned, sworn to the overthrow of British rule in India, had arrived in Tashkent and, with Bolshevik assistance, begun to disseminate anti-British propaganda. They were currently busy preparing inflammatory pamphlets and other literature in a number of languages, the purpose of which was to spread the gospel of Lenin beyond Russia's Asiatic frontiers. It was already known to the Raj intelligence chiefs that certain Indian revolutionaries, who had once staked all their hopes in the Germans and Turks, had now turned to Moscow for help in driving the British out of India. But Bailey's on-the-spot intelligence showed them already to be at work, and pinpointed Tashkent as their base of operations.

And they were not the only new arrivals at this time to be noted by Bailey. Alarmed by reports of blood-letting and anarchy, Moscow had despatched a team of ideological troubleshooters to Tashkent the moment the rail link was reopened. Their task was to set the Bolshevik house there in order along more orthodox lines. For the gory goings-on in this Central Asian backwater were beginning to give the new revolutionary gospel a bad name.

Some of the new Soviets which were springing up everywhere had very uncertain concepts of what Marxism-Leninism was all about. North of the Caspian, at Suizran, a proclamation had been issued ordering the nationalisation of women. All the best and most beautiful women, it declared, had hitherto belonged to the bourgeoisie, while the peasants and workers had had to put up with the second best. This was unfair, and from now on all women were to become public property. 'This was too much for Lenin and the Bolsheviks at the centre,' Bailey wrote afterwards, 'and the order was withdrawn and possession of even a copy was forbidden.' While no less revolutionary or ruthless than the local Tashkent commissars, the new advisers from Moscow were at least more sophisticated.

One of them, Bailey reported – a former Tsarist consul in India named Bravin – had been put in charge of co-ordinating the insurrectionary activities of the Indian revolutionaries, but now had a new job as Moscow's first ambassador to Afghanistan. Every effort, Bailey warned, was being made by the Bolsheviks to woo the Afghans, and members of a mission from Kabul had been garlanded with flowers and greeted with artillery salutes. Cut off as he was from the outside world, Bailey had no way of ascertaining how much of what he was passing on was new, and how much was already known to Delhi. News of Moscow's overtures to Afghanistan – whose proximity to the North-West Frontier of India made it an ideal base for Bolshevik infiltration or even invasion – had in fact already reached the desks of Bailey's chiefs from another source.

Ever since his withdrawal from Russian territory to Meshed, General Malleson had been vigorously engaged in trying to sabotage attempts by the Bolsheviks to gain a political or military toe-hold in Afghanistan. Throughout the 1914–18 war, despite the urgings of senior court officials to throw in his lot with the Germans and Turks and declare a Holy War against the British, King Habibullah of Afghanistan remained strictly neutral. And following the Russian Revolution he resolutely refused to have any dealings with the Bolsheviks, whom he regarded as blasphemous heathens out to destroy Islam. 'The friendly attitude of Soviet Russia', Moscow protested, 'met with a sharp rebuff.' But very shortly afterwards, in February 1919, they got their chance when Habibullah was shot dead by an assassin, and his third son Amanullah succeeded him after a brief family struggle. Amanullah, who had ambitious plans to reform the country, soon showed himself willing to treat with his new northern neighbours, to the alarm of Delhi.

But shortly after coming to the throne, he had suffered a severe setback at the hands of the British. Spurred on, some claim, by Moscow, he had embarked on an ill-fated invasion of northern India. Beset by troubles within the army, and among the powerful mullahs who opposed his reformist zeal, he saw this as a way of uniting the country behind his rickety throne. Moreover the prospects of victory appeared to be good – or so he had been led to believe. For he had been receiving highly optimistic reports from his agents in India that the whole country, but especially the North-West Frontier Province and the Punjab, was a powder-keg of discontent. It only needed a spark to set it off. The moment his troops crossed the frontier, they had assured him, the entire native population would rise against their war-weakened British oppressors and rally in millions to the Afghan flag.

Amanullah's invasion took place in May 1919, and has now become known as the Third Afghan War. It was timed to coincide with uprisings on the North-West Frontier and in the Punjab. But the British had got wind of these and largely forestalled them. The Afghan forces were driven back across the frontier in a few weeks, leaving them badly mauled. The speed of the British victory – won in cruel heat and over punishing terrain – owed much to the use of aircraft whose bombs and machine-guns had a devastating effect on Afghan morale.

Realising his terrible miscalculation, based on wildly exaggerated reports from his agents, Amanullah hastily sued for peace, insisting that it had all sprung from an unfortunate misunderstanding. If he had been expecting help from the Bolsheviks, he was sadly disappointed. None had been forthcoming. The last thing Moscow sought at that moment was an armed confrontation with Britain. What encouragement – if any – they had given Amanullah to attack India is not known. But hawkish frontier officers like Major Blacker – Bailey's former companion in Tashkent, now engaged in Bolshevik-watching from Meshed – had no doubts whatever about their complicity.

Whether or not Amanullah had hoped for Soviet support in his hour of need, he did not allow this to sour his relations with the Bolsheviks. While conducting peace talks with the British, he also managed to maintain a flirtation with an only-too-eager Moscow. Lenin, beset by massive problems of his own, even found time to write to the Afghan leader to congratulate him on his heroic stand against British imperialism, declaring that the Afghans had been singled out for 'a great and historic task'. Their destiny, he told Amanullah, was 'to unite all the enslaved Muslim peoples' and deliver them from their oppressors. A friendly Afghanistan, as both Moscow and Delhi were aware, would serve as an ideally situated base from where the gospel of violent revolution could be carried into India when the moment was right.

The British, thanks to Malleson's network of agents, kept a close watch on the comings and goings of secret emissaries between Kabul and Tashkent, as well as on wireless traffic between the two governments. But anxious less Amanullah, stung by the humiliation of his defeat, should throw in his lot with the Bolsheviks, they conceded to the Afghans in the peace treaty remarkably generous terms, including recognition of Afghanistan as a fully independent kingdom. In achieving this most satisfactory outcome from a position of defeat, the Afghans had merely done what they had always done – played one powerful neighbour successfully off against another. General Malleson, for one, was convinced that the Afghans would see British magnanimity simply as weakness. He was determined therefore to spoil the Bolsheviks' game, and keep them out of Afghanistan.

'It became our task', he recounted afterwards, 'to do everything possible to prevent the consummation of Afghan and Bolshevik plans for an offensive and defensive alliance.' Not a very likeable man, Malleson was an undisputed master of the dirty tricks side of intelligence work and an expert on frontier politics. A fellow officer once described him as 'clever as a fox . . . the Devil Incarnate' – and loathed by everyone. He was soon to give both Bolsheviks and Afghans good cause to loathe him too – that is if they ever realised that it was he who was sabotaging their efforts to achieve amity. Addressing the Royal Central Asian Society in London in 1922, after his retirement, Malleson described the tactics he employed from his base at Meshed:

'Having, through numerous agents in both camps, a fairly accurate notion of what was going on, and of how these two interesting parties were seeking how best to take each other in, we made it our business to keep each side unofficially informed of the perfidy of the other. The Afghans about this time, hearing that there was a serious and promising anti-Bolshevik rebellion throughout Ferghana, were gauche enough to send special emissaries there with letters and presents for the leaders of the insurgents. This information we felt it our duty to bring to the notice of the Bolsheviks.'

At the same time, an Afghan mission had visited Moscow, where it had been warmly welcomed by Lenin, Trotsky and other senior Bolsheviks. Its members returned home exultant at having obtained promises of arms, money and even aircraft, and the restitution of Afghan territory expropriated by the Tsarists. This was seen by the Afghans as a sign that the Bolsheviks must be badly in need of their friendship. They therefore began to take liberties. Malleson soon learned that an armed Afghan force had entered Soviet territory without Moscow's knowledge or permission and had reached the oasis town of Merv, while Amanullah's agents and mullahs travelled regularly back and forth between the two countries.

All this was drawn to the attention of the Bolsheviks, who sent Red Army troops to patrol the border and despatched a senior commissar to Merv and Ashkabad to find out what the Afghans were up to. While he was there he was involved in an unfortunate incident with an Afghan officer, and the result was that the Bolsheviks sent reinforcements to the frontier. Alerted to this by Malleson, the Afghans did likewise. This, in turn, was drawn to the attention of the Bolsheviks. And so it went on.

As a result of all this, deep suspicions about Kabul's intentions began to trouble Moscow. Malleson told his audience: 'The promised help in money and arms was delayed, and finally actually countermanded altogether, because they had become at any rate partly convinced that the Afghans were fomenting a huge pan-Islamic rising throughout Central Asia against them.'

Now that its purpose had been achieved, the general felt able to reveal more details about his little-known operation to an audience which included two officers – Colonel Redl and Major Blacker – who had taken part in it. He recounted:

'I had some most excellent officers, speaking numerous languages. I had agents up to a distance of a thousand miles or more, even in the government offices of the Bolsheviks. I had relays of men constantly coming and going in areas which I deemed important. There was hardly a train on the Central Asian railway which had not one of our agents on board, and there was no important railway centre which had not two or three men on the spot. Travellers of every sort and description were cross-examined at scores of different places . . .'

*　　　*　　　*

To Bailey in Tashkent it had become obvious that the British were not aiming to drive the Bolsheviks out of Central Asia. He was simply wasting his time there, and at considerable risk to his life. After all he had been through, it must have been a great disappointment to him, for he was still totally convinced that were a small British force to march on Tashkent, even at this late stage, Bolshevik rule would collapse. He determined to get away as soon as possible. Already a plan had begun to form in his mind.

There were only two feasible escape routes. The most obvious was to try to leave by the way he had come, crossing the frontier into China and thence making his way to Kashgar. This was the route by which Nazaroff, after months of wandering, eventually made his escape, though Bailey only learned of this long afterwards in a letter from Nazaroff which is now in my possession. He knew that this exit was very closely watched and guarded by the Bolsheviks, and that his chances of getting through the numerous checkpoints undetected would be minimal. Many other fugitives had been picked up while attempting this route, including at least one of his own couriers. Moreover, with the breakdown of law and order, it was known to be plagued by armed bandits.

The only other possible way out was across the remote and ill-guarded Persian frontier to Meshed. Provided one could obtain the necessary papers, the first half of the journey could be done in comparative comfort by rail. If one left the train at the small town of Kagan, which was firmly in Bolshevik hands, one could try to reach Bokhara, some ten miles away and still vigorously maintaining its independence. That was assuming that the Emir's officials would let one in. From the relative safety of Bokhara, one would commence the final and most gruelling stage of the escape – a three-hundred-mile dash across the great Karakum desert to the Persian frontier, and freedom.

It was this route that Bailey decided to take, being marginally the less dangerous of the two. But how was he, a wanted man, going to get hold of a permit to leave Tashkent and take the train to Kagan? And even if he reached Kagan, how would he explain to the authorities there why he wanted to cross the political no-man's-land to the Emir's forbidden capital?

With his usual resourcefulness, Bailey hit upon a solution to both problems. It was one of almost unbelievable daring. He had discovered from a Serbian contact working for the Cheka that the Bolsheviks were greatly alarmed by rumours emanating from Bokhara that British officers were being used there to train the Emir's troops. Another rumour claimed that an entire regiment of Indian troops was stationed in a heavily guarded camp outside the capital. Anxious to establish the truth, the Bolsheviks had despatched a succession of spies to Bokhara. In all there had been fifteen. But one after another they had been caught by the Emir's highly efficient secret police – and strangled. Bailey now volunteered to be the sixteenth. It was hardly a job for which there would be much competition.

The assignment, which involved being recruited into the Bolshevik secret service, was negotiated for him by his Serbian police contact, a man named Manditch. Manditch was one of a handful of trusted individuals in Tashkent who knew who Bailey really was. It was he who had tipped Bailey off the previous year when he and Tredwell were due to be arrested. An ex-lieutenant in the Austrian army, he had managed to worm his way into the confidence of the Bolsheviks, and now enjoyed both their trust and a comfortable existence. Indeed, he was just about to get married to a local girl.

At first Bailey had been extremely suspicious of him, assuming him to be an *agent provocateur*. For it was hard to see why he should risk everything, including his life, to help a British officer he had never even met before. But the reason soon became clear. Despite his privileged position, he had no wish to spend the rest of his life in Tashkent. Neither had his fiancée. Like so many others at that time, Manditch was merely going along with the system, awaiting his opportunity to escape. If he could be helpful to Bailey, then Bailey might be useful to him when the need arose. In the event, this was exactly how it worked out.

Manditch went to see the head of the Bolshevik intelligence service, a cunning and much feared individual named Dunkov, and told him that an Albanian friend of his was prepared to go to Bokhara and try to discover what the British were up to. On the assumption that Dunkov himself would want to interview and brief the volunteer, Bailey and Manditch had together devised an elaborate cover story for him, complete with documents and photographs, showing him to be an Albanian army clerk named Joseph Kastamuni. For they had discovered that no one in Tashkent spoke this obscure language.

By a stroke of luck, Bailey was spared the ordeal of a searching interview with his new chief, for he and Manditch had run into Dunkov in the street, and the briefing had taken place as they strolled along together. The head of the secret service gave his new recruit his orders there and then: 'We are very anxious to get definite news of affairs in Bokhara as soon as possible. You must go at once and see what truth there is in these stories of British officers. Our information is so detailed that we are sure there is something going on. Time is of great importance and you must start at once. In fact, there is a train going tomorrow and I will have your documents made out immediately so that you can catch it.'

Dunkov's plan was quite straightforward. Bailey and Manditch would travel to Kagan together. There Manditch would remain while Bailey, or rather Kastamuni, made his way to the mud-walled Bokharan capital and endeavoured to pry out its secrets. These he would communicate to Manditch by whatever means he could, before returning to Kagan when he had learned all there was to learn. That, anyway, was how Dunkov saw it. Their own plan, it is hardly necessary to add, was rather different.

They left Tashkent on October 15, 1919. Manditch had in the meantime got married, and somehow managed to get permission to take his bride with him. Before departing, Bailey was able to see and thank most of those who had risked their lives for him during his months on the run, including the plucky Miss Houston (who was later to make her own dramatic escape into Persia). But most of his friends he would never see again, or even learn what had become of them. After several last-minute hitches, Bailey, Manditch and his new wife finally made their way to the railway station. Bailey wore a coarse woollen suit cut in local Bolshevik style, and to his hat was pinned a red star with hammer and sickle, the badge of the Red Army. His documents consisted of a permit to travel to Kagan, which could be shown to anyone, and an identity card marked SECRET, which only Cheka and other security officials could see.

The train arrived a day and a half late, and had no passenger coaches. The three of them pushed their way through the huge crowds on the platform and managed to find themselves a corner of an already packed goods wagon. Two days later they reached Samarkand, where there was a further long delay. This gave Bailey the chance to slip into town and see the remains of Tamerlane's famous capital with its gleaming, blue-tiled mosques and tombs, then looking sadly neglected. In the bazaar he bought a bunch of the largest grapes he had ever seen and hastened back to the railway station. But it was another seven hours before the train finally left for Kagan, which they reached three days after leaving Tashkent. Here, with difficulty, they managed to obtain a room in the only hotel, which all three of them had to share.

Also staying in the hotel, just across the corridor, was a leading Indian revolutionary, wanted by the British on sedition charges, named Mahendra Pratap. During the war, encouraged by the Germans, he and a fellow-revolutionary called Barka-tullah (to whose presence in Tashkent Bailey had already alerted Delhi) had set up an Indian republican government-in-exile in Berlin. Their aim was to rule an independent India after the defeat of Britain and her allies. Following Germany's collapse, however, they had thrown in their lot with the Bolsheviks. To gain the ear of Lenin, with whom he had a number of meetings, Mahendra Pratap had posed as an Indian prince of great influence.

He and Bailey (whom he never dreamed was an Englishman in disguise) had a long discussion about British rule in India, and Pratap's plans for ending it. Bailey listened patiently, aware that the authorities at home were extremely interested in the Indian's movements and intentions. But he found the conspirator's ideas so bizarre that, like Lenin before him, he was unable to take them seriously. The Emir of Bokhara, whom the Indian was in Kagan trying to see, had refused to have anything to do with him, so he was on his way now to Kabul to try his luck with Amanullah.

The story of Bailey's brief career in the Soviet secret service now took an even stranger turn. During their overnight stay in Kagan an urgent, coded telegram was delivered to them. It was from the Chief of the Bolshevik General Staff in Tashkent, and ordered: 'Please communicate all information you have regarding Anglo-Indian Service Colonel Bailey.' Ludicrously, Bailey was being asked to keep a look-out for himself. He and Manditch hurriedly concocted a reply reporting that a European, disguised as a native but answering Bailey's description, had been spotted some weeks earlier leaving Afghanistan with some companions. It was believed that the party was heading for Ferghana. Malleson himself could hardly have improved on that. For to the Bolsheviks it must have appeared that the double-dealing Afghans had been sheltering the British masterspy all along. But wherever he was now, he was nowhere near Bokhara.

By now the other Bolshevik agents staying in the hotel had heard of the secret mission this Albanian was about to undertake for Dunkov. 'They asked Manditch', Bailey wrote later, 'how I proposed to get into Bokhara, a walled city with every gate guarded and all who entered, especially Europeans, thoroughly searched and questioned.' Manditch replied that it was so secret that even he did not know. The other agents looked at Bailey in sympathy as (in his own words) 'a very brave man who, for the Soviet cause, was about to meet an unpleasant death in Bokhara.' After all, had not fifteen of their colleagues already tried and failed?

In fact, before leaving Tashkent, Bailey had managed to

obtain a letter of introduction from the Bokharan consul to his opposite number in Kagan. It had been acquired through mutual friends on a solemn promise that Bailey was not a Bolshevik. Thanks to this letter Bailey was able to obtain from the consul in Kagan a sealed note which was his visa to enter Bokhara. The following day, having discarded their Bolshevik-style suits, he and Manditch hired a horse-drawn *tarantas* and set off on the ten-mile journey to Bokhara, leaving Mrs Manditch temporarily in Kagan. If everything proceeded according to plan, they intended to arrange for her to join them later that day. It was the last the Bolsheviks were ever to see of Bailey.

In addition to his visa, he had concealed on him two letters of introduction, one in his watch and the other in a box of matches. Both were extremely compromising to Bailey as well as to their senders. To safeguard the latter, their signatures were in invisible ink. The texts simply declared: 'Trust this man and do whatever is possible for him.' Even Manditch did not know about these letters, although he knew enough about Bailey to have had him shot on the spot had he wished.

Meticulous to the last detail, Bailey had earlier despatched a courier to Malleson in Meshed, four hundred miles to the south-west, asking him to try to arrange with the Emir a safe passage for him through Bokhara. Unlike so many previous ones, this message had got through, and Malleson had been able to advise Delhi: 'The Emir has given me his promise that he will do all in his power to assist Lieut-Colonel Bailey should he come into Bokharan territory.'

But it soon transpired that the Emir's orders had not been passed down the line. On presenting themselves at the city gates, Bailey and Manditch were regarded with the deepest suspicion by armed officials there. With good reason the Bokharans were paranoid about Bolshevik agents, and the place swarmed with the Emir's own spies and informers. Finally, on the strength of Bailey's visa, both men were allowed to enter the Muslim holy city where, only a few decades earlier, two British officers had been put to death by the Emir for refusing to embrace Islam. But their troubles were still far from over. While Bailey was being interviewed by the official whose job it was to vet all strangers arriving in the city, he heard angry shouts from the courtyard where Manditch was awaiting his turn.

'You're a brave man,' a voice was yelling, 'but you won't get back this time.' Bailey dashed out to find that someone had recognised Manditch as a Bolshevik agent and was threatening to have him arrested. Bailey managed to prevent his accuser from calling the police, and produced the two letters of introduction to convince him that they were not Bolsheviks, but rather fugitives fleeing the vengeance of the Cheka. Eventually, their anti-Bolshevik credentials were accepted, and Mrs Manditch was allowed to join them.

Meanwhile, to explain his absence to his colleagues back in Kagan, Manditch had managed to smuggle out a message to them advising: 'Am engaged on dangerous work. Will not be able to communicate further for a week at least.' He had hopefully added: 'Am urgently in need of money. Please send 40,000 roubles immediately.' Although the message was acknowledged by his unsuspecting colleagues, needless to say the money never arrived.

It occurred to Bailey that once established in Bokhara, with the Emir's blessing, he would be well placed to supply to Meshed regular intelligence about what was going on in Bolshevik Central Asia, just as Etherton was from Kashgar. He had sent a message via Malleson proposing this, but had failed to get any reply. Malleson, though, through one of his agents, had learned of Bailey's arrival in Bokhara and telegraphed the news to the Viceroy. 'There are risks in getting away from Bokhara,' he added, 'but it is done every day, and the risk of remaining there is even greater.'

To stay on in Bokhara, Bailey himself soon realised, would be both foolish and dangerous. His real identity was already known to a number of people there, and it would only be a matter of time before the Bolsheviks discovered too. Pressure might then be put on the Emir, whose own position was anything but secure, to hand him over. Kidnapping even was not out of the question. He therefore abandoned any idea of staying on, and began to prepare for the long journey across the desert to the Persian frontier.

By the time they were ready to leave, the party had become far larger than Bailey had intended, and now included seven White Russian officers who had been given permission by the Bokharan authorities to travel by the same route. His original party had been small and mobile, and had included, besides himself and Mr and Mrs Manditch, two Indian Army NCOs. The latter had been sent to the Emir by Malleson on special duty with a camel caravan laden with supplies, almost certainly rifles, although Bailey does not say so. They should have returned long before, but the Emir had been reluctant to see these two excellent men go. He had argued that the Indian Army was so large that these two men would not be missed. It was almost certainly their presence which had led to rumours reaching Bolshevik ears of British officers being used to train the Emir's army. Bailey had also had to take on guides to steer them between wells during their twenty-day journey, the only map he had being one torn from a Victorian travel book.

Secrecy about their departure was vital, he realised, for were the Bolsheviks to get wind of this, ambush was almost certain. He therefore kept the date on which he intended to leave secret until the very last moment, warning his party to be on stand-by as they would only get an hour's notice.

They left on the night of December 18, 1919. Everyone wore Turkoman dress, including huge black sheepskin hats, and grey *khalats* over their own clothes. Being thus dressed, they might not be molested by the murderous bands of armed robbers which roamed the desert, since it would be assumed that they too were Turkoman brigands. This was vital, for they had only seven antiquated rifles between the seventeen of them and could not risk a shoot-out. But it was to work against them, too, for their appearance frightened away the peaceable nomads from whom they had hoped to buy most of their food. As a result they were often desperately hungry, and their ponies dangerously weakened by lack of fodder.

It was bitterly cold, and in one blizzard five inches of snow fell, obliterating what few landmarks there were. Their guides proved to be hopeless, moreover, constantly losing the way, until, on the eleventh day, in the very middle of the desert, they admitted to Bailey that they were completely lost. The situation looked very serious. But then later that day, by a miracle, they came upon a small shepherds' encampment where they bought three sheep. Using the cleaning-rods of their rifles as makeshift skewers, they roasted chunks of the flesh and devoured them immediately. 'We had had practically nothing to eat for several days except the ponies' food, which we either parched or boiled according to the individual taste,' Bailey recounts. The shepherds, who had been terrified at the sight of such a large party, also made them fresh bread, while they were able to draw water for both men and ponies from the well. This, amazingly, proved to be seven hundred and fifty feet deep, and had the shepherds not been there with their own rope Bailey's party would have been unable to reach the water. Without this chance encounter, he wrote afterwards, they would all undoubtedly have perished.

Because of the proximity of a Bolshevik garrison town, they could not take the most direct route towards the frontier, but had to steer further west, travelling at night and navigating by the stars. Then at last, on January 6, 1920, they saw by first light a range of snow-covered mountains in the distance. Bailey knew that they lay in Persia. He recounts: 'The feelings of all of us at the sight of a free land, even in the distance, is hard to describe.' Some ten miles further on, as they topped a ridge, they suddenly saw below them the rush-lined Tedzhen river which marked the frontier between Russia and Persia. But as they looked down at this last remaining barrier between themselves and freedom, they realised that they had been spotted.

'My first inclination', wrote Bailey afterwards, 'was to ride on at once before any possible enemy could make preparations.' But there was no sign of a bridge, and the guides were unable to say where it could best be forded. The men who had spotted them, who were too far off to identify, had now vanished. If they were a Bolshevik border patrol, as Bailey feared, or even a party sent specially to intercept him, then they were almost certainly positioning themselves for an ambush. There was little time to lose.

The first shots rang out as they neared the river. Bailey had sent one of the Indian NCOs to gallop ahead to try to find a good crossing point, while the rest of the party moved forward more cautiously. When the Indian was half way to the river, he called out, signalling with his arm while continuing to advance at a gallop. Not understanding what he was trying to tell them, Bailey himself galloped forward to join him. The Indian told him that he had spotted some men hiding in the reeds on their right. At that moment the ambushers opened fire, fortunately hitting no one.

Bailey's immediate fear was that the Persian villagers on the far side of the river would think that they were being attacked, and try to prevent his party from crossing. Taking the NCO's rifle, he ordered him to cross the river and tell the villagers that they were not being attacked. By now the rest of the party, at full gallop, had reached the river bank and were beginning to cross. Those with rifles, once across, began to fire on the ambushers to cover the withdrawal of the others. The Bolsheviks, peering up from among the rushes in their large sheepskin hats, made conspicuous targets. Amazingly, none of Bailey's party was hit, although Mrs Manditch, who had been thrown from her pony, had to run to the river bank where one of the Russian officers lifted her into his saddle.

Once Bailey's party were all safely across, the firing ceased on both sides, as if by tacit agreement. Their only loss had been a saddle-bag full of Bokharan silk dresses belonging to Mrs Manditch. Later, through binoculars, Bailey observed the Bolsheviks examining the contents of the bag. Feeling sorry for

Mrs Manditch, Bailey arranged for a messenger from the village to cross the river and ask the Bolsheviks how much they wanted for the return of the dresses. But the Bolsheviks, two of whose men had been wounded, were in no mood for such frivolity, and fired an angry shot after the messenger when he was galloping back to the river.

After seventeen hair-raising months, with his life perpetually at risk, Bailey was once more on friendly soil. He had not achieved what he would have liked, but the policy-makers at home had ruled this out. Nonetheless, he had had no end of an adventure, and had become something of a legend in Soviet Central Asia. So much so that the Bolsheviks felt it necessary to dispose of this British super-spy once and for all. He had been killed, they announced, in a skirmish on the Persian frontier, and had been given a full military funeral. Nor, as we shall see, was Colonel Bailey the only British officer they had good reason to wish dead.

7 'To Set the East Ablaze'

Back from the outer darkness of Bolshevism – if not quite from the dead – Colonel Bailey found himself an instant hero. Here was just the tonic an exhausted nation needed. Given up for lost, he had suddenly and miraculously reappeared, disguised as a Turkoman tribesman. Single-handed, and over many months, he had outwitted the villainous Bolsheviks, even concealing himself within the ranks of their own secret service. His final escape through the legendary cities of the ancient Silk Road was one of the most romantic that anyone could remember. It was better even than Buchan.

The newspapers at home naturally made much of it – as much, that is, as could be told. For apart from delicate political considerations, the lives of brave men and women whom Bailey had left behind were still at stake. *The Times* headlined the story: A CENTRAL ASIAN ROMANCE, and reported that Bailey had reached Delhi. The *Daily Telegraph* headlined it: BRITISH OFFICER IN BOLSHEVIK ASIA . . . AMAZING ADVENTURES. If these adventures had not achieved very much, no one minded, or even noticed. He had pulled a fast one on Lenin and Trotsky and their bloodthirsty, revolutionary mob, and that was the main thing.

But although for many Bailey will always remain the last player in the Great Game, there were other British officers still matching their wits against the Bolsheviks in this shadowy, undeclared war on India's frontiers. With Malleson's ungentlemanly activities we are already familiar. However, from Kashgar all this time Etherton too had been closely monitoring Bolshevik moves, and wherever possible spoiling their game. Like most British-Indian officers he was imbued with a deep distrust of the Russians which now amounted to little short of paranoia.

A man of abounding energy and an appetite for intrigue, he harnessed these to such effect against the Bolsheviks that before long they were to put a price on his head. In the Soviet order of villainy, Major (later Colonel) Etherton rates only a little below Bailey. This is not really surprising, for during his four years as British Consul-General in Kashgar he was to wage a remorseless, almost personal, war against the Bolsheviks.

Now approaching forty, he had served a rugged apprenticeship in the Australian gold-fields (which he had chosen in preference to Sandhurst) before riding with Kitchener's Fighting Scouts in the Boer War and ending up in an Indian Army frontier regiment. It was while serving with the Garhwal Rifles that he was chosen to join the Bailey mission.

His credentials for intelligence work in Central Asia were exceptional. Before the war, as a young subaltern, he had made a bold and dangerous journey through innermost Asia, gaining first-hand experience of the tribes and terrain. It had taken him the best part of a year and had resulted in a book called *Across the Roof of the World*. After crossing the Pamir to Kashgar, he had traversed the northern arm of the Silk Road around the fringes of the Taklamakan desert to the Mongolian frontier. Travelling northwards through Mongolia, he had finally entered Russia and taken the Trans-Siberian Railway home. It was to prove an invaluable blooding for his role at Kashgar.

From the moment he took over from Sir George Macartney he began to build up a network of agents and to send back to his chiefs in Delhi and London a steady stream of intelligence, all of which had to be carried by special runner through the Karakoram passes to India. For at that time Kashgar had no radio-transmitter, although messages could be sent by morse over the Chinese telegraph line to Urumchi, and thence to Peking. However, by January 1918 a wireless receiving set had been installed which was to prove invaluable for intercepting Bolshevik radio traffic between Tashkent, Moscow and elsewhere. One early scoop apparently obtained by such eavesdropping, shortly after the station began operating, was that of Osipov's murder of his fellow-commissars and abortive uprising.

Leafing through Etherton's now long-forgotten intelligence reports one can see the extent of his multifarious anti-Bolshevik activities. These ranged from monitoring the strength and state of alertness of the Bolshevik garrisons across the frontier, to burning bundles of inflammatory literature intercepted by him *en route* from Tashkent to India. He also maintained a close watch on the movements and activities of Bolshevik agents in Chinese Turkestan (or Sinkiang, to use its correct name). For, like Afghanistan, there was a danger of this being used as a thoroughfare for infiltrating revolutionaries and even arms into northern India. Ever since Tsarist days the Russians had sought to dominate Chinese Turkestan by every means short of actual invasion, and there seemed no reason to think that the Bolsheviks would be any different. Etherton was determined, at all costs, to keep them out.

Officially, as Consul-General, he was there to protect the rights of British-Indian subjects in Chinese Turkestan. These were mostly Hindu traders and money-lenders living in the oasis-towns at the eastern end of the Silk Road – a consular 'parish' roughly the size of France and Spain combined. This widely scattered business community, which had every reason to fear any Bolshevik penetration of Sinkiang, was to provide Etherton with a ready-made spy network.

'The system', he wrote afterwards, 'worked well and enabled me to keep in touch with almost every house and family of note in the country, and no move of importance could be made without it being known.' In addition to having his agents in every town and village in Sinkiang, he also had a small staff under him at Kashgar. This included a Vice-Consul, British wireless monitors, a chief clerk, an assistant clerk, a Chinese secretary and numerous orderlies and servants. To protect it in the event of trouble, this lonely British outpost had an escort of thirty sepoys commanded by an Indian officer who were changed annually.

Originally, when Sir George Macartney had first arrived

there, the consulate had consisted of a modest-sized native house surrounded by a garden. It was known as *Chini Bagh*, or Chinese Garden. In 1913 this had been demolished and a twenty-roomed European-style residence, surrounded by a high protective wall, built in its place. But the unofficial name of *Chini Bagh*, and the old garden so lovingly designed and cared for by Lady Macartney during her seventeen years there, had both been retained. Before the 1914–18 war, this very English home set in remotest Central Asia had been an oasis of comfort for rare European travellers. These had included Sir Aurel Stein and Albert von Le Coq, those two famous rivals for the sand-buried treasures of the Silk Road.

In Etherton's time, however, the cool rooms and shady gardens were to become a sanctuary for a different kind of traveller – men and women fleeing from Bolshevik rule, and often carrying valuable intelligence with them from across the frontier. He was quick to hear of Paul Nazaroff's arrival in Kashgar, and the Russian was to prove a valuable source of intelligence during his four years there.

With his limited resources, it was impossible for Etherton to keep a watch over all the passes leading into Sinkiang from Soviet territory. The only way to prevent these from being used to infiltrate agents or arms through Sinkiang into India was to frighten the Chinese into stepping up their own border security lest Bolshevik agitators should enter the country and undermine their rule. Etherton, who was on good terms with the Chinese authorities, even suggested more effective procedures which they might take at their frontier posts, and was soon able to report that these were being adopted and troop reinforcements sent to help carry them out. In future everyone crossing the frontier from Soviet territory would be thoroughly searched, he advised Delhi. 'A certain number of Bolshevik agents did get through,' he wrote afterwards. 'But with the intelligence service at my disposal they were rounded up and either incarcerated or deported.' One he even succeeded in getting the Chinese to execute, he was able to inform his chiefs.

The Bolsheviks, for their part, were pressing the Chinese to be allowed to open consulates in Sinkiang, and demanding the surrender and handing over of those who still remained loyal to the Tsarist cause, including the staff of the Consulate-General in Kashgar, over which the Imperial Russian flag continued to flutter as though nothing was amiss. But Etherton, a formidable individual, was determined to sabotage this Bolshevik move. A toe-hold of any kind in Sinkiang would bring them that much nearer to India's frontiers.

He warned the Chinese that the consulates would be used to foment trouble among the Muslim population, already restless, and undermine their own minority rule. Etherton was secretly convinced that Bolshevik rule might not be wholly unwelcome to the Muslims, since in their eyes it could hardly be worse than the corrupt Chinese colonial administration under which they were suffering. Anyway, he so alarmed the Chinese about what would follow if they let the Bolsheviks in that it was not until three years after his departure from Kashgar that Moscow was allowed to reoccupy its own Consulate-General there.

Two further attempts by the Bolsheviks to gain a foothold in Sinkiang, this time using trade missions, were also thwarted by Etherton who succeeded in getting these turned back at the frontier. A move to outflank him by sending a mission in from next-door Afghanistan, headed by Mahendra Pratap, the Indian revolutionary whom Bailey had met in Kagan, was similarly repulsed. But in Etherton's view Chinese resistance to Bolshevik demands 'would not have lasted a week' had he not been there to stiffen their resolve. It was hardly surprising that the Tashkent newspapers clamoured for the death of 'the bloodthirsty British consul' at Kashgar. In view of this, it must have been with some satisfaction that, on July 14, 1920, Etherton was able to reassure his chiefs that 'so far we have kept Kashgaria clear of Bolshevism'.

But if Etherton was winning his one-man crusade against the Bolsheviks in remote Sinkiang, everywhere else the tide had turned in their favour. Right across the far-flung Civil War battlefield the remnants of the White armies were now in full retreat before the military prowess of Trotsky, supported by some thirty thousand ex-Tsarist officers who had thrown in their lot with the Reds. Refugees, both soldiers and civilians, were now beginning, in ever increasing numbers, to pour across China's frontiers, especially into Sinkiang. Many were reduced to begging for scraps of food, and to eating rats and tortoises to survive. In northern Sinkiang, close to the Russian frontier, there were said to be fifty thousand of them, including Annenkov, the celebrated Cossack general, and more than a thousand of his troops. Armed with machine-guns, artillery and two armoured cars, they were proposing to continue the war against the Reds from Chinese territory.

In Urumchi, the provincial capital, Governor Yang Tseng-hsin at once saw the danger and acted swiftly. In doing so, the wily but able ruler prevented the horrors of the Civil War from spilling over into Sinkiang, as they were shortly to do into neighbouring Mongolia. Apart from the immediate risk of the Bolsheviks invading his province to annihilate the Whites while they were re-grouping, he foresaw an even greater danger – that of Annenkov's refugee army taking over Sinkiang by force of arms and making it their permanent home. So, luring the unsuspecting general to Urumchi for talks, Yang ordered him and the three officers accompanying him to be seized and bound hand and foot. Then all four were thrown into a dungeon. There Annenkov languished for months – in chains, it is said, and liberally supplied with opium to sap his will. Thus deprived of his leadership, his demoralised troops were easily disarmed and interned.

*   *   *

Meanwhile, far away in Moscow, something had taken place which was to have repercussions throughout the world. On March 2, 1919, fifty-two leading revolutionaries, including Lenin and – briefly back from the battlefield – Trotsky, had met within the walls of the Kremlin to lay the foundations of the

Communist International, which was to become better known as the Comintern. Its avowed aim was to overthrow, by any means, all existing governments, and replace them with a world Soviet. This revolutionary process would begin, they were convinced, in defeated and demoralised Germany, and then spread like a forest fire across a Europe weakened and exhausted by war. The task of the Communist International, through its network of agents, would be to ignite that fire and keep it well ablaze. For unless they could seize Europe, and especially Germany, their own revolution would have little hope of surviving the hostility of the imperialist powers.

Before they dispersed, the delegates rose from their seats and solemnly sang the new hymn of the Comintern, the now famous *Internationale*. They left the Kremlin convinced that Europe was about to go up in flames, and that before very long the world would be theirs. So confident of this was Grigori Zinoviev, the revolutionary hero chosen by Lenin to mastermind the Comintern's operations, that in the first issue of its journal he rashly forecast that 'in a year the whole of Europe will be Communist'.

However, despite some early but short-lived successes – most notably in Hungary – it soon became clear that no such thing was going to happen in Europe. Admittedly it had been touch and go, and in a secret memorandum to his colleagues at the Paris Peace Conference in March 1919, Lloyd George, the British Prime Minister, had warned:

The whole of Europe is filled with the spirit of revolution. There is a deep sense not only of discontent, but of anger and revolt . . . The whole existing order in its political, social and economic aspects is questioned by the masses from one end of Europe to the other . . . There is a danger that we may throw the masses of the population throughout Europe into the arms of the extremists whose only idea for regenerating mankind is to destroy utterly the whole existing fabric of society. These men have triumphed in Russia . . .

The greatest danger, he went on, would be if Germany

turned Communist and threw in her lot with the Bolsheviks. This would place 'her resources, her brains, her vast organising power, at the disposal of the revolutionary fanatics whose dream is to conquer the world for Bolshevism by force of arms'. Nor was he alone in such fears. Field Marshal Sir Henry Wilson, the British Chief of Staff, noted grimly in his diary: 'We are sitting on top of a mine which may go up at any minute.' He was particularly alarmed by the unrest in the British Army which had led to mutinies at home and overseas. 'We dare not', he warned the Cabinet, 'give an unpopular order to the troops.'

But when the hoped-for revolution failed to materialise in Europe, Lenin was forced to reconsider his strategy. Aware that there was widespread unrest in the East, particularly in India, he began to turn his attention there. As long before as 1882, Engels had prophesied a revolution in British India. Lenin had always believed that the liberation of the oppressed peoples of Asia and Africa would follow the revolution in Europe. He still did. But he began to reason that if the European powers could be divested of their colonies, or their minority rule there be made untenable, then this would so undermine them economically that revolution at home would be inevitable. 'The East', he exhorted, 'will help us to conquer the West. Let us turn our faces towards Asia.'

To set the East ablaze now became the clarion call of the Comintern, with India as the starting-point of a conflagration which would destroy imperialism. For Britain, then still the foremost imperialist power, was seen by Lenin as the main obstacle to his dream of world revolution. 'England', he declared, 'is our greatest enemy. It is in India that we must strike them hardest.'

Because this represented a deviation from orthodox Marxist theory, which was then still sacrosanct to the Bolsheviks, the Comintern's second congress, held in the summer of 1920, was faced with the task of resolving it. Only then could detailed plans be worked out for launching a campaign of subversion and insurrection in Asia. But here Lenin had a problem. Neither he nor any of the other leading revolutionaries had any first-hand experience of conditions in the colonial territories, any more than Marx himself had. Who better to help them than one of those they sought to liberate from Britain's yoke?

Prominent among the Asian delegates at the congress was a tall young Indian revolutionary with burning eyes named Manabendra Nath Roy (although, like so many of those present, this was not his real name, which was Bhattacharya). Described in an Indian Government intelligence report as 'a most dangerous conspirator . . . ambitious, energetic and unscrupulous', he was by far the most experienced and sophisticated of the Indian revolutionaries, and the only one whom Lenin was prepared to take seriously.

Highly intelligent, and from a well-known Brahmin family, Roy had begun his revolutionary career as a teenage terrorist in a fanatically anti-British secret society in his native Bengal. Its plans for the violent overthrow of the Raj were financed by means of armed robbery, but on the outbreak of war its leaders had turned hopefully to Germany for supplies of weapons. Roy was involved in trying to smuggle a shipment of these to Calcutta when the plot was uncovered by the British, who raided the offices of a bogus firm called Harry and Sons, which the conspirators were using as a front. Meanwhile the promised consignment of arms which Roy was in Java awaiting had failed to materialise.

Wanted for treason now by the British authorities, Roy fled via Japan and China to the United States, then still neutral, disguised as a bearded West Indian Catholic priest. But very soon he was wanted too by the American police and was forced to flee across the border into Mexico. There he was talent-spotted by a senior Comintern agent, Mikhail Borodin, who initiated him into the heady mysteries of Marxism and the secrets of professional revolutionaries. Together the Indian and the Russian, now close friends, founded in Mexico the first communist party outside Russia. Both men were destined to rise to high positions in the clandestine world of the Comintern, and both were fated eventually to fall from grace under Stalin.

On Lenin's personal invitation, and travelling under an alias, Roy reached Moscow in April 1920. Lenin, who had received excellent reports of him from Borodin, asked to see the young Indian firebrand on the eve of the second Comintern congress. Here, perhaps, was the man he was looking for to lead his crusade in the East. Here, maybe, was the Soviet Greenmantle.

Roy recalls in his memoirs his first encounter with the great revolutionary leader as he came forward, hand extended, to greet his nervous young guest in his barely furnished Kremlin office: 'Nearly a head shorter, he tilted his red goatee almost to a horizontal position to look at my face quizzically. I was embarrassed, did not know what to say. He helped me out with a banter: "You are so young! I expected a grey-bearded wise man from the East." '

The ice was broken as Roy managed to splutter out a protest at Lenin's disparagement of his twenty-seven years. Lenin laughed, instantly putting the Indian more at ease in the presence of this legendary figure who was changing the world. Although too overwhelmed to recall much of their first meeting, Roy was struck by the impish smile which often crossed Lenin's face, contradicting the universally held belief that he was a cold and inhuman fanatic. At that first brief meeting Lenin told him of his dream of mobilising the oppressed and exploited masses of Asia into a vast revolutionary movement. But he confessed that, having no knowledge of the East, he needed Roy's cooperation in helping him to shape his strategy. This would be presented to the congress in a document which, he believed, would become a landmark in the history of the world revolution.

With that, a bulb on Lenin's desk glowed briefly, and the interview was over. Taking Roy by the arm, Lenin led him to the door just as another visitor, clutching a bulging briefcase under his arm, was arriving. It was none other than Zinoviev, head of the Comintern, and regarded by many as Lenin's heir (not least by himself). Already he wielded enormous power in

Russia. Lenin introduced Roy to the man who was to be his new chief. His hand, the Indian noted, was limp and clammy, and he wore baggy trousers. His face was rather sensitive, and he spoke in a high-pitched voice. Yet this was the voice which could rouse a mob to a frenzy of excitement. Trotsky, himself a spellbinding orator, dubbed him 'the greatest demagogue among the Bolsheviks'. Stalin called him 'an orator of extraordinary power' – before having him liquidated.

A few days later Roy listened to him addressing a May Day rally from a platform in Red Square after keeping the crowd waiting for an hour. Roy recounts: 'At last he arrived, perfunctorily apologised for being late, mounted the platform and let loose a terrific torrent of words. This was my first experience of revolutionary oratory. I marvelled at the performance.'

Although the Bolsheviks had far from given up hope of fomenting revolution in Europe, two full sessions of the second congress were devoted to resolving the ideological question of how to apply Marxist revolutionary doctrine to the East. A special committee was appointed to formulate a policy which would then be submitted to the entire congress. It was as a member of this that the young Indian revolutionary took his fellow delegates' breath away by daring to question Lenin's own analysis of the colonial problem.

Some accounts suggest that their disagreement took place publicly. But in his memoirs, published in India after his death, Roy makes it clear that it was in private. He recounts: 'The delegates whispered, mostly in awe, that the young Indian upstart had dared question the wisdom of Lenin and cross swords with the master of polemics. But Lenin's attitude was very kind and tolerant. In the beginning he appeared to be amused by the naïveté of a novice. But before long he was impressed by my arguments, and could not dispute the authenticity of the facts I cited.'

Roy has been accused by his critics of intellectual arrogance, but no one has ever questioned his courage. He always said what he believed, and yet managed to survive. He and Lenin disagreed on two issues. One was about how much importance should be placed on revolution in the East. Both set much store by it, but while Roy argued that revolution in Europe depended wholly now on their first liberating the colonies, especially India, Lenin saw it more as a means of hastening the process.

Their other disagreement was over the question of whether the Comintern should co-operate with non-Marxist liberation movements, particularly in India. Roy argued that such movements were not truly revolutionary, but bourgeois at heart, and would merely restore the status quo after overthrowing colonial rule. Lenin contended that the Indian communist party, which had not yet even been formed, would be small and weak and unable to reach the masses and thus challenge the colonial power. For reasons of expediency, therefore, temporary alliances would have to be forged with such nationalist movements, and power seized from them once they had served their purpose.

Lenin had already prepared a thesis setting out his arguments on these doctrinal issues – issues of deep complexity, which I have greatly simplified here, but which continue to exercise Marxists today, and constitute what is known as 'the national and colonial question'. Copies of Lenin's thesis had already been issued to all committee members when Roy challenged it. But genuinely impressed by the Indian's arguments, as well as by his courage, Lenin invited him to prepare a separate paper. He told the startled delegates that Roy's arguments had made him a little less confident about some of his own. He proposed, therefore, that they should debate both documents. Amendments were subsequently made to each paper before the two were put before the full congress for discussion. A tactful Dutch delegate from the Netherlands East Indies argued that the two theses, as amended, were not in disagreement. A vote was held, and as one commentator put it: 'The congress, relieved to take this view, cheerfully adopted both.'

In fact Lenin's thesis, predictably, now became official Comintern doctrine, whereas Roy's supplementary thesis was quietly forgotten, although his prestige had been greatly enhanced by the episode. With ideological issues now more or less resolved, plans for the liberation of Asia could proceed. But first there took place a bizarre event which Roy was to christen irreverently 'Zinoviev's circus'.

8 'The Army of God'

'Of all the strange things which have happened in the last few years,' declared *The Times* of London on September 23, 1920, 'none has been stranger than the spectacle of two Jews, one of them a convicted pickpocket, summoning the world of Islam to a *jihad*.' The newspaper's wrath, not to say its anti-semitic tone, had been prompted by a bold and provocative opening move by the Comintern in its new bid for the hearts and minds of Asia.

In an attempt to rally the Muslim masses of the East to its crusade against the imperialist powers, and against Britain in particular, it invited one thousand eight hundred delegates of some twenty nationalities from the Middle East and Central Asia to a week-long rally at Baku, on the Caspian Sea. The two Jews referred to were the hosts – Grigori Zinoviev, head of the Comintern, and Bela Kun (or Cohen, as *The Times* pointed out), another leading revolutionary. Which was the pickpocket the writer did not say, but his venom was directed principally against Zinoviev.

For it was Zinoviev, in a spellbinding opening oration, who had called on Muslims everywhere to join the *jihad*, or Holy War, against their imperialist oppressors. The delegates had responded with wild enthusiasm, it was reported from Baku, drawing their swords and brandishing their revolvers and echoing his call for the liberation of the East. The uproar had been such that Zinoviev was unable to continue for several minutes. Three times the tumultuous applause was followed by the playing of the *Internationale*. According to the official record, Zinoviev told the delegates:

'Comrades! Brothers! The time has come when you can start on the organisation of a true and holy people's war against the robbers and oppressors. The Communist International turns today to the peoples of the East and says to them: "Brothers, we summon you to a holy war, in the first place against English imperialism!" (Stormy applause. Prolonged hurrahs. Members of the congress rise from their seats and brandish their weapons . . . The cry rings out "We swear it!").'

After several minutes of thunderous applause, Zinoviev continued: 'May today's declaration be heard in London, in Paris, and in all the cities where the capitalists are still in power. May they heed this solemn oath sworn by the representatives of tens of millions of toilers of the East, that the rule of the British enslavers shall be no more in the East, that the oppression of the toilers of the East shall be no more!'

So frenzied was the response to this that when at last he could make himself heard he had to appeal for calm, and order delegates to resume their seats. Many of them were dressed in ethnic costume, while some had made hazardous journeys to reach Baku, not long back in Bolshevik hands. More than two-thirds professed to be communists, but Zinoviev himself, writing afterwards in the Comintern journal, described the majority as 'non-party'.

Despite the euphoria, much of it obviously stage-managed, Zinoviev's appeal to Muslim aspirations was not without its dangers. For, if not handled carefully, Pan-Islam could be double-edged. Many of the delegates came from the newly-conquered former Tsarist territories of Central Asia and the Caucasus. There they had quickly learned that, despite all the slogans and promises, self-determination did not apply to them, only to other people's colonies. They had learned, moreover, that under their new, all-white rulers some were more equal than others. The Bolsheviks, it had become clear, regarded the Muslims as their subjects. Indeed, this was officially admitted, and was certainly known to Lenin, for Georgi Safarov, his special emissary to Central Asia, was in no doubt as to what was going on.

'It was inevitable', Safarov wrote later, 'that the Russian

revolution in Turkestan should have a colonialist character. The Turkestani working class, numerically small, had neither leader, programme, party nor revolutionary tradition. It could not therefore protest against colonial exploitation . . . For this reason the dictatorship of the proletariat took on a typical colonialist aspect.'

Once the razzmatazz was over and the serious discussion had begun, this disillusionment with the reality of Bolshevik rule began to be reflected in some of the speeches. Some delegates are said to have been openly critical of the Bolsheviks' colonial attitudes. But quite how far they went, and who they were, will never be known, for – or so it is claimed – they were struck from the record or drastically edited. But officially, the congress was hailed as a resounding success. As a final symbolic act before departing, the delegates had attended a funeral ceremony for the twenty-six Baku commissars who – with British connivance, the Bolsheviks claimed – had been executed in the desert by their White Russian captors, and whose bodies had been brought back to their home town for burial.

The Congress, in fact, had achieved very little, although its proceedings had been watched anxiously by the British through their agents among the delegates. For at this time, the entire Indian sub-continent, particularly its Muslim population, was seething with unrest, causing the authorities considerable anxiety. Muslim feelings had been inflamed by the humiliating dismemberment of Turkey's empire by Britain and her allies after the war. This had been exacerbated by fears about the future of the Caliphate, traditionally invested in the person of the Turkish Sultan. The British, it was whispered, were planning to abolish it, while the breaking up of the Ottoman Empire, it was believed, would anyway deny the spiritual leader of all Muslims access to the Holy Places of Islam. To add to Delhi's worries, Mahatma Gandhi and his supporters had decided to back their Muslim brothers by means of a massive nationwide campaign of non-cooperation. And if that were not enough, there had been the Amritsar massacre, when British troops shot dead some three hundred and eighty unarmed Indian demonstrators.

But if British fortunes in India were at a low ebb, things were beginning at last to look up for the Bolsheviks in Asia. Their prestige throughout the East had been considerably boosted by the failure of the Allied Intervention, and their ultimate triumph in the Civil War. Following the withdrawal of Malleson's troops from Russian soil, the oasis towns of Turkestan had fallen one by one to the Red Army, now under the able command of Mikhail Frunze. In February 1920 his troops had occupied the semi-independent Khanate of Khiva, just south of the Aral Sea, declaring it a People's Republic. That September, nine months after Bailey had sheltered there, the same fate befell Bokhara. After four days of fighting, and a vain plea by the Emir for British help, the Red Flag had fluttered from its picturesque, mud-walled citadel. The Emir had fled to Afghanistan, 'dropping favourite dancing boy after favourite dancing boy in his flight' – as one writer wryly put it – 'in the hope of thus retarding the advance of the pursuing Red Army'.

Although Soviet fortunes had picked up in Asia, in Europe they had suffered a serious reverse. Not only had the revolution failed to materialise there, but a last-ditch attempt to impose it by force of arms had resulted in humiliating defeat, and the headlong flight of the Red Army – part of which was commanded by Stalin. It happened in the autumn of 1920. After driving an invading Polish force from the Ukraine, where it had tried unsuccessfully to set up an anti-Bolshevik government, triumphant Red Army troops had crossed the frontier and advanced rapidly into Poland, Russia's age-old foe.

Here, Lenin believed, was his chance to carry the revolutionary banner at bayonet-point into Western Europe. For if Warsaw, with the help of the Polish workers, could be prised from the grasp of its capitalist rulers, who knew where it might not end? Comintern agents in Europe immediately set about trying to mobilise general support for popular uprisings. However, all they were able to achieve was a refusal by British railwaymen to handle munitions being shipped to the belea-guered Poles.

Despite warning voices inside the Kremlin, Lenin ordered the Red Army, its lines of communication now stretched to the limit, to seize Warsaw. But at the eleventh hour, when Red patrols had already reached the suburbs, the army was routed by the tactical genius of Marshal Pilsudski, aided by French staff officers under General Weygand. The Bolsheviks suffered some 150,000 casualties, and many more in the ensuing flight. Lenin had miscalculated badly. The Polish workers had not rallied to their would-be liberators. Worse, they had flocked patriotically to the colours of Marshal Pilsudski.

That autumn the long-awaited revolution in Europe must have seemed further away than ever to the disappointed men in the Kremlin, most of all to Lenin himself. But one man not in the least dispirited was the Indian revolutionary Roy. He had been convinced all along that the world revolution must begin in Asia and not in Europe. Burning with hatred for the British who occupied his homeland, and impatient for action rather than empty slogans, he set to work on a bold and grandiose plan aimed at both restoring Bolshevik fortunes and ending British rule in India.

With the backing of Lenin and the Revolutionary Military Council, headed by Trotsky, he proposed to recruit and train an army in Central Asia, and to invade and seize part of India. Roy knew full well what had happened to King Amanullah's ill-planned and ill-equipped attempt the previous year. But his own force would be far better armed and prepared than King Amanullah's. The Red Army instructors who were to train it had some three years of Civil War experience behind them, and in planning the invasion they would be able to draw on the military genius of men like Trotsky and Frunze, even if there was to be no direct Russian participation. For Roy's army would be recruited from disaffected Indian Muslims. Incensed by what they saw as Britain's harsh treatment of Turkey, and fearful for the future of the Caliphate, they had begun to leave

India in thousands, crossing into Afghanistan on their way to Turkey to fight the British, then still occupying Constantinople. But many of them, now hungry and destitute, had found themselves stranded in Afghanistan, without the means to proceed further.

The invasion (provided the co-operation of King Amanullah could be obtained) would be accompanied by waves of fanatically anti-British tribesmen, armed by Moscow, and thirsting for revenge after their humiliating defeat in 1919. Simultaneously, carefully orchestrated 'popular' uprisings would take place in India which, in turn, would spark off a chain reaction. As a liberating army, the invasion force – which was to be called 'The Army of God' – would thus advance further and further into India in the wake of these anti-British uprisings.

If the invasion was to be launched through Afghanistan – and there was really nowhere else – then the co-operation of King Amanullah was clearly crucial. As Lenin pointed out when Roy first put the plan to him, Amanullah was an opportunist, not a revolutionary. Ultimately he would always sell himself to the highest bidder. They must have no illusions about that. As a non-elected autocrat, moreover, he probably had more in common with the British than with the revolutionary ideals of the Bolsheviks. Nonetheless the strategy of revolution called for the exploitation of every opportunity. Moscow's representative in Kabul, it was agreed, would be given the delicate task of softening up King Amanullah.

On obtaining Lenin's go-ahead, Roy immediately began work while the rest of the Comintern hierarchy attended the Baku congress. The Indian had opposed this from the start, arguing that it could only serve the cause of agitation, which alone was not enough to bring about a revolution in the East. He recalls in his memoirs: 'Notwithstanding the temptation of being star of the show, I refused to join the picturesque cavalcade to the gates of the mysterious Orient. Lenin smiled indulgently on my cussedness; Zinoviev was angry at the audacity of the upstart crossing his will; Radek [Secretary to the

Comintern] ridiculed my precocious seriousness. It might not yield any lasting results, but why forgo the fun of a picturesque show which was sure to give the then British Foreign Secretary, Lord Curzon, some sleepless nights.'

Even his old friend Borodin, now back in Moscow from Mexico, had been exasperated by his lack of discipline – the highest Bolshevik virtue – while Chicherin, the aristocrat-turned-revolutionary, now Russia's Commissar for Foreign Affairs, had sat up into the early hours trying to change the mind of this stubborn Indian. Men and women had been liquidated for a good deal less than this, even in those early days before Stalin's grim reign began. But Roy enjoyed the patronage of the only man who counted, Lenin himself. While he had such support, he was inviolable. He was Lenin's chosen Greenmantle. With luck, when the time was right, he might set the East ablaze for them.

A fellow Indian revolutionary, who later deserted the Bolshevik cause, has left this description of Roy at that time. Writing in *The Times* of February 25, 1930, Abdul Qadir Khan recalls a 'tall, slim man with dark Bengali features and burning eyes, rather handsome and with a certain grace'. But while courageous and determined, he was also 'self-important and ill-tempered in discussion . . . and vehement in seeking to impose his opinions on others'. Indian Government intelligence assessments were considerably less flattering, and they could only assume that Roy must have somehow mesmerised the Bolsheviks with his gift for self-aggrandisement. While there was undoubtedly some truth in this, Lenin knew that he had very little to lose by giving Roy his head. Moreover, another thought was beginning to take shape in the mind of the Revolution's supreme strategist.

Meanwhile, so depleted were the Bolshevik armouries after three years of civil war, that even with Lenin's backing Roy had difficulty in obtaining arms in the quantities he needed. However, by the beginning of the winter of 1920 his convoy of weapons and instructors was ready to leave Moscow for

Tashkent, which had been chosen as the best location for training the secret liberation army. Already it was a busy centre for the dissemination of anti-British propaganda.

If Roy's own account of this extraordinary affair is to be believed – and no one has ever questioned it – the party left in two heavily-armed trains. One, consisting of twenty-seven coaches, contained an arsenal of rifles, revolvers, machine-guns, light artillery, ammunition, stores and field equipment, including wireless sets. It was escorted by two companies of Red Army troops, lest it fall into the wrong hands during the two-thousand-mile journey across regions in which armed White Russian bands still roamed. The second train, on which Roy himself travelled with the Red Army instructors and other staff, was even more heavily guarded. Two of its wagons were weighed down with gold coins and bullion, and a further ten carried dismantled aeroplanes. The Revolutionary Military Council had not, it seems, forgotten the lessons of the ill-fated Afghan invasion the previous year, when the RAF light bombers had left an indelible mark on the memories of the tribesmen. Camouflaged machine-guns were positioned on the roofs of the wagons carrying the treasury and Roy's warplanes. Seven other coaches were filled with military personnel.

Moscow was aware of the irregularities which had gone on in Turkestan in the name of Bolshevism, and one of Roy's tasks, as a member of the three-man Central Asiatic Bureau of the Comintern, which was to have its headquarters in Tashkent, was to ensure that the correct ideological line was pursued in future.

On reaching Tashkent in mid-November, he and his Red Army colleagues set to work at once to lay the foundations of the secret military school, complete with firing ranges and class-rooms for political indoctrination, where the first recruits of the all-Indian 'Army of God' would be trained for their great crusade. Details, even now, are sketchy, but the school's principal function seems to have been to produce officers and NCOs. The next step – provided Amanullah's co-operation could be obtained – would be to open a base in Kabul, and a number of forward operational bases on Afghanistan's frontier with India. The main task force, it appears, would be recruited from among the thirty thousand able-bodied and anti-British Muslims who had crossed into Afghanistan and were now stranded there. On arriving in Tashkent Roy found he already had a number of excellent recruits, trained in frontier warfare. These were deserters (he does not say how many) from the Indian Army, mostly Pathans, who were now trained by Red Army instructors in the use of machine-guns and light artillery, with which, they said, the British would not trust them.

While his Red Army team worked on setting up the school, Roy was able to pursue the other task with which he had been entrusted, that of speeding the de-colonisation of the Tsar's former territories along the correct ideological lines. One of the more bizarre of his responsibilities was that of 'liberating' the ex-Emir of Bokhara's harem, which was evidently proving too much for the local Bolsheviks. On his advice a proclamation was issued declaring that the Emir's four hundred wives were now divorced from him and were free to leave and marry whom they wished. Roy recounts:

'I felt that the proclamation would be a temptation for the soldiers, because the inmates of the harem were all good-looking and mostly young women. It was further declared that any soldier who would take a former inmate of the Emir's harem for his wife and settle down in peaceful domestic life, would receive a grant of land and some cash to cultivate it.'

Although there was no lack of interest among the soldiers, the wives seemed in no hurry to leave the luxury of their quarters for the uncertain world outside. The authorities were thus faced by a stalemate. Drastic measures were called for. It was decided that those soldiers who had responded to the proclamation would be allowed to enter the harem and choose themselves wives, provided there was no rowdyism or violence. Roy describes the scene:

'The storming of the harem took place under strict vigilance, and nothing unpleasant happened. The *begums*, of course, behaved like scared rabbits, but the sight of the husky young men scrambling for them must have made some impression on them. Able-bodied young men seeking their favour was a new experience to women whose erotic life naturally could not be satisfied by a senile old man. At the end it was a pleasing sight – the secluded females happily allowing themselves to be carried away by proud men.'

While in Bokhara, Roy received a report that a group of Indians had been captured by Turkoman tribesmen after crossing from Afghanistan into the Soviet Union. It turned out that they were Muslims on their way from India to Turkey where they hoped to fight for Kemal Ataturk against the British and other infidel forces occupying parts of Turkey. Fortunately General Frunze was still in Bokhara following its capture, and he ordered a Red Army detachment to be sent up the Oxus with a gunboat on a rescue mission. The Indians, some seventy of them, were freed and brought back to Bokhara where Roy was waiting for them. They were in a deplorable condition, starving and in rags, and had been kept tied up. When first freed they were so weak that they were hardly able to move.

Once they had recovered from their ordeal, Roy set about trying to recruit them. He pointed out the futility of their mission to Turkey, explaining that Kemal Ataturk had a fully-trained army of his own and would have no use for a handful of Indians with no military experience. 'I advised them', he recounts, 'to abandon their wild goose chase and settle down in Central Asia to be trained politically and militarily for future revolutionary activity in India.' Some fifty of them agreed to enlist in Roy's liberation army, but the remaining twenty, fanatical Muslims, insisted on proceeding to Turkey. Roy never discovered whether they survived the perilous journey, but his fifty volunteers travelled back to Tashkent with him, already wearing Red Army uniforms.

One of Roy's biggest problems was that of preventing news of his invasion plan from reaching the British. Once enrolled in the military school, recruits were forbidden to visit the bazaar, because some of the Indian traders who had not fled the Revolution were suspected of having pro-British sympathies, if not actual links. One day a British spy was found actually living among the recruits in the hostel, known as India House, where they were billeted. He was a tall, handsome Pathan, with black beard and turban, named Maulana. Roy reported his suspicions about the man to 'bloody Peter', the Cheka chief who had been sent to Tashkent by Moscow to liquidate spies and counter-revolutionaries. Maulana was followed, and it was noticed that he spent much of his time in the bazaar with Indian traders suspected of having pro-British sympathies.

After two Indian revolutionaries from Kabul had positively identified him as a known British agent, he was seized and searched. A large sum of Indian currency was found on him. The previous evening he had been seen in the bazaar with some of the recruits from the military school. When they were searched, sums of money were found on them too. 'The case', Roy wrote, 'was conclusive enough for the revolutionary justice of those days.' Maulana was sentenced to be shot. But a problem now arose. Because great revolutionary hopes were placed on the Indians, the possible repercussions if they executed one began to worry the Bolsheviks. No senior official was willing to take the responsibility of ordering the death sentence to be carried out.

Even the veteran revolutionary Molotov, then visiting Tashkent, refused to give the order. 'Molotov', sneered the Cheka chief, 'seems to be afraid of Allah's wrath.' The next day Molotov, later to be Soviet Foreign Minister, called on Roy to discuss the problem. 'Was it advisable', he asked, 'to kill an Indian comrade?' Roy pointed out that the man was certainly no comrade and, moreover, was a British spy. Finally, he recounts, he was forced to give the order himself. 'The daring Maulana was accordingly dealt with the next morning,' he wrote. To avoid any trouble among the Indians, both the arrest and execution were kept very secret. 'Not a single soul except those directly concerned with the affair knew anything about it,' Roy added. It was agreed with 'bloody Peter' that no action would be taken against the recruits known to have received money from Maulana.

Whether or not Maulana really was a British agent will probably never be known. His name does not appear in the secret intelligence files of the day. But on February 10, 1921, Colonel Etherton reported to his chiefs that 'several of my best agents' had disappeared recently in Soviet Central Asia. Maulana could well have been one of them.

*   *   *

Ever since the October Revolution there had been a growing awareness in India of the threat posed by what Churchill called 'the bacillus' of Bolshevism. That had been one of the reasons for sending Bailey to Tashkent. It was hoped that he would be able to discover there Lenin's precise intentions towards British India. Very soon, as the India Office files show, a steady stream of anxious telegrams was passing between the Viceroy and London, as fears of Bolshevik plans for a Soviet India grew. On June 18, 1919, London had signalled the Viceroy:

'There have been numerous indications recently that Bolsheviks are conducting organised propaganda in the East with special object of subverting authority of British Government . . . Have you considered whether special precautions are required to prevent Bolshevik agents from entering India either by sea or across land frontiers, and what measures do you contemplate for countering propaganda?'

To this the Viceroy, Lord Chelmsford, replied: 'All authorities concerned are alive to the importance of intercepting Bolshevik agents and literature . . . But with our vast frontier we must rely in the main on the evil being tapped at its source by means of intelligence systems at all chief centres of Bolshevik activities. . . . We ourselves are attempting to set up one such intelligence agency at Tashkent, now apparently most active centre where India is concerned.'

Just who was involved in the latter operation is not clear,

though the Viceroy was probably referring to the activities of Etherton's agents in Tashkent, for at that time Bailey had more or less been given up for lost. The passes leading into northern India and other overland approaches, the Viceroy assured London, were being closely watched, as also were India's many seaports. Were everything else to fail, he added, and Bolshevism gained ground in India, then force would have to be used to combat it.

On October 18 of the same year (just as Colonel Bailey was preparing to enter Bokhara) the Viceroy advised London that so far there had been few signs of Bolshevik activity within India. Were it to surface, however, it would be in a different guise from that manifested in Europe. It would, moreover, attach itself to any source of discontent or grievance it could find. One such grievance vulnerable to exploitation, he warned, would be among Indian Muslims roused to anger over Turkey. This was drafted exactly a year before Roy, with his Red *jihad*, set about doing just that. The Viceroy further warned London that he was 'not yet armed to combat it satisfactorily', although urgent measures were being taken to remedy this.

In January 1920, a special intelligence unit was set up in India to combat Bolshevism and monitor the activities of Comintern agents both at home and overseas. But it frequently found its work hampered by uncertainty over the Cabinet's current policy towards the Bolsheviks. Even the Viceroy on one occasion was forced to seek guidance on this after reading conflicting Reuter telegrams.

Another early difficulty arose from the lack of knowledge of the nature and aims of Bolshevism. To remedy this, a small library of books on the subject was hastily despatched to India from London. It included seventeen works on the theory and practice of Bolshevism, in English, French and German, and a detailed analysis of its implications in the Islamic world, specially prepared for the Director of Intelligence by 'an English Muslim'. This literature was particularly needed by those engaged in counter-propaganda, who endeavoured to besmirch the new creed and thus deter would-be converts. A word of caution on this was offered in an internal memorandum of March 1921. 'Great care', it warned, 'has to be taken not to overdo this matter of propaganda for fear of exciting . . . an unhealthy interest in the question in quarters where little or nothing may be known regarding it.'

Other clandestine work which the new intelligence bureau co-ordinated or carried out included the discreet reading of suspects' mail, the interception and decoding of Bolshevik wireless messages, and the penetration of Indian nationalist groups suspected of having links with Moscow. One very effective measure taken in connection with the latter was the banning of rouble notes from circulation in India, on pain of confiscation and prosecution, thus thwarting efforts by Roy's agents to purchase support. A close watch, too, was kept on Indian revolutionaries and revolutionary groups abroad, including the self-styled Provisional Government of Free India, then in exile in Kabul, and of course Roy himself.

Around this time a number of curious stories began to circulate about Bolshevik moves against India. One, reported by *The Times*, claimed that four hundred Indians, trained in agitation and armed with quantities of Soviet gold, were on their way to India to spread the Bolshevik gospel and overthrow British rule there. Another, attributed to a high-ranking Comintern official, claimed that a Soviet propaganda school in Samarkand had turned out some three thousand trained agitators, a quarter of them Indians who would shortly be returning to their homeland to preach the new creed. Already, it was claimed, Bolshevik schools had been opened in Delhi and Benares, under the very eyes of the British.

Such stories were clearly intended by Moscow to cause alarm in India. Significantly, they coincided with a change in Lenin's foreign policy strategy, and may well have been designed to put pressure on the British Government to open trade talks with Moscow. His revolutionary crusade in Europe having so far failed, Lenin now found himself desperately in need of vital plant and supplies with which to rebuild Russia's shattered economy. These could only be obtained in the West, and that meant a hostile Britain. Lenin, it appears, planned to try for the best of both worlds. By stepping up pressure on India, he might succeed in wringing concessions out of Britain – an old Tsarist game – without having to abandon his dreams of a Soviet India.

Certainly there were no signs of any let up by either side in the undeclared war for India. Etherton, at his lonely forward base in Kashgar, worked remorselessly to counter every Bolshevik move, and to maintain a continuous flow of intelligence on their machinations in Central Asia. Well pleased with his efforts, his chiefs signalled him on February 8, 1921: 'Government of India consider it advisable, in view of anticipated increase in Bolshevik activity in Ferghana, Semerechia, Chinese Turkestan and Pamirs in early summer, that intelligence organisation in this area should be strengthened by placing at your disposal for period of six months a King's commissioned Indian officer as intelligence officer. Government of India would be glad of your views by telegraph.'

Not only was the overworked Etherton grateful for this, but he also requested replacements for the agents he had already lost behind Bolshevik lines. All, he said, should speak Turki and Persian and 'be more or less accustomed to secret service'. They would have to use disguises and be prepared to take risks.

Meanwhile, as the clandestine struggle between Briton and Bolshevik continued, some thousand miles to the east one of the most blood-stained episodes in Central Asian history was about to commence.

9 The Bloody Baron

While Roy was planning the downfall of the British in India, elsewhere in Asia agents of the Comintern were already busy spreading the heady new revolutionary gospel. Early in 1920, Ivan Maisky, later to become the Soviet ambassador in London, had made a secret visit to Mongolia, then in the tyrannical grip of a Chinese general known as 'Little Hsu', where he established contact with a small group of Mongolian revolutionaries determined to rid their country of alien rule. A return visit to Moscow by the Mongolians – carrying a message for Lenin in the hollowed-out handle of a riding whip – had led to the setting up of a Mongolian People's Revolutionary Government in exile, just across the Soviet frontier. But how, without dragging the Red Army into an unwanted war with China, were a handful of Mongolian revolutionaries to drive out a greatly superior force of Chinese? It was at this moment that fate played into the hands of the Comintern, delivering Mongolia to them on a plate as the first country, after their own, to turn Communist. It happened like this.

In the tumultuous times which followed the Bolshevik Revolution and the Russian Civil War, Lenin was not the only one who dreamed of setting Asia ablaze. In the ancient caravan cities of Central Asia lesser messiahs were at work preaching rival creeds. In the early 1920s, two such visionaries appeared, each aspiring to found a great post-war empire in Asia. One was a Russian, a Buddhist, who believed himself to be the reincarnation of Genghis Khan. The other was a Turkish general who saw himself as heir to Napoleon. Both were virulently anti-Bolshevik.

The first to try his luck was the Russian, a madman named Baron Ungern-Sternberg. Today he would simply have been certified as a psychopath and locked up. But in the desperate days of the Civil War he had won renown among the White armies as a soldier of extraordinary – if reckless – courage, as well as ferocious cruelty. Truth and legend about the 'Mad Baron' are so inextricably mixed that it is difficult to be sure where one ends and the other begins. So much so, that one would-be biographer in the 1930s was forced to admit defeat after months of research and settle for a fictionalised account of the Baron's unsavoury life. Even his physical appearance presents problems. One contemporary remembers him with blue eyes, another with grey. One describes his hair as being red, another as yellow. One insists that he was tall, another that he was of average height. A fellow White Russian who met him in Mongolia in 1920 describes his appearance thus:

'A small head on wide shoulders, blond hair in disorder, a reddish bristling moustache, a skinny exhausted face like those on the old Byzantine ikons. Then everything else faded from view save a big, protruding forehead overhanging steely sharp eyes. These eyes were fixed on me like those of an animal from a cave.'

One officer who served under him recalls: 'He was tall and slim, with the lean white face of an ascetic. His watery blue eyes were steady and piercing. He possessed the dangerous power of reading people's thoughts . . . His broad forehead bore a terrible sword cut which pulsed with red veins. His white lips were closed tightly, and long blond whiskers hung in disorder over his narrow chin. One eye was a little above the other.'

Roman Nicolaus Fyodorovich von Ungern-Sternberg, to give him his full name, was born in 1887 of a long line of Baltic soldier-barons. They were descended, he claimed, from Attila the Hun. Over the centuries they had been crusaders, pirates and soldiers of fortune, and had founded the city of Riga as their stronghold. Fighting was the family's principal business, and so it became that of the latest in the line. But like almost everything about him there is more than one version of this. One says that he began as a cadet in the Imperial Russian Navy but, finding life too tame, ran off at the age of seventeen to fight in the Russo-Japanese War. Another maintains that he was expelled from naval college and that by the time he reached the Far East – on horseback across Siberia – the war was all but over.

Whatever the truth, in 1908 he obtained a commission in a Cossack cavalry regiment, and when hostilities broke out between Mongolia and China in 1911 he found himself, on secondment, commanding Mongol horsemen. Like T.E. Lawrence with his affinity for the Arabs, the young Ungern-Sternberg found himself strongly attracted to the Mongols and their vast empty land. During his four years there he even adopted their religion, Lamaistic Buddhism, and came to believe in soothsayers and the occult.

From 1914 to 1918 he fought with the Tsarist armies against the Germans, displaying the ferocious courage and leadership for which he was to become famous. He ended the war as a Major-General, aged only thirty-three and festooned with decorations, including the highly coveted Cross of St George. But despite this his military career had been blighted by a series of scandalous episodes, including frequent duels with fellow officers. As one writer on this period recounts: 'He had not the slightest rudiments of common decency or military discipline . . . Only his reckless courage prevented his being cashiered by various commanding officers under whom he had served . . . When Ungern-Sternberg entered a café other occupants retired, for he was an expert with his gun. In his drinking bouts he slew many of his own officers.'

His madness may well have been congenital, or may even have been the result of the terrible sabre cut across his skull. In any case, the sadistic side of his character seems to have come into its own during the Civil War, when barbarism became the norm. Unnumbered thousands of innocent people, including women and children, were slaughtered at this time, and Ungern-Sternberg's own wife and child are reputed to have been among the victims. If true, this may explain the passion to exterminate Bolsheviks which now possessed him.

After the collapse of the White armies, Ungern-Sternberg found himself in Siberia, now swarming with bands of marauding Cossacks and others, living off the land like brigands. Without a leader, it was only a matter of time before they would be rounded up by the Red Army and exterminated. However, an ambitious plan began to form in the tortured, half-demented brain of the baron. It centred on his beloved Mongolia, now occupied by the Chinese. With an army recruited from ex-White troops and from the Mongols themselves, he would drive the Chinese out of Urga, the capital, and back into their own country. Then, with the Mongol tribes behind him, and the blind Bogdo Khan – or Living Buddha – restored to the throne, he would proclaim a Greater Mongolia. This would be the rallying point for the final stage in his dream – the recreation of the empire of Genghis Khan, whose reincarnation he believed himself to be. At the head of an ever-swelling army, he would sweep across Russia, freeing his people from Bolshevik rule as he rode.

He immediately set about recruiting his task force. A former White officer, Dmitri Alioshin, has left us a vivid description of the baron as, whip in hand and wearing a cherry-red Chinese jacket and blue Imperial Russian Army breeches, he inspected a batch of recruits:

'He would stop at each man separately, look straight into his face, hold that gaze for a few moments, and then bark: "To the army", "back to the cattle", or "liquidate". All men with physical defects were shot until only the able-bodied remained. He killed all Jews, regardless of age, sex or ability. Hundreds of innocent people had been liquidated by the time the inspection was closed . . . His Buddhist teachers taught him about reincarnation, and he firmly believed that in killing the feeble people he only did them good, as they would be stronger beings in their next life.'

But ill-equipped, hungry and without funds, Ungern-Sternberg's crusaders needed more than sadistic discipline and his ferocious leadership to weld them into a serious fighting force. They also needed arms, money and food before they could march on the holy city of Urga with any real hope of capturing it. These, however, were not slow in coming.

The baron's benefactors were the Japanese. Deeply hostile to the Bolsheviks, and suspicious of Moscow's intentions in Asia, the Japanese had been one of the most active of the Interventionist powers. In Siberia they had been the mainstay of the White cause during the Civil War. With the collapse of anti-Bolshevik resistance, all of a sudden, new strategies became crucial if the Red tide was to be halted in Asia. Pinning their hopes on the 'Mad Baron', the Japanese promised him their full support. Precisely what this amounted to is uncertain, but it appears to have included weapons, funds and professional advisers – 'some tens of Japanese officers', was Ivan Maisky's estimate at the time.

With their own post-war Asiatic ambitions in mind, the Japanese had for some time been preaching a creed of their own invention – 'Pan-Asianism', or 'Asia for the Asians' – conveniently tailored to include themselves. Their backing of the baron's plans for a Greater Mongolia (which they had earmarked as a Japanese protectorate), and his holy war against the Bolsheviks, fitted very neatly into their designs for an empire in Asia. They had little to lose and much to gain by backing him.

Estimates vary considerably as to the size and composition of the force which Ungern-Sternberg led into Mongolia in the autumn of 1920. All those who took part in this bizarre campaign are now long dead, but Maisky, writing in 1921, put its strength at around six thousand. Of these, he says, some four thousand were White Russians, and the rest Mongols and other Asiatics. Alioshin, on the other hand, puts the total at only twelve hundred. The force was accompanied by a number of Buddhist soothsayers to whom Ungern-Sternberg could turn for advice. A Mongolian princess – the baron's new bride – also joined the march. Finally, Alioshin tells us, the Dalai Lama in nearby Tibet sent seventy of his finest warriors to act as bodyguard to this great new saviour who would rid Central Asia of both Bolsheviks and Chinese.

A wave of terror and blind panic now began to sweep across the country as the 'Mad Baron' started his advance on Urga. The reputation he had earned for horrifying and indiscriminate cruelty and sadism travelled ahead of him, alarming the Chinese garrison occupying the Mongolian capital, although it greatly outnumbered his force. Alioshin recounts how even his fellow-countrymen tried to flee before the baron's freebooters:

'In barbaric luxury and glory, Ungern moved through Mongolia, and by the middle of October began hostilities against the Chinese at Urga . . . Meanwhile, Russian refugees, like mice in a burning building, ran back and forth in despair looking for an escape. But it could not be found. The north was blocked by the Communists, the south by the dreaded Gobi Desert. The west was closed by an impenetrable and hostile Tibet. To the east were four thousand miles of travel between them and Manchuria.'

Those who did escape told appalling stories of the baron's atrocities. Alioshin continues:

'They related, for example, how the village of Buluktai was burned with the inhabitants locked in their huts; how Captain Vishnevsky was whipped to death; how the baron had strangled Colonels Lihachev and Yahontov; how his adjutant had killed Korotkov just to get his young and pretty wife; how Dr Engelgard-Esersky was burned alive at the stake.'

Sickened by all this, one of the baron's officers, a Captain Rujansky, decided one night to desert with sixty-eight of his men. A party of fierce Chahars – a Mongol warrior tribe – was sent off in pursuit. They returned with grisly evidence of their success, a sack filled with the fugitives' ears. 'Rujansky's beautiful wife', Alioshin relates, 'was given to the Chahars as a reward. She went insane and died in agony.' No one, he tells us, was spared, not even children. Bolsheviks and Jews, however, were the principal victims of the baron's atrocities, most of which are too horrifying to describe here.

By mid-October 1920 his force had reached Urga after marching nearly half way across a land the size of France, Germany, Italy and Britain combined. On the way scores of recruits, mostly the remnants of the broken White armies, had flocked to his banner. They had little choice. For most of them it was their only hope of survival, with the terrible Mongolian winter approaching and every other man's hand against them. Remembering how his fellow officers had once sought to get him cashiered, the baron now seized the opportunity to avenge himself. He reduced a number of former officers to the ranks, placing them under the men they had once commanded. Alioshin remembers:

'The former Russian officers were dressed in rags, with pieces of leather tied to the soles of their feet. Unshaven and dirty, cynical and cunningly cruel, they were lost to the world. Death was always welcome to them, and they fought like devils. Although utterly neglected, they were the cementing force that united the whole army.'

Finally, on October 26, Ungern-Sternberg launched his attack on Urga, after his Mongol soothsayers had declared it a propitious day. But they must have seriously misread the oracle bones. According to one account, the attackers ran into a withering cross-fire as they approached the capital under cover of darkness. Not only were the Chinese clearly expecting them, but they were well dug in and better armed. They also greatly outnumbered the attacking force. After suffering heavy casualties, the baron's men were driven back.

Undeterred, and still convinced of his divine mission, Ungern-Sternberg withdrew to some nearby hills where, amid severe snowstorms, his soothsayers once again consulted their oracle bones. The gods kept them waiting for five days, during which the baron's men suffered appallingly from the cold. Then, on October 31, came the signal that the moment was auspicious for an attack. But again they were beaten back by the Chinese. Two further attempts, according to Alioshin, were also repulsed. Even the baron was now forced to admit that it would require a stronger force than his present one to take the capital. He withdrew his army eastwards along the Kerulen river towards China, hoping to recruit fresh troops from the riff-raff of ex-White soldiery still roaming the area in armed bands. For some inexplicable reason the Chinese garrison commander chose not to pursue and destroy the baron's army. It was an error of judgement which was to cost him Urga.

The baron's initial setback had encouraged some of the more faint-hearted of his men to desert his cause at the earliest opportunity. Characteristically, he quickly put a stop to the rot by devising fiendish ways of punishing those who were caught. One of these was to roast them slowly by lowering them onto a fire from a tree. When Colonel Hiro Yama, commander of the Japanese detachment, decided that he had had enough and sought sanctuary with the Chinese at Urga, the baron sent the garrison a message warning them that he was a spy. When the Japanese reached Chinese lines he was arrested and executed. But not only deserters were killed. Those too badly wounded to fight were quietly disposed of by poisoning.

By January of 1921, Ungern-Sternberg felt able to advance once more towards the holy city. As before, there are no reliable figures as to the size of his force, but to judge from the outcome it must have been a far more formidable one than the first. In Urga, meanwhile, the Chinese had tightened their grip, imprisoning the blind and elderly Bogdo Khan, or Living Buddha, in his hill-top palace. Life became increasingly more repressive, and food and other shortages more acute. As word of the baron's advance reached Urga, he and his troops were seen by many there as deliverers. But they were in for an unpleasant shock – as were two car-loads of fleeing Jews who were unfortunate enough to be caught by one of the baron's patrols. 'All were lynched with great gaiety,' Alioshin recounts, their money being appropriated for the crusade's funds. Many of the early revolutionaries were Jewish, and therefore to Ungern-Sternberg Bolsheviks and Jews were synonymous.

His plan of attack was simple and, despite his earlier defeat, based on his arrogant assumption that one determined Russian soldier was worth ten ill-trained and half-hearted Chinese. From divine sources his soothsayers had learned that the Living Buddha would regain his liberty on February 1, and that their victory would be complete by February 4. The baron therefore decided that the assault would be launched under cover of darkness on the night of January 31. First, however, in the hope of saving precious ammunition and of swelling the ranks of his army for the coming anti-Soviet crusade, he had sent a message to the Chinese inviting them to join forces with him against the Bolsheviks. This had been rejected out of hand. If the baron wanted Urga, then he must be prepared to die for it.

Scorning the carefully prepared plan of one of his senior officers, Ungern-Sternberg now gave his orders for the attack. Addressing his men in his strange, high-pitched voice, he sent small groups of them into the hills surrounding Urga with orders to light huge fires as soon as darkness fell. This was intended to deceive the defenders into believing that they were completely cut off by overwhelming odds. 'It must be admitted,' Alioshin wrote, 'the sight was magnificent. It created an impression that there were almost a hundred thousand Russians.' According to Alioshin, the baron had only one thousand seven hundred men, while in Urga there were twelve thousand Chinese.

The main body of the baron's force, under cover of an artillery barrage, was ordered to storm the Chinese barracks, the defenders' principal stronghold. Another force was to attack simultaneously from the south, while a third, consisting of two hundred and fifty Russians and sixty Tibetan warriors, would secretly scale the Bogdo Ul, or holy mountain, setting free the Living Buddha. With him safely in their hands, the baron reasoned, they would enjoy the support of the entire Mongol population which would thus welcome them as liberators.

But on the night of the attack things started off badly for the baron's men. Although they were in position before midnight, the very high winds had delayed the arrival of the artillery, which was drawn by oxen. As a result it was already dawn by the time the batteries were ready to open up on the Chinese positions, and the enemy had spotted the baron's men and begun to shell and machine-gun them. This had caused the Mongol units, which were fortunately held in reserve, to flee in panic.

The attack, nonetheless, was pressed home with grim determination. Urga promised the attackers everything they lacked: food, clothing, ammunition and a dry, warm place to sleep in after months in the open, exposed to snow, rain and the cruel wind. If they could not take Urga this time, they knew that few of them would survive the rapidly worsening winter. Despite the heavy fire now directed against them, the main assault group quickly managed to capture two enemy field guns which were immediately turned at close range and with devastating effect on the Chinese themselves. Meanwhile the party sent to free the Living Buddha had successfully stormed his palace after taking the Chinese defenders by surprise. While fierce hand-to-hand fighting continued on the holy mountain, the old man was led out into the palace courtyard and helped by Buddhist priests into the saddle of a pony. According to one account, more than a thousand Chinese were killed in the fighting for the palace and quantities of machine-guns, ammunition and grenades captured. The latter were rushed to the main battlefront where they were quickly brought to bear on their previous owners. By early afternoon the baron's men, their morale running high, had gained the upper hand. Some two thousand of the Chinese, unused to such savage fighting, had already fled the battlefield.

But now something happened which very nearly cost the baron his victory. This time the predictions of the soothsayers had so far proved right. The Living Buddha was safely in his hands and victory lay within his grasp. But the gods had ordained that this would not come about for a further three days, not until February 4. The baron was unwilling to risk their wrath. He immediately ordered a ceasefire while his troops consolidated themselves, thus enabling the Chinese to do the same as they desperately awaited the arrival of reinforcements. However, during the night, one of the baron's men inadvertently – or possibly even intentionally – fired a rocket into the sky. Alioshin recounts what followed:

'Immediately the Chinese opened unsystematic and mad shooting. Machine-guns began their dreadful clattering. The temptation was too great and, contrary to orders, we dashed forward into the battle. The baron was carried away by the mad impulse also, as we saw him galloping on his white horse in front of our lines, directing us towards the enemy's barbed wire.'

While the attackers engaged the Chinese in hand-to-hand fighting, using bayonets, their cavalry attacked the defenders from the rear. Soon huge fires were burning in the Chinese quarter of the town – the work, it appears, of saboteurs. By the light of these, the Russians could see that they were now right under the walls of the Chinese barracks. The main gates were immediately blown open with grenades, and the triumphant attackers, lusting for Chinese blood, poured in. A massacre of the demoralised garrison now followed. Alioshin, the sole participant to leave an account of the fighting, describes the scene:

'Mad with revenge and hatred, the conquerors began plundering the city. Drunken horsemen galloped along the streets shooting and killing at their fancy, breaking into houses, dragging property outside into the dirty streets, dressing themselves in rich silks found in the shops. In front of the Chinese banks, lines were formed, where each man was given the right to plunge his bloody hand inside the strong boxes and get what his luck would bring him. Some were fortunate enough to drag out gold coins and bullion. Some were less fortunate and got silver, while many found only paper currency and bank notes, which they immediately threw into the streets as worthless.'

Wherever they could be found hiding, Jews were killed, their womenfolk first being raped. Russians who had been imprisoned by the Chinese were freed, and kissed and embraced their liberators. Many of the attackers were now so drunk that one Cossack began killing his own comrades, until he himself was shot dead. One particularly sadistic Russian, Alioshin tells us, liked strangling old women 'because he enjoyed seeing them quiver under the grip of his fingers as he broke their necks'. A Dane called Olsen, who courageously protested at the horrifying outrages he had witnessed, was dragged through the streets by a rope attached to a galloping horse until he was dead. One of the Russians who had been released from prison was shot on the spot when he injudiciously asked for a horse – just in case Ungern-Sternberg was forced to withdraw. A baker's boy suspected of Bolshevik sympathies was baked alive in his own oven. Young women were raped to death by whole squadrons of Mongol cavalry. Others offered to give their bodies in exchange for the lives of their menfolk – 'but as often as not', Alioshin recounts, 'were cheated in the end'. According to one account, 'innumerable men, women and children of all ages, races and creeds were hacked to bits and bayoneted and shot and strangled and hung and crucified and burnt alive' as for three nightmarish days the Mongolian capital was given over to murder and revenge.

Then, without warning, on the fourth morning the baron suddenly called a halt to the orgy of bloodshed, rape and plunder which had been his men's reward. He ordered that anyone who so much as laid a hand on a local, or touched anyone's property, would be hanged, while drunkenness would be punished by flogging. A number of unfortunates whom the order did not reach in time were hanged from the doorways of shops they were caught pillaging. Ferdinand Ossendowski, a Polish geologist who arrived in Urga at this time, describes how two Cossacks and a Mongol soldier were hanged outside one shop for stealing brandy. Shortly afterwards the owner went to plead with the baron to have the corpses cut down, as no one would come into his shop while they still hung there, and he was losing valuable business.

Ungern-Sternberg's Mongol scouts now warned that several thousand Chinese troops were approaching from the south, in two groups. These were the reinforcements which had been asked for by the Chinese garrison, and they appeared totally unaware that Urga had fallen. They thus became easy victims for the Cossacks sent to ambush them. An order had been given by the baron that no prisoners were to be taken, and over a thousand Chinese were slaughtered in the snow twenty-five miles outside Urga. A similar fate befell the second group. The few who managed to escape were very soon to die of thirst or cold in the Gobi desert. Meanwhile a third column was reported approaching from the north. These were the Chinese deserters who had been refused entry earlier by the Bolsheviks when they had sought sanctuary across the frontier. Their intentions appear not to have been clear, but the baron was taking no chances and sent a detachment of Cossacks to deal with them. After a brief battle, the Chinese surrendered, whereupon the baron ordered the officers to be killed, and the men to be incorporated in his army.

Ossendowski, while on his way to Urga, had crossed the spot where this action was fought and saw the corpses still lying there: 'The killed showed terrible sword wounds; everywhere equipment and other debris were scattered about. The Mongols, with their herds, moved away from the neighbourhood and their place was taken by the wolves which hid behind every stone and in every ditch as we passed. Packs of dogs that had become wild fought with the wolves over the prey.'

By this time news of the terrible disaster at Urga had reached Peking, and at once the northern warlord Marshal Chang Tso-lin was ordered to march against Sternberg. This he agreed to do with the greatest reluctance, and only on condition he was paid ten million Mexican gold dollars (a coinage then widely used in China). But after receiving three million in advance, he promptly approached the baron with a business proposition, uniquely Chinese.

If Ungern-Sternberg would agree to retreat before his advancing forces, Chang promised to pay him six hundred thousand dollars. Sternberg, according to one account, rejected this as being insufficient, and in return demanded a million dollars. However, this does not quite ring true, for the baron was a soldier, if nothing else, and lusted for glory, not for personal wealth. Moreover he was hardly short of funds, for he had already looted millions from the Mongolian state coffers. To have agreed to evacuate Urga, furthermore, would not only have meant sacrificing his dreams of a Greater Mongolia, but would also have robbed him of his base for the invasion of Russia.

Perhaps he simply intended to relieve the warlord of his money, and then renege on the deal. Perhaps the whole story is apocryphal. In any event their two armies never met, and it now fell to the Bolsheviks to try to rid the world of their appalling fellow-countryman.

10 'An Avenue of Gallows'

Convinced of his own military genius, Baron Ungern-Sternberg now boasted that he would plant 'an avenue of gallows', stretching all the way from Mongolia to Moscow, from which he would swing Bolshevik and Jew alike. While his troops prepared for the great crusade, which he promised would destroy Bolshevism for ever, the baron himself earnestly consulted the soothsayers, and issued numerous proclamations, each more boastful than the last. Finally, on May 27, 1921 he declared himself Emperor of all Russia.

In the meantime, much had been happening elsewhere. For a start, Lenin's strategy of wringing concessions from the British Government by exerting pressure on India had begun to bear fruit. In mid-March a deal had been struck between London and Moscow which enabled the Bolsheviks to buy from Britain desperately-needed plant and supplies hitherto denied them by the Allied blockade. But it offered them considerably more than that. Known officially as the 1921 Anglo-Soviet Trade Agreement, it also conceded to the fledgling republic, then still an outcast among nations, partial recognition by the greatest of the imperialist powers. To the nervous men in the Kremlin, further intervention by the Allies now seemed less likely.

The agreement was signed by Lloyd George, the British Prime Minister, despite strong opposition from Bolshephobe members of his coalition cabinet, including Winston Churchill, then Secretary of State for War, and Lord Curzon, the Foreign Secretary. As a *quid pro quo*, however, he demanded from Moscow a guarantee that all secret intrigues or other harmful activities against India would cease forthwith.

So that there could be no possible room for misunderstanding, and to remind Moscow that the omnipresent British secret service knew of everything that was going on in Tashkent and elsewhere, a peremptory note was handed to the Soviets at the signing ceremony. This accused them of seeking to bring about the overthrow of British rule in India. It also named certain 'notorious Indian seditionists', including Roy, who were known to be trying to foment violent revolution in India – either from inside Soviet territory or, with Moscow's encouragement, from Afghanistan. It further accused the Bolsheviks of trying to negotiate secretly with the Afghans for permission to transport arms and ammunition across their territory for use against British India. Finally the note insisted that the ending of all such activities – and particularly those in which Roy was currently engaged from Tashkent – was 'an essential corollary' to the signing of the agreement.

So it was that Lenin was obliged to call off Roy's grandiose plan for the invasion of India, and order the closure of the military school in Tashkent. For anxious to reap the immediate benefits of the new agreement, he wished to be seen to be adhering to his side of it. And with men like Etherton and Malleson around, it was proving impossible to keep anything secret for very long. Yet, as the British were shortly to discover, Moscow was conceding less than it might appear.

Because there were no formal diplomatic relations between the two governments, and therefore no exchange of ambassadors, it was agreed that instead each should appoint an official trade agent to reside in the other's country. Eager to start business as soon as possible, Moscow had opened in London a branch of Arcos Ltd, the official Soviet trade agency. At the same time the British security services, who were strongly opposed to the agreement, opened a file labelled 'Violations of the Russian Trade Agreement'. It was not to remain empty for very long.

The abandonment of Roy's plan in no way meant an end to the Comintern's designs on British India, as he himself recounts in his memoirs. 'The work initiated in Tashkent', he wrote, 'would henceforth be done more elaborately, on a larger scale, in the Communist University for the Toilers of the East, to be founded in Moscow in the near future.' The twenty-two most promising students from Tashkent – those who showed real revolutionary aptitude and grasp of the new ideology – were therefore brought to Moscow.

The problem now arose of what to do with the remainder, most of whom had turned out to be rather more trouble than they were worth. They had, wrote Roy, 'refused persistently to be trained as intelligent revolutionary propagandists', believing themselves to know the business better than their professional Bolshevik instructors, and even questioning his own authority. The majority (Roy does not say how many there were in all) now expressed a wish to return to India. But while not sorry to be rid of these failures, Roy had no wish to see them fall straight into the hands of the British the moment they crossed the frontier. For a start, they knew too much. So they were taken in small groups and, with the help of the Bolshevik border guards, infiltrated secretly across the frontier at various points. 'Once they were on the other side of the Russian border they were to depend on their own wits,' Roy wrote. 'In any case, we did not feel in any way responsible for what might happen to them.'

But despite Moscow's assurances that the Tashkent operation was being shut down, it appears that not all those sent home to India in this manner were allowed to go to waste. One of the returning Indians, who reached Peshawar in February 1922, told his British captors that he and his party had been given £1,400 and six rifles and made to promise that they would undertake clandestine work in India. They also brought with them letters addressed to northern tribal leaders urging risings against British rule along the frontier. The rest of Roy's failures, it would seem, just quietly disappeared, all thoughts of revolution forgotten, and only too grateful to be home. Others simply surrendered to the authorities. But these men, to be fair to Roy, had never had much stomach for insurrection. His star pupils, now receiving advanced training in Moscow, had still to take the field.

Officially, if only to give themselves a short-term gain, the

Soviets had acceded to British demands. Roy, Britain's particular *bête noire*, had been withdrawn from Tashkent, and his school shut down, even if its activities were merely switched elsewhere, safely out of reach of Etherton's ears. But it would appear that the British may well have been tricked even over this. For according to one contemporary witness, Tashkent continued to be used by the Bolsheviks as an insurrectionary centre, albeit in great secrecy.

Alexander Barmine, then a young Soviet official, reports finding it still flourishing late in 1921, some months after its supposed closure. In his memoirs, published after his defection, he describes how he went to an address he had been given in Tashkent for an organisation calling itself the Pan-Hindu Revolutionary Committee. As there was nothing to indicate that he had arrived at the right house, he asked a shoeshine boy lounging on the steps where the committee's headquarters were. 'He could tell me nothing', Barmine recalls. 'He was not interested in revolutionary committees and had no special desire to conquer India. But in trying to make him understand me I had raised my voice. An angry face with large eyes and a little black beard appeared at a window just above our heads. Its possessor laid a finger to his lips when he saw me and made a sign to enter by a neighbouring door.'

Coming down to meet Barmine, he told him: 'This is the committee. But why the hell are you shouting so loud? The committee doesn't exist officially. The Government has promised the English to dissolve it.' Barmine, who was himself involved in secret service work for Moscow, adds that the centre had done little more 'than take in its signboard, rename its publications, and give its military school a more innocent name'. Despite Moscow's policy of appeasement towards Britain, Barmine insists, Lenin had far from abandoned his plans for a Soviet India.

As with so much that was going on at that time, it is hard to know who or what to believe. However, the distinguished British historian of this period, E.H. Carr, accuses both sides of double-dealing. In his mammoth *History of Soviet Russia* he maintains that both the British and Soviet governments, 'undeterred by the agreement, continued to regard the activities of their own agents as legitimate retaliation or legitimate self-defence, and those of the other party as unprovoked aggression'. The only significant difference between them, he adds, was that 'while the British departments mainly responsible for the conduct of Anglo-Soviet relations at that time would willingly have seen the agreement break down, the corresponding Soviet authorities merely wanted to see how far they could go without causing a break'.

Whatever the truth, within six months of the agreement being signed, a blazing row broke out between the two governments. India, predictably, was at the centre of it. The 'violations' file opened by the British counter-intelligence services had been filling up. On September 7, 1921, Lord Curzon penned a tetchy protest to Chicherin, the Commissar for Foreign Affairs, enumerating alleged breaches of the agreement by Moscow. These included anti-British activities in India and other parts of Asia, and inflammatory utterances made by senior Bolshevik officials, including Stalin.

'In 1921,' one of the chiefs of the Comintern's Eastern Department was alleged to have declared, 'we are already taking the offensive against the foundations of capitalism in India.' Another Comintern official was alleged by Curzon to have boasted that they would shortly have a revolutionary base close to India from which British rule could be effectively undermined. To those responsible for the defence of India, this could only mean Afghanistan where, Curzon claimed, Dr Abdul Hafiz, a well-known Indian anarchist, had opened a bomb-making factory with the help of the Soviets.

Curzon's temper was not improved by the discovery, shortly after his note had been delivered, that some of the intelligence on which it was based was faulty, as Moscow was quick to point out. Nonetheless, the broad truth of his allegations could hardly be disputed. But here the Bolsheviks produced their trump card. Replying to the British charges, of which they naturally denied all knowledge, they disarmingly washed their hands of any responsibility for the activities or utterances of officials of the Comintern. This was an independent body, they claimed, with worldwide membership, which happened to have its head-quarters in Moscow. While some senior Soviet officials were also Comintern officials, this latter role was performed in their capacity as individuals. It was hardly necessary for Moscow to remind Lord Curzon that the agreement made no mention whatsoever of the Comintern or its activities.

Lord Curzon was not a man to take this lying down. Quickly firing off a second note, he pointed out that the Comintern's leadership included both Lenin and Trotsky, 'the two most prominent members of the Russian Government'. This, he insisted, established 'so close an identity between the two bodies that each must be answerable to charges against the other'. Furthermore, the Comintern had been set up in Moscow 'under the protection of the Russian Government, from which it draws constant support and resources'. His note concluded with words which, for sheer rudeness, can seldom have been surpassed in diplomatic exchanges. 'When the Russian Govern-ment desire to take some action more than usually repugnant to normal international law and comity,' he wrote, 'they ordinarily erect some ostensibly independent authority to take the action on their behalf . . . The process is familiar, and has ceased to beguile.'

There the matter rested, for the time being anyway. Mean-while, in far off Kashgar, news of the Anglo-Soviet agreement had come as a bombshell to Colonel Etherton. For it was to put a stop to his personal war against the 'Red scum', as he called the Bolsheviks. But after being advised of the British Gov-ernment's prohibition of all such anti-Soviet activities, he informed his chiefs: 'I am not relaxing vigilance in any way with regard to Bolshevik designs against India and the East in general. But my enquiries and investigations have to be conduc-ted with great circumspection.'

*   *   *

By the spring of 1921, in the Mongolian capital, Baron Ungern-Sternberg was almost ready to launch his crusade against what he described in one of his proclamations as 'the criminal destroyers and defilers of Russia'. For all Bolsheviks and Jews, together with their families, there was only one punishment – death. Or, as this specialist in barbaric methods of execution put it with relish, death 'in various degrees'.

The baron's last strange days in the Mongol capital are described most graphically by Dr Ossendowski, the Polish geologist, in his memoir *Beasts, Men and Gods*. He recounts how he accompanied Ungern-Sternberg on a visit to a Buddhist temple to pray for victory over the heathen Bolsheviks. Passing between the low benches where the saffron-robed lamas sat in prayer, they approached the great altar. There, by the glow from the flickering butter-lamps, Ossendowski could discern sacred vessels of gold and silver. Behind the altar hung a heavy curtain of yellow silk bearing Tibetan characters. The priests now drew this aside.

'Out of the dim light from the flickering lamps', Ossendowski recalls, 'gradually appeared the great gilded statue of Buddha seated in the Golden Lotus. The face of the god was indifferent and calm, with only a soft gleam of light animating it . . . The baron struck the gong to attract the Great Buddha's attention to his prayer, and threw a handful of coins into a large bronze bowl. And then this great scion of crusaders closed his eyes, placed his hands together before his face, and prayed.'

He remained there motionless for about ten minutes. Twisted around his left wrist, the Pole noticed, was a string of black Buddhist prayer-beads. Finally the baron rose. He turned to his companion with a frown and said: 'I do not like this temple. It is new, erected by the lamas when the Living Buddha became blind. I do not find on the face of the golden Buddha either tears, hopes, distress or the thanks of the people. They have not yet had time to leave their traces . . . We shall now go to the old Shrine of the Prophesies.'

He next led the way to a small building, blackened with age, with huge copper prayer-wheels either side of the entrance. Inside, in the gloom, sat two lamas reciting sutras. Addressing them in his strange, high-pitched voice, he ordered: 'Cast the dice for the number of my days.' Two bowls were hurriedly fetched, each of them filled with dice. The baron and Ossendowski looked on tensely as these were spilled onto a table. In silence they added up the total. The baron was the first to speak. 'One hundred and thirty!' he said. '*One hundred and thirty days*!'

The oracle of the Shrine of Prophesies had spoken. Baron Roman Nicolaus Fyodorovich von Ungern-Sternberg, descendant of Attila the Hun, would-be conqueror of Central Asia and the whole of Russia, was being given just four months and seven days in which to carry this out. Then – extinction. Seemingly unperturbed, the baron now moved to the altar on which rested an ancient figure of Buddha carved from stone. Standing silently before this, he began once more to pray, ceasing only when dawn broke over the holy city.

As the fateful day chosen by the soothsayers for the launching of the crusade approached, the baron became more and more preoccupied with sorcery. One night he took Ossendowski to the *yurt*, or tent, of a Mongol prince who had fought against both the Germans and the Bolsheviks with him. A woman celebrated among the tribes for the accuracy of her prophesies was sent for. Squatting down before the baron she stared for a while into his face. Then, drawing a small bag from her sash, she took from it some dry grass and the bones of a bird. She began to utter unintelligibly and to toss handfuls of grass onto the brazier, filling the *yurt* with a soft fragrance. With a pair of small bronze tongs she now placed the bones one by one on the glowing coals. As they blackened, she removed them from the brazier and examined them carefully. Her face now began to show fear, and her body to convulse. Finally she spoke: 'I see . . . I see the God of War . . . His life runs out . . . horribly . . .

After it a shadow . . . black like the night . . . Beyond it darkness . . . Nothing!'

For the first time the baron seemed shaken, and bowed his head. Her revelation over, the sorceress collapsed and was carried from their presence by servants. When she was gone, the baron rose and began to circle the brazier, whispering to himself. Then, suddenly, he began to address them. He would die, he said, for Karma had so decided. But this did not matter: 'The cause has been launched and will not die. The tribes of Genghis Khan's successors are awakened. Nobody shall extinguish the fire in the heart of the Mongols. In Asia there will be a great State from the Pacific and Indian Oceans to the shore of the Volga. The wise religion of Buddha shall run to the north and the west. It will be the victory of the spirit . . .'

A new conqueror would arise, he told his awe-struck audience, who would be even greater than Genghis Khan. He would rule until 'from his subterranean capital shall emerge the King of the World'. But first Russia must 'wash herself from the insult of revolution, purifying herself with blood and death'. Finally, as dawn was breaking outside, he told them: 'My moment has now come. In a little while I shall leave Urga.' He then shook hands with them all. 'The door of the *yurt* slammed shut and he was gone,' Ossendowski recounts, adding: 'I never saw him again.'

*　　　*　　　*

In India meanwhile, a new figure had appeared on the political scene who broke all the rules of revolution laid down in the Comintern textbooks. By sheer charisma he had succeeded in uniting the aspirations of India's millions into a mass movement which, for a time, embraced Hindu and Muslim alike. The phenomenon of Mahatma Gandhi who, clad only in a loin cloth, was to take on the full might of the Raj, still defies Marxist explanation and occupies their theoreticians.

At first the Bolsheviks had hoped to make use of Gandhi's immense popularity for their own ends, but eventually he was to prove as much a threat to their ambitions for a Soviet India as he already was to British rule there. Back in February 1919, using passive resistance tactics he had successfully tested while living in South Africa, Gandhi had launched a civil disobedience campaign which united Hindus and Muslims against the authorities. (He had won Muslim support by embracing their cause over the harsh treatment meted out to Turkey by the Allies after the war.) Gandhi's other far-reaching achievement of this period had been to transform the Indian National Congress, whose leadership he had assumed, from what was little more than a debating society for the intelligentsia into a nationwide political party for the masses.

For a full account of the Indian freedom movement the reader must turn elsewhere, for it is outside the scope of this book. Sufficient to say, while the Bolsheviks were agonising over doctrinal difficulties, Gandhi had seized the initiative, thereby stealing a march on Roy. However, Roy was not a man to give in easily, and if he did not frighten Gandhi, he would continue to send shivers down British spines, as we shall see.

* * *

On May 27, 1921, Baron Ungern-Sternberg moved his forces northwards into Soviet territory. All the signs, his soothsayers had assured him, pointed to an overwhelming victory. In Urga's temples special services were held, with hundreds of lamas praying for the baron's forces – or so they told him. More likely, sickened by his sadistic rule, they prayed for his defeat. His troops, flushed by their earlier victories against the ill-trained Chinese, expected only half-hearted resistance from their Red Army adversaries. The Bolshevik soldiers, the baron promised them, would desert in thousands and flock to his own banner. But if they believed this, they were in for a shock, as was the baron himself. His long stay in Urga had given the Bolsheviks time to concentrate their forces along the Soviet-Mongolian frontier, and now they were ready for him.

Several battles ensued. In one, lasting six hours, the attacking

Red Army cavalry was finally driven off, triumphantly pursued by a squadron of the baron's own horsemen. But the Bolshevik commander proved more than a match for the baron who, for all his fanatical courage, had regularly failed his tactical examinations. For the cock-a-hoop Whites raced headlong into a carefully laid ambush, as Dmitri Alioshin, the only man to leave an account of the fighting (Dr Ossendowski was very sensibly on his way to Peking), recounts.

'We were in the middle of the forest when the Reds opened deadly fire,' he wrote. 'Our men were swept from their feet like grass before a scythe. Men and horses were piled together in bloody heaps.' By late evening those who had managed to escape regrouped in a valley six miles from the Russian town of Kyakhta. Just inside the Soviet frontier, it was the headquarters of the Mongolian People's Revolutionary Government in exile. That night the baron ordered his men to attack and capture the town early the next morning. But the Red Army troops rose even earlier, striking without warning, and from two directions simultaneously.

'In great panic, half asleep and barely dressed, our men ran headlong,' Alioshin recalls. An entire battery of artillery, many machine-guns and quantities of ammunition were thus allowed to fall into Red Army hands. During the ensuing flight, and although wounded, the baron courageously tried to rally his men. Meanwhile his main force found itself encircled by the Bolsheviks. Numerically superior and better armed than their adversaries, the baron's men nonetheless panicked. Alioshin describes the rout. 'The Whites threw away their heavy ammunition, artillerymen cut loose their horses from the guns, the hospital personnel abandoned their wounded, men in charge of our transport left ammunition and food, and all dashed madly into the hills.'

His situation was so bad now that the baron had no choice but to withdraw from Soviet territory into Mongolia, and try to regroup before launching a fresh attack. Here they were joined by two Mongolian regiments from Urga and White units which had been held in reserve. Their second foray into Soviet-held territory proved rather more successful. They caught the Bolsheviks by surprise, wiping out what Alioshin, in his book *Asian Odyssey*, claims was an entire Red Army division, although he gives no casualty figures to justify this. 'With the exception of some hundred men,' he tells us, 'all the Reds perished in the fierce battle.' He adds: 'We shot every prisoner.'

Another victory followed, this time against the 35th Bolshevik Cavalry Division (although he more likely means squadron). Alioshin writes: 'The prisoners were forced to dig large communal graves at which they were subsequently lined up. Machine-gun fire was directed upon them, and they fell into the fresh grave. The lucky ones were killed instantly, but those who were only wounded were buried alive when we filled the grave with earth.'

With a hint of relish (after all, he was one of the baron's freebooters himself), he tells us: 'The Red nurses were given to soldiers hungry for women's bodies. All died during the endless humiliation.' But by now the Bolsheviks had begun to rush reinforcements up to the front, including aircraft. Once again the baron's forces were driven back into Mongolia. There was no returning to Urga, however, for this was now in Bolshevik hands. They had been invited in as liberators by their puppets, the exiled Mongolian People's Revolutionary Government. It was a strategy with which the world was soon to become familiar. So it was that Mongolia became Moscow's first client state, and the second country to turn Communist. Baron Ungern-Sternberg had made it easy for the Russians. Mongolia had been handed to Lenin on a plate.

But the baron's own fate, so graphically foretold by the sorceress, had yet to be decided. Even he now recognised that he could not win, and that his men's belief in his genius had finally deserted them. Escape was now their only hope, for avenging Red Army troops were closing in on them. Ungern-Sternberg decided to make a break for it and head westwards towards Chinese Turkestan with the remnants of his force.

There other defeated White troops had sought refuge from Bolshevik wrath.

His head bowed, the baron rode silently at the head of his broken and demoralised army. But even now they left a trail of atrocities, pillage and destruction behind them. 'The baron', Alioshin tells us, 'had lost his hat and most of his clothes. On his naked chest numerous Mongolian talismans and charms hung on a bright yellow cord.' So horrifying was his appearance that people were afraid even to look at him. Some of his disillusioned soldiers now began to plot against this madman who had brought them so much misfortune.

One night, when the baron was asleep in his tent, they opened fire on him with a machine-gun at point-blank range. To their amazement, he dashed out of his tent, leaped on his horse and galloped off into the darkness. But after a while he suddenly reappeared, covered with blood, to confront the mutineers. Such was the effect of his presence, even in defeat, that his men stood momentarily rooted to the spot, terrified by the prospect of the retribution which must surely follow. Then, summoning up his courage, a captain named Makeev drew his revolver and fired a shot at the baron. It missed, but realising that he cold hope for no further loyalty from these men, the baron wheeled his horse around and before anyone else could fire at him, vanished into the night.

Everywhere he turned now, even from his once most trusted units, he met with hostility. Finally, Alioshin tells us, 'bleeding, exhausted and helpless, Baron von Ungern-Sternberg slid from his saddle and fell to the ground unconscious.' He was to remain there, badly wounded, and tormented by ants, until he was discovered by the Mongolians. The remnants of his army, after an orgy of blood-letting and revenge in which the now maddened Cossacks hacked to pieces the most detested of the baron's officers, managed to escape into China. Among them was Alioshin. (Attempts to discover what finally became of him – if that was even his real name – have proved abortive, for the records of his publishers were destroyed during World War II.)

After coming upon the wounded baron out on the plain, the Mongols debated among themselves what to do with the man whose insane dreams had ruined them all. No one dared shoot him in cold blood, for they were convinced that he was immortal and enjoyed divine protection. There was only one solution they could think of. So there could be no possible risk of his escaping, and bringing further suffering to their land, several of the most fearless of them rode out to where he lay with a length of rope and bound him hand and foot. Then, in terror of divine retribution, they quickly galloped off.

The following day, writhing about trying to shake off the ants, he was found by a Red Army patrol, apparently by chance. Not recognising him at first, and unsure whether he was friend or foe, they asked him who he was. 'I am Baron von Ungern-Sternberg,' he screamed at his captors, or so it is said, whereupon they retreated to a safe distance to confer. Possibly, buried deep in the Red Army archives, there lies the patrol commander's report of the baron's capture. But, as always when writing about Sternberg, especially so many years afterwards, it is well-nigh impossible to separate truth from legend.

Even *The Times* carried a report on September 13, 1921, that the baron was being exhibited 'as a monster' at the stations of the Trans-Siberian Railway *en route* for trial in Moscow. In fact, at that very moment he was being tried on a series of charges, all carrying the death penalty, before the Soviet Supreme Court at Novosibirsk, in Siberia. He was accused, among many other things, of trying to overthrow the Soviet Government, plotting to restore the monarchy, butchering vast numbers of innocent people, and perpetrating the most barbaric atrocities. One American report describes the scene: 'It was an extraordinary trial. Hundreds of workers, peasants, soldiers – Russians, Siberians, Mongolians and Chinese – jammed the courtroom. Thousands more stood outside in the street. Many of these people had lived through Ungern's reign of terror. Their brothers, children, wives and husbands had been shot, tortured or hurled into the boilers of locomotives.'

Showing no signs of fear at the fate awaiting him, the baron challenged the right of a 'people's court' to try him. He told his Bolshevik accusers: 'For a thousand years Ungerns have given other people orders. We have never taken orders from anyone. I refuse to accept the authority of the working class.' Defiant to the end, he denied none of the charges, telling the court that he had killed so many people because they were 'too Red'.

Needless to say, the judges found the baron guilty on every charge. Sentenced to death a dozen times over, he was put before a Red Army firing squad on September 15, 1921 and shot – just one hundred and thirty days after the dice had foretold his fate that strange night in the Shrine of Prophesies at Urga.

The Bolsheviks, of course, had little time for divination, even in those outlandish parts. Otherwise they might have been forewarned by the soothsayers of another storm brewing in the East – one, moreover, which threatened to engulf the whole of Russian Central Asia and rob them of their newly-won empire there.

The execution of the 'Mad Baron' in a muddy prison yard that chill autumn morning brought to a close one of the most bizarre and bloody episodes in modern Central Asian history. But although the Civil War, which had left an estimated ten million dead, was finally over, even now the Bolsheviks were not fully masters in their own house. In the mountains and valleys of southern Turkestan peace still remained a long way off.

Skulking in their lairs in the Ferghana Valley region, and in Eastern Bokhara, were bands of fanatical Muslim freedom fighters who had sworn on the Koran to rid their homeland of the godless Bolsheviks – and indeed of all Russians. These were the *basmachi* – half patriot, half brigand – with whom, three years previously, Colonel Bailey had vainly tried to make contact from his bee-farm refuge.

The uprising had largely been of the Bolsheviks' own making, sparked off originally by the Tashkent Soviet's brutal sacking of the ancient Muslim town of Kokand in 1918. This act had alienated the entire Muslim population of Central Asia. The Bolsheviks' subsequent neo-colonialist attitudes had finally dashed any hopes among the native population that the Revolution was intended to benefit *them* as well as the European Russian settlers who had taken it over.

Within weeks of the Kokand massacre, *basmachi* bands had been formed in almost every town and village in the surrounding areas. If their leaders lacked experience of modern warfare, they made up for it in other ways. Like the Pathans of the North-West Frontier, the *basmachi* displayed fanatical courage, great endurance and possessed an intimate knowledge of the Central Asian terrain. They also enjoyed the wholehearted support of the local Muslim population, so crucial in partisan warfare. Furthermore, the movement was gaining strength all the time, as each fresh blunder by the Bolsheviks swelled its ranks with eager new recruits. At one time, it has been estimated, there were as many as twenty thousand *basmachi* in the field, although many of them were part-time rebels: peasants by day and guerrillas at night.

What the movement did not have was a united front and a single, charismatic leader. As with the *mujahidin* in Afghanistan today, there was rivalry and distrust among the individual groups and leaders. They came from different tribes and had no political programme as a basis for co-operation. Even with their common Turkic origin, shared faith and purpose, they found it impossible to achieve a unified strategy or command. As a result, their operations against the Bolsheviks were largely uncoordinated, and limited to laying ambushes, carrying out sabotage and assassinations, and other partisan-type activities.

On the other hand, the troops sent against them were all that the Red Army, then still hard-pressed in the Civil War, could spare. Their commanders were inexperienced, while their men were unused to either the climate or the terrain. Many died of illness, particularly malaria. At one time, it has been estimated, nearly ninety per cent of the men in some units were suffering from malaria. In those early days, moreover, the Tashkent Bolsheviks were totally isolated from Moscow and only concerned with their own survival. They made no attempt to woo the Muslim population, or even to play off one tribe against another. Their tactics were brutal, inept and counter-productive.

But then, as the Civil War began to draw to an end, the tide started to turn against the ill-armed *basmachi*. With the defeat of the White Russians, more and more battle-experienced Red Army troops were freed for transfer to the Central Asian front, including Mikhail Frunze, a commander of exceptional ability. Following his arrival in Central Asia in February 1920 the days of the *basmachi* seemed numbered. They found themselves forced to surrender, one after another, the towns and villages they controlled in the agriculturally rich Ferghana Valley region. In a clever move, Frunze brought in Muslim units of the Red Army from the Caucasus to help subdue their rebellious co-religionists. This proved surprisingly effective, and many of the rebels surrendered their arms, some even joining the Red Army ranks to fight against their erstwhile comrades. (It is interesting to note that when, sixty years later, Moscow tried to repeat this tactic in Afghanistan, it was to fail miserably.)

In spite of these reverses, the *basmachi* were still far from beaten. From their secret hideouts in the mountains they kept up the struggle against these new-style colonialists with their blasphemous creed. 'Russians Go Home' and 'Down with the Infidels' became the cry. Now and again the Bolsheviks would play into their hands with a move – like Frunze's seizure of Bokhara, the holiest city in Central Asia – which intensified Muslim hostility and swelled the *basmachi* ranks. At such times even the Muslim units of the Red Army showed signs of rest-lessness, numbers of soldiers deserting to the rebels. Thus, throughout 1920 and 1921, the struggle continued, with Frunze trying hard to undermine the *basmachi* cause by making conces-sions to the local populace, while stepping up military pressure against the guerrillas.

Then, in the autumn of 1921, in a bid to break the *basmachi* for good and woo the Muslim masses to the Bolshevik cause, Lenin himself decided to take an enormous gamble. The man he chose to carry out his plan was a former Turkish general named Enver Pasha. Although his name is all but forgotten today, at that time it was certainly one to conjure with. For Enver, as absolute ruler of the Ottoman Empire while still only in his mid-thirties, had led Turkey against the Allies during the war.

Despite his humble origins (his father was a bridge-keeper and his mother a despised layer-out of the dead), Enver had enjoyed a brilliant, and at times romantic, career. Through sheer ability and ambition, he had risen from penniless subal-tern, through Staff College in Constantinople, to play a leading role in the Young Turk revolution of 1908. Political intrigue was second nature to him. On the eve of the uprising, and disguised as a lemonade vendor, he had given the Sultan's secret police the slip and led a march of young officers on the capital. This had caused one leading British statesman to liken him to Garibaldi.

On the outbreak of World War I, at the age of thirty-two, the handsome Enver was appointed Turkey's Minister of War and promoted to Major-General. Small and dapper, and of mercurial temperament, he was as agile as a panther and said to be the finest fencer in the Turkish Empire. At the dinner table he was charming, polished, gallant and highly articulate in French and German. Daring in action, he was a familiar figure to his troops in his tall (to give himself added inches) astrakhan hat and immaculate uniform. Proud, vain, headstrong, chivalrous and cunning – all these epithets have been applied to the flamboyant Enver.

But with the defeat of Turkey, his fortunes naturally took a heavy fall. As head of the triumvirate which had led the nation to disaster and the loss of its huge Middle Eastern empire, Enver was forced to flee the country to save his neck from the hangman's noose. Sentenced to death in his absence by a Turkish court seeking a scapegoat for the nation's misfortunes, his first sanctuary was Berlin where he had once had powerful friends. But Germany too was a defeated nation. Realising there was little he could do from there to regain the post-war leadership of Turkey, and fearful of falling into the hands of the odious British, he flew secretly to Moscow at the invitation of Lenin, who was then busy gathering likely prospects under his roof.

It was here that the Indian revolutionary Roy, himself then still a contender for Lenin's ear, first met Enver. Accompanied by his friend Borodin, he called on the Turkish leader in his apartments in the Soviet state guest-house overlooking the Kremlin. 'We were received with oriental courtesy, followed by a sumptuous tea party', Roy recalls. 'The famous Turkish leader was still rather young, most probably under fifty. Though not above middle height and somewhat on the plump side, he was a handsome man. Dressed in a tight-fitting uniform, he spoke in elegant French . . . The flow of his polite salon conversation, enlivened by occasional bravado, did not give me any opening for a serious talk. It was clear that he was not at all disposed to talk business with a stranger who had no official status.'

Roy noticed several large diamond rings on Enver's fingers, while Borodin's first words as they descended the staircase afterwards were to ask his friend whether he had observed that the Turk wore a corset. It is clear that both took a dislike to Enver. In Roy's case this was hardly surprising, for at this stage Lenin had not yet approved his plans for the invasion of India, and it was clear that Enver had similar aspirations.

Enver's proposal to Lenin, when it came, was breathtakingly simple. Through his prowess as both soldier and revolutionary, he would deliver British India to the Bolsheviks in exchange for their help in restoring him to power in Turkey, which by now was in the grip of one of his former colonels, Mustapha Pasha, better known today as Kemal Ataturk. Enver intended first to seize Chinese Turkestan and, having forcibly ejected the Chinese, to establish a Muslim republic there as a base. From there (and not from Afghanistan, as Roy proposed) a full-scale holy war would be launched against British India.

One finds oneself wondering, uncharitably perhaps, whether Roy did not somehow leak this rival plan of Enver's to the British in a deliberate attempt to strangle it at birth. It could, of course, have been simply the result of careless talk. But certainly British intelligence got wind of it, as the political and secret files show. According to one of their Indian agents in Moscow: 'Enver Pasha and other Turkish leaders are organising and training a big Turkish and Tartar army in East Turkestan for the invasion of India.' In the event, the British were unable to take it seriously. After all, had anything like this really been brewing in Chinese Central Asia, it would hardly have escaped the attention of Colonel Etherton in Kashgar.

Roy claims in his memoirs to have guessed from the start what Enver's real game was. The Turk, he believed, had no more time for Bolshevism than Lord Curzon had. However, a temporary alliance with Moscow could help him towards realising his own secret dream. This was to found a great new Pan-Turkic empire, stretching from Constantinople in the west to Chinese Turkestan and Mongolia in the east, which would unite all the peoples and tribes of Turkish ancestry. It would also embrace Russian Turkestan, enabling him – in Roy's words – 'to carve out of the fallen Tsarist Empire a kingdom for himself and perhaps his descendants'. Nor, as it turned out, were Roy's suspicions so far out.

Nonetheless, while wary of Enver, and having him closely watched, Lenin believed that this charismatic figure, who still enjoyed a considerable following among Muslims, might in due course prove valuable. So far Kemal Ataturk, in his new capital Ankara, was showing himself to be friendly towards his Soviet neighbours, and gratifyingly hostile towards the British, whom Moscow wished to see dislodged from their age-old position in the Middle East. But were this formidable and unpredictable ruler to turn against them for any reason, then the ambitious Enver might prove a valuable card for them to have up their sleeve.

Anyway, he could hardly be asked to leave the safety of Moscow at that juncture, for as Roy points out, 'his fanatical admirers would accuse the Soviet Government of having delivered the greatest son of modern Asia to the vindictiveness of British imperialism.' On the other hand, Roy claims – and there is no corroboration of this – that at one time the Bolsheviks actually considered disposing of their awkward guest. It was no secret, he tells us, that Enver and his Turkish entourage made full use of the Moscow black-market, a crime punishable by death under the Soviet penal code. 'Bloody Peter', the Cheka chief – writes Roy with hardly disguised relish – would happily have attended to the rest if called upon. But Chicherin, the Commissar for Foreign Affairs, would have none of it, for it would have caused an international scandal 'if Enver Pasha simply disappeared from Moscow'.

Whatever the truth of all this, Enver's political fortunes reached a low ebb on March 16, 1921, when Moscow finally signed a treaty with his arch-foe Ataturk. But he somehow managed to conceal his resentment from his hosts, for, having no illusions about the motive for Lenin's hospitality, he had by now made up his mind to double-cross the Bolsheviks. There are (as so often) several versions of what followed. But it appears that the unsuspecting Lenin despatched him to Central Asia hoping that he would exert his considerable influence on the local Muslim population and thus woo them away from the *basmachi* – a sort of Greenmantle in reverse.

Enver arrived in Bokhara, now firmly in Bolshevik hands, on November 8, 1921. It was the first time he had set foot in this fabled city. There, unknown to his Russian hosts, he managed to make secret contact with the local *basmachi* leaders. According to the Turkish historian Ahmed Togan, who was himself at that time with the *basmachi*, Enver was deeply affected at finding himself in the cradle of the Turkish race, sitting cross-legged among the men he was to lead against the Bolsheviks. For this was the very eve of what he believed to be his historic destiny.

The next morning, in Turkish officer's uniform, he rode eastwards with twenty-four trusted followers, some of them his own staff, the rest local *basmachi*. His hosts believed that he was off on a hunting expedition, though they would have been dismayed had they realised who was to be his quarry. But it was not long before they discovered. The wily Turk, it dawned on them too late, had double-crossed them, and was now preparing to launch a full-scale holy war against them. Nor was it long before the Muslim populace awoke to the fact that a celebrated general was in their midst who was not only a world figure, but a Turk like themselves.

The extraordinary news sent a thrill through the ranks of the embattled *basmachi*, giving them fresh heart for their long-running struggle with the Bolsheviks. Enver, now suddenly in his element, rode on in triumph eastwards from Bokhara, gathering fresh recruits by the thousand, and making contact with the other *basmachi* leaders. He knew that his first task was to unite under his own command the numerous groups, whether Uzbek or Turkoman, Kirghiz or Kazakh. He sent messengers as far afield as Khiva, Samarkand and Ferghana to invite *basmachi* leaders there to join forces with him, and mount a co-ordinated offensive against the Bolsheviks.

He also sent emissaries to the deposed Emir of Bokhara, himself now a fugitive from the Bolsheviks. Delighted at finding so powerful and renowned an ally, the Emir at once proclaimed him the Commander-in-Chief of all forces opposing Bolshevik rule in his former kingdom. Enver went even further, declaring himself to be the 'Commander-in-Chief of All the Armies of Islam' and, through his marriage to the Sultan of Turkey's niece, 'Kinsman of the Caliph, the Representative on Earth of the Prophet'. He next had a great gold seal made, bearing all these titles. Finally he announced his intention of founding a new Turkish empire in Central Asia, once he had driven out the Bolsheviks.

Enver's victories now began to multiply. On February 14, 1922, with two hundred ill-armed guerrillas, he captured the important town of Dushambe, in present-day Tajikstan. It represented a major victory, the one he needed to consolidate his reputation and establish his right to the overall leadership of the *basmachi*. A daring raid on the holy city of Bokhara followed, in which heavy casualties were inflicted on the Bolsheviks, although opinions are divided over whether Enver was personally involved in this operation. Nonetheless, it gave *basmachi* morale, already beginning to soar, a considerable fillip, and shook the Bolsheviks badly. As word of these successes spread, more and more recruits flocked to Enver's standard, even if the concept of Pan-Turkism he preached was beyond the grasp of most of them.

Enver's rapid progress had been watched with interest all this time by King Amanullah of Afghanistan who began to see him as the vehicle for the realisation of his own dream – a Central Asian confederacy, with himself at its head. Amanullah now entered into secret correspondence with Enver, and began to supply him with arms and – ostensibly as 'volunteers' – with trained military personnel. Bolshevik spies very soon discovered this, and a strongly-worded note was sent to Kabul demanding an end to Amanullah's support for the *basmachi*, as well as for the ex-Emir of Bokhara, to whom he had given sanctuary. Confident, however, that before very long the Bolsheviks would be driven out of Bokhara by Enver, and his fellow Emir be restored to his throne, Amanullah ignored their protest and continued to supply Enver with aid.

By the spring of 1922, Enver had some seven thousand troops under his command, and controlled much of the former kingdom of Bokhara. His anti-Bolshevik operations were carried out through a command structure built on German lines, with a staff which included a number of experienced Turkish officers. The Bolsheviks, greatly alarmed at the turn of events, now despatched a ten-man 'peace' delegation to Bokhara to try to negotiate with the renegade. But Enver neither trusted them nor sought peace. His reply was uncompromising. 'Peace', he informed them, 'is only acceptable after the withdrawal of Russian troops from Turkestan soil. The freedom fighters, whose leader I am, have sworn to fight for independence and liberty until their last breath.'

In the midst of this, Ahmed Togan, the Turkish historian serving with the *basmachi*, heard that Moscow was planning to send one hundred thousand more troops to Central Asia to crush Enver for good if their peace initiative was rejected. He sent an urgent message to Enver urging him to come to terms with them. But his warning arrived too late. Enver had already sent off his reply – and followed it with an ultimatum demanding that all Red Army troops be withdrawn within fifteen days from Turkestan, as well as from the former Muslim states of Bokhara and Khiva. There could be no turning back now, though in any case Enver was never a man given to doubts. The Bolsheviks, stung to fury by the insolence of the Turk's ultimatum, did not even bother to answer it. They began instead to prepare for an all-out assault on his stronghold.

*   *   *

In Moscow, all this time, the work of spreading the gospel of Marxism-Leninism through the East had been proceeding apace. Roy was to play a considerable part in it. On his return to Moscow from Tashkent, he had been sent by Lenin to discuss with Stalin their future strategy in Asia. Roy recalls his meeting with Stalin, who was wearing Red Army uniform. His long greatcoat and peaked cap, the Indian noted, made him look much taller than his actual height of five feet six inches. His pock-marked face bore a friendly grin and, as they talked, he smoked a pipe which he stuffed with crushed cigarettes, paper and all.

The newly founded University for the Toilers of the East, Stalin explained to Roy, was to come under the direction of the Eastern Department of the Comintern. Its function would be to train revolutionaries for work in Asia, especially India. Roy himself was to be appointed its first Political Director. There was little point, Stalin went on, in supplying the nationalist movements in India and elsewhere with weapons or money, for at the moment they were politically immature and without any revolutionary ideology. They must first be taken in hand by trained revolutionaries. The University for the Toilers of the East had been founded to produce such men.

It hardly needed to be said, Stalin added, that the nationalists would never be allowed to come to power after the colonialists had departed. At the right moment, the Moscow-trained insurrectionaries would foment civil war from which they would emerge triumphant. There was nothing new in this to Roy. 'One could learn all that from any textbook of Leninism,' he wrote years later. 'But to have the revolutionary gospel expounded personally by the Man of Destiny was a privilege.' He had learned much, too, from his experience in Tashkent, even if it had ended in disappointment. He recounts: 'A year and a half ago I had left Moscow with great expectations. The experience in Central Asia was very valuable . . . The contact with a cross-section of the Indian masses dispelled some of my earlier illusions, and gave me a realistic view of the latter. I was convinced that the Indian revolution was still a long way off, and an uphill path lay ahead.'

News of Gandhi's civil-disobedience campaign, which reached Moscow in the middle of 1921, had raised hopes in the Comintern that India was on the eve of revolution. But Roy urged caution, pointing out that Gandhi's ideas, far from being revolutionary, were positively reactionary. Even the normally cautious Chicherin had begun to believe that the Indian revolution might be imminent, and asked Roy whether he was not being needlessly pessimistic. In the event Roy proved right. After a furious mob had burned down a police station, killing twenty-two officers, the violence-deploring Gandhi called off his campaign, just as the British were beginning to count their last hours. The Government of India breathed again. 'He gave us a scare,' the Governor of Bombay, Sir George Lloyd, admitted to an American journalist. 'You cannot go on arresting people for ever – not when there are 319,000,000 of them.'

Moscow, however, was furious with Gandhi, despite Roy's warning. His suspension of the campaign just when it seemed that he had succeeded in inflaming India's restive millions against British rule was seen as 'a betrayal of the revolutionary rank and file by the non-revolutionary and reactionary leadership'. Even Roy was disappointed. He wrote in *Vanguard*, his revolutionary sheet intended for secret distribution in India: 'We maintain that there was a splendid opportunity for a national uprising, but this was missed because there did not exist in the country a revolutionary party which could lead the masses to an offensive with courage and determination. One opportunity is lost. Another will come . . .'

It was an eventuality which Moscow had already begun to

prepare for. By the summer of that year the first of the graduates of the University for the Toilers of the East were ready to be infiltrated across the frontier. Their mission was to set up revolutionary cells in India and to penetrate the existing nationalist movements. The first four of Roy's Moscow-trained agents set out from Baku and, travelling individually, succeeded in entering India on false passports from Persia. Two of them, until they were trapped by the British authorities and jailed, had dutifully embarked on their clandestine task. But their two companions promptly vanished, never to be heard of again, either by the British or by their Comintern chiefs. In all probability, like some of their former colleagues from the ill-fated Tashkent school, they had decided to settle for the quiet life.

The following spring, ten more Indians set out, but they were quickly picked up after entering the country across the Pamir. Others were despatched that autumn, but most were arrested on arrival. By now the British were becoming increasingly well-informed about the movements of Roy's infiltrators, largely through the interception of their mail and the skilled interrogation of those they apprehended. According to Sir David Petrie, head of the Indian Government's anti-Bolshevik operations, Roy's correspondence was being 'extensively read' at this time, albeit without him realising it. Writing in the confidential handbook *Communism in India*, he reveals: 'It has been an unfailing source of information of proved accuracy as to the movements of men, money and literature.'

In addition to this, Roy faced numerous other difficulties in his efforts to create an effective organisation behind British lines. Not only were there deep rifts dividing the various nationalist factions both inside India and in exile abroad, but there was also fierce resentment felt by many of his rivals at his claim to represent revolutionary India at the Bolshevik court, not to say jealousy at his having won the ear of Lenin. Another obstacle was the sheer size of the country in which he was endeavouring to organise a revolution, virtually from scratch. It was a formidable task that Roy had taken on, and at times, one suspects, he must have despaired, as agent after agent fell into British hands.

An early setback had been the arraignment of the first batch of Moscow-trained *apparatchiks* to be picked up by the British after their arduous crossing of the Pamir. They were charged, under section 121-A of the Indian Penal Code, of 'conspiring to deprive the King-Emperor of his sovereignty over India'. Seven of them were jailed for periods of up to five years with hard labour, while two others who turned King's evidence were set free. It was the first of three such conspiracy trials involving Comintern agents which were to be held in India during the 1920s, and used by the British to demonstrate that Moscow was continuing to disregard the pledges of the Anglo-Soviet treaty.

But if Roy was making little headway, it was not for want of trying. On December 21, 1922, under the headlines BOLSHEVIK PLAN FOR INDIA . . . A REVOLUTIONARY PRO-GRAMME . . . GRIEVANCES TO BE EXPLOITED, *The Times* of London disclosed the contents of a highly inflammatory pamphlet outlining Moscow's blueprint for a Soviet India. Large numbers of these had been mailed to India by Roy – 'the notorious Indian Communist', as *The Times* called him – on the eve of the annual conference of the Indian National Congress. He demanded 'complete national independence' for India, the disbanding of the Indian Army, the scrapping of all direct taxes, nationalisation of public utilities, and the abolition of landlordism – 'all large estates being confiscated without any compensation'.

With such a programme, Roy declared, Gandhi's policy of Swaraj, or Home Rule for India, would no longer remain 'a vague abstraction'. He called for a campaign of nationwide disobedience under which, he promised, the authority of the Government, and of the landlord and capitalist class, would break down, and thus precipitate what he called 'the final stage of our struggle'. All copies which the authorities could get their hands on were immediately seized, and possession of it made a criminal offence. However, the detailed account in *The Times* was at once telegraphed by Reuters in London to India where it was widely published in the press.

The pro-British, Anglo-Indian newspapers used it to hint at sinister connections between the leaders of the Indian National Congress and Moscow. Finding certain superficial similarities between the two documents, *The Englishman* of Calcutta insinuated that the programme of C.R. Das, the Congress leader (Gandhi, at that time, was in jail), had been produced in collaboration with Roy. The Allahabad *Leader* condemned Roy's programme as being deliberately designed to appeal to 'the cupidity and self-interest of the masses', while the *Statesman* of Calcutta denounced him as 'a blackguardly ruffian'. The Allahabad *Independent*, however, turned its wrath on Reuters, accusing it of playing 'a deep game' whose purpose was to injure Congress by stigmatising it as a body 'depending for its inspiration on Bolsheviks', and so alienate it from the sympathy of employers, landlords and the professional classes.

But in the end, apart from generating a good deal of publicity for his cause, and infuriating the British authorities, Roy's clarion call to the Indian masses achieved little. Indeed, it may even have restrained Congress from adopting a more radical plan of action for fear of being accused of following the Bolshevik blueprint. Certainly *The Times* believed that the disclosure of Roy's plan had had a 'sobering' effect on some of the more extreme Congress leaders and members. But India's real extremists – the terrorist and underground nationalist movements – wanted from Moscow, not Roy's views, but arms and money. They had plenty of views of their own. In fact, a certain amount of money had got through, but being India this had not always ended up in the hands of those for whom it was intended. One large sum which had been successfully smuggled across the frontier had been used by one of Roy's agents to build himself a house.

Stalin, who had been placed in charge of the Comintern's eastern operations by Lenin, was now becoming increasingly impatient at Roy's lack of results. According to *The Times* of January 1, 1923, a top-secret and highly critical memorandum signed by Stalin had been circulated among members of the ruling Politburo. Its view of the progress being made in Asia, and particularly in India, contrasted sharply with the praise being lavished at that very moment on Roy at the Comintern's Fourth Congress. Far from having achieved 'valuable results' in India, as delegates were being assured, Roy and his colleagues had so far failed to achieve anything.

The secret memorandum – numbered 647/5, according to *The Times* – went on: 'It has now been realised that Communism is completely unacceptable to the Hindus in their present state of development, and independence is a condition which must precede it. Our propaganda agents did not realise this and did not report it, and continued to work on completely the wrong lines.'

Assuming that the memorandum is authentic, one man who could have told them all this from the start was Gandhi. Temporarily out of action in a Poona jail, where he was serving twenty-two months of a six-year sentence for sedition, he had written in his weekly *Young India*: 'India does not want Bolshevism. The people are too peaceful to stand anarchy. They will bow the knee to anyone who restores order. Let us recognise the Indian psychology . . .'

But following the Bolshevik conspiracy trial, and now the publication of Roy's Marxist blueprint for India – both of which proved Moscow's total disregard for its pledges of non-interference – the British Cabinet was spoiling for a row. Since Lord Curzon's earlier exchange with Moscow over Roy's activities, there had been a change of government in Britain. Lloyd George's coalition had been replaced by a Bolshephobe Tory administration, and with Curzon back in his previous Cabinet post as Foreign Secretary an explosion was inevitable.

12 Curzon's Ultimatum

The killing or taking alive of Enver Pasha in Soviet Turkestan had meanwhile become a top priority for the Bolsheviks. More and more troops were switched to the Eastern Bokharan front, and spies were sent in to try to infiltrate the *basmachi* movement and discover the whereabouts of Enver's secret headquarters. As the weeks passed, the Turkish general's poorly armed and greatly outnumbered forces were gradually forced back onto the defensive. Enver's great dream of an empire in the heart of Asia was rapidly beginning to crumble. Without substantial support from outside – and this had not been forthcoming – he knew he now stood no hope of defeating the Bolsheviks. Indeed, it would only be a matter of time before they cornered him.

On the night of June 14, 1922, Enver suffered a major defeat when he attacked a force more than twice the size of his own. General Kakurin, the Bolshevik commander, estimated that Enver had no more than three thousand troops, while his own totalled some eight thousand and enjoyed both artillery and cavalry support. Many of those who had originally flocked to Enver's banner, sensing the way the wind was now beginning to blow, slipped away to their villages or joined other *basmachi* bands. For all his reputation and charisma, he had never managed to win the following of the whole movement. From the start, some of its leaders had resented and resisted his claim to its overall command.

The well-commanded and co-ordinated Bolshevik forces now began to work their way eastwards, driving the *basmachi* before them. One by one they took back the towns and villages captured by the rebels. Enver, his forces ever more depleted by casualties and desertions, was forced to withdraw towards the Pamir. Concessions (albeit only temporary) extended to the hitherto hostile population by the Bolsheviks began to take effect. The *basmachi* were no longer welcome in many villages, thus depriving them of food and other essentials. Many of them were forced back into banditry.

King Amanullah, realising that he had backed the wrong horse, withdrew his aid, including his 'volunteers'. Enver, and those who had remained loyal to him, now knew that nothing could save them from annihilation, except flight into Afghanistan or across the Pamir into Chinese Turkestan. But neither the word flight, nor surrender, was in the proud Turk's vocabulary. He would fight it out to the bitter end.

On July 25, Enver sat at the foot of a tree and wrote to his wife. It was something he had always tried to do, even from the battlefield. This letter was written from the village of Satalmis, only fifty miles from the Afghan frontier, and in what is today Soviet Tajikstan. The Red troops, he wrote, were pressing his exhausted men remorselessly. Dushambe had already fallen. The defensive position he had prepared near the village had proved useless, for his irregular troops knew nothing of trench warfare. The day's wounded had been evacuated, giving him a few moments to write. 'The weather is very depressing,' he told her. 'There is an odd sort of fog. The sun doesn't shine through. There is no movement among the enemy.'

Aware that the end must now be close, he added: 'I commend you and the children to the Oneness of God, my dear heart.' He finished: 'Well my little one, I must end this letter. Along with the wild flowers I send you every day from here, I enclose a little twig I broke from the elm tree under which I slept.' On that tree, he told her, he had carved her name. It was the last she was ever to hear from him.

Death came to Enver ten days later, on August 4, 1922. He died as one would expect a Turkish soldier to die – with ferocious courage. Outgunned and outnumbered, he could have escaped into Afghanistan with no loss of honour. Yet he chose instead to attack once again a greatly superior force, perhaps hoping to rout it by the sheer violence of his onslaught.

That morning, with a handful of his friends and followers, most of them Turks, he had been celebrating Bayram, the Muslim Feast of Sacrifice, in the village of Abiderya. It was to be their last headquarters. By a miscalculation of the Muslim calendar, the villagers had observed the feast the previous day, and the ground was still drenched with the blood of the sheep they had slaughtered. Enver now gathered his men before the mud-built house in which he was staying for an exchange of the traditional gifts and greetings. All of them knew that their position was now utterly hopeless, the Bolsheviks having all but surrounded them. This was the last time they would be together. Sevket Aydemir, Enver's Turkish biographer, describes that sad farewell: 'Enver recited the Bayram prayers to his remaining soldiers and gave them each a little money. For the officers, or so they relate, he had nothing. He gave them instead a document, a certificate of their rank, bearing his seal and signature, in memory of their common struggle. There was one for each of them.'

Suddenly, in the middle of the proceedings, a message reached them warning that three hundred Red troops were approaching the village. Moments later gunfire was heard, as Enver's outposts opened up on them. He at once drew his sabre and leaped into the saddle. Then, according to survivors, he rode straight towards the enemy. Those of his men who had horses followed hotly after him. Aydemir gives an account of their charge which, for sheer reckless courage, must rival that of the Light Brigade: 'The suicidal onslaught by those twenty-five horsemen, naked swords in hand, in the face of machine-gun fire from Commander Kulikov's detachment, caused momentary confusion among the enemy. The nearest machine-gun was actually silenced, but two others continued to direct heavy fire at the charging horsemen.'

Enver, who was leading, was the first to fall. He plunged from his grey horse Dervish which, also hit, sank slowly to its knees before rolling over. Enver's companions too went down in the terrible hail of machine-gun fire. Within minutes it was all over, leaving the hillside strewn with the dead and dying, both men and horses. One or two survivors managed to crawl away unnoticed. Eventually they reached the village with news of what had happened, only to find that the *basmachi* had melted away.

Kulikov's men began to examine the corpses, stripping them naked in their search for papers or identification. But one of the dead puzzled them. He was dressed in a buttoned khaki tunic, similar to those worn by Turkish officers, and German lace-up field boots, but his breeches and fur hat were of a type with which none of them was familiar. His sabre too was different, and he carried field-glasses of foreign make. In one of his pockets they found some letters, including a half-finished one, while from his tunic had fallen a small Koran. Examination of his corpse showed that he had been hit seven times (some accounts say five). Unsure of this stranger's identity, Kulikov despatched all his possessions and papers to Tashkent for scrutiny by experts.

With that, he and his men hastened on in their pursuit of the *basmachi*, leaving Enver's body lying on his blood-soaked clothes. There, two days later, a passing mullah came upon it, and at once realised whose it was. A party of villagers immediately set out to bring back his and his companions' bodies for Muslim burial, now that the Bolsheviks had gone. As preparations for the funeral were being made, word spread quickly that Enver's body had been found. Mourners – some say as many as fifteen thousand – began to converge from miles around to pay homage to this man who had come from so far away to fight for their cause.

They buried him beneath a walnut tree, in an unmarked grave beside the river at Abiderya, in the cradle of the Turkish race. It was just as he would have wished. Every year, it is said, on the anniversary of Enver's death, the sons and grandsons of some of those who fought and died with him visit his lonely grave to pay their secret respects. A few come from as far away as Turkey.

It was soon realised in Tashkent that the mysterious officer was none other than Enver Pasha. There was naturally great rejoicing. But it was weeks before definite news of his death reached the West. On December 2, 1922, four months after that reckless charge, Arthur Ransome, then Moscow correspondent of the *Manchester Guardian*, revealed to the outside world the epic story beneath the blazing headline: THE LAST ADVENTURE OF ENVER PASHA. So ended another dream of an empire astride the Oxus. Two such dreams had now been shattered, each amid considerable bloodshed. But they would not be the last.

*   *   *

Although the *basmachi* movement did not die with Enver, their moment had now passed. Without his professional leadership they could never again be a threat to Moscow's rule in Central Asia, although for several years more they continued to harass the Bolsheviks from their secret hideouts in the mountains. But in the meantime trouble of a different kind was brewing elsewhere for Russia, this time with Great Britain.

On May 8, 1923, Lord Curzon sent an ultimatum warning Moscow that unless, within ten days, it withdrew all its agents operating against British interests in Asia, or anywhere else, trade relations between the two countries would be terminated forthwith. The British note, splenetic in tone, enumerated a whole series of alleged violations of the trade agreement by the Bolsheviks, including the continued infiltration of trained agitators into India. The agitators, it claimed, had been helped across the frontier by Soviet military and other officials 'by a circuitous and difficult route' in order to avoid detection. The ultimatum also charged that large sums of money had been paid by Moscow into the coffers of the British and Indian Communist parties. It cited, as evidence, an instance in which a number of £100 notes issued by Lloyds Bank in London to a Soviet trade official had later been found in the possession of revolutionaries held in India.

Conceding that there had been a slight curtailment in the

activities of Bolshevik agents against India following the previous British protest, the note charged that these 'pernicious
activities' had recently been 'vigorously resumed'. The Soviet
Minister in Teheran especially had been 'tireless' in fomenting
trouble in India, while some two-thirds of the budget of the
Soviet legation in Kabul, it was alleged, was devoted to a similar
purpose. The examples enumerated, the note concluded, were
'but a few selected examples among many scores of similar
incidents'. Unless, within ten days of its receipt, Moscow com-
plied fully and unconditionally with Britain's demands, this
time the Anglo-Soviet Trade Agreement would be regarded as
terminated.

'Such a note sent by one Great Power to another would,
before 1914, have meant war,' declared the *Daily Herald*, then
regarded by many on the right as the dupe (or perhaps worse) of
Moscow. 'Today,' it went on, 'the only hope of avoiding a
rupture of relations is that the Soviet Government may display,
in the face of provocation, a restraint which the Tsar's ministers
would certainly never have shown.' However, Curzon's angry
warning was welcomed by those, including a large section of the
press, who, all along, had opposed having anything to do with
the Bolsheviks. *The Economist* saw the ultimatum ('not a model
of moderation') as evidence that the new Tory administration
was planning to end the agreement.

Moscow was momentarily stunned by Curzon's bombshell,
with its all-too-short fuse. The Bolshevik leaders had not fully
appreciated the significance of the change of government in
Britain. Nor could they really see what the fuss was about. After
all, they were doing nothing they had not already been doing for
several years. While deciding how to act, they denounced the
ultimatum as a package of false charges. Addressing the Moscow Soviet, Chicherin declared that the British Government
was composed of extreme reactionaries, who were convinced
that Lenin's deteriorating health had seriously weakened the
Soviet Government, making this a favourable moment for its
overthrow.

Referring to India, he told his audience that the liberation movement was gathering momentum in the East. The British, he said, 'dream of secret agents when they are faced with the effects of an historical process'. The Soviet people felt a profound sympathy for others fighting for their freedom, but Lord Curzon remained 'at the bottom of his heart the Viceroy of India'. He could only see historical inevitability in the light of an anti-British conspiracy.

The official Soviet reply was delivered on May 13, five days before the expiry of the ultimatum. It denied categorically all charges of anti-British intrigues in the East. Referring to the evidence of this cited in the British note (much of it, incidentally, obtained from radio intercepts), the Soviets insisted that 'similar material is at the disposal of all governments'. Were this to be used 'for creating conflicts', then friendly relations between governments could hardly be maintained. As an illustration of what they meant by this, the Soviets claimed to have 'plenty of reports and documents' to prove that British agents were active on the borders of Soviet Central Asia, and giving assistance to the *basmachi* in Turkestan and Eastern Bokhara.

The British, the Soviet reply went on, could hardly expect Moscow to have no policy of its own in the East, and everywhere to 'support English aspirations'. Yet, though the Soviets had no intention of losing face, either domestically or internationally, the tone of the reply was generally conciliatory, for Moscow was most anxious to maintain its crucial trade links with Britain. A number of concessions were therefore offered in areas in which it had previously refused to budge, including the payment of compensation to Britons who had suffered as a result of the October Revolution.

Meanwhile lobbying hard in London against a break in relations was the Soviet trade representative, Leonid Krasin. He warned, in a newspaper interview he gave on the day the Soviets delivered their reply, that if a split occurred between the two governments there could be 'catastrophic consequences' which it was 'impossible to foresee'. For one thing, he pointed out,

Moscow would no longer be obliged to refrain from anti-British intrigue in the East.

Although the hawks would have welcomed a break with the Soviet Union, which they still believed could be brought to its knees by means of an economic boycott, other commentators were unable to see how Britain would benefit. British exports to Russia, they pointed out, had doubled in value between 1921 and 1922, and would merely be taken over by her commercial rivals. The severance of trade relations, moreover, would give Moscow a free hand in pursuing her ambitions in India and elsewhere, while robbing Britain of any means of applying pressure on her.

Finally, after an extension of the deadline, the Soviets yielded on what the British Cabinet saw as the 'pivotal issue' upon which the fate of the agreement rested. After first protesting that this greatly extended and altered their obligations under the original agreement, the Soviets agreed to sign a declaration aimed at curbing once and for all their activities in India and elsewhere. Carefully drafted in Whitehall so as to include not only the Comintern but also any future Soviet-supported organisations they might be tempted to launch, this stated:

> In view of complaints which have been made, the Soviet Government undertakes not to support with funds or in any other form persons or bodies or agencies or institutions whose aim is to spread discontent or to foment rebellion in any other part of the British Empire . . . and to impress upon its officers and officials the full and continuous observance of these conditions.

After at first refusing, Moscow also agreed to transfer its representatives in Teheran and Kabul elsewhere. It was soon discovered, however, that the two men were to be moved anyway, as a result of similar complaints about their activities from their host governments. Nonetheless, both sides secretly congratulated themselves on the final outcome. Curzon confided to a friend that he believed he had 'won a considerable victory over the Soviet Government', and that he expected them to 'behave with more circumspection for some time to come'.

For their part, the Bolsheviks had skilfully averted the rupture in relations which the British had seemed determined to provoke. They knew perfectly well, moreover, that there was no possible way in which Curzon or anyone else could police their new undertaking. Just how little notice they were to take of these pledges, we shall see. For them a Soviet India remained the ultimate prize in Asia, and Moscow had no intention of abandoning its hopes of achieving this, however long it took.

The failure of Roy to ignite the Indian powder-keg may have disappointed his masters in the Kremlin, but it appears not to have harmed his revolutionary reputation. In the mid-1920s, Roy was still seen by the Soviets as a sort of Marxist Mahdi who, when the moment arrived, would help them to set the East ablaze. Although a Soviet India seemed as far away as ever, Roy continued to dream up new strategies for outmanoeuvring the British in India, and implanting secret revolutionary cells behind their lines.

One of these was his two-party trick. The idea was to establish two organisations there. One would be legal and there for all to see. The other would be illegal and secret. The latter – a small but active Communist cell – would operate from inside the legal party. It would be controlled by the Comintern, which meant Roy himself, and would consist of hard-core, Moscow-trained revolutionaries. The legal, or 'front' organisation, would be called the Workers' and Peasants' Party. The Comintern-directed cell, which would be the real Indian Communist Party, would make full but covert use of the 'front' party's nationwide organisation and would recruit its most promising members.

There was, in fact, already an Indian Communist Party. It functioned openly, and disclaimed all connections with Moscow or the Comintern. This organisation, Roy warned his adherents, was really a stooge party run by British *agents provocateurs*, its real purpose being to try to find out who the Indian Communists were. However, the British security services had no need to go to such lengths, for they continued to obtain most of what they required through the regular reading of Roy's mail. And here they found India's climate on their side, since at times it rendered invisible ink only too visible.

Yet India, while still the ultimate prize, was not the only Asiatic country that Moscow had in its sights. By now, the long arm of the Comintern stretched as far eastwards as China, as well as into French Indo-China and the Dutch East Indies. China, plagued by civil war and famine ever since the overthrow of the Manchus in 1911, had long been seen as a candidate for Comintern conversion. Not only was it desirable in itself, but it was also seen by the Kremlin's strategists as a stepping-stone to India. Hitherto, Afghanistan and Persia had been the traditional invasion routes. But finding themselves blocked there, the Bolsheviks now decided to abandon them in favour of China as – in the words of Zinoviev, head of the Comintern – 'the central starting-point for action in India'. A new and somewhat unwieldy slogan was added to the Comintern's armoury of maxims – 'Via Revolutionary China to the Federal Republic of the United States of India'.

Bolshevik links with China dated from 1920, when secret Comintern emissaries were sent to make contact with fledgling Communist groups there. Until then the two countries had been isolated from one another by the Civil War, although in 1919 the new Soviet Government had won considerable sympathy among educated Chinese by voluntarily renouncing most of the treaty privileges forcibly obtained by the Tsarists. What is more, they had loudly denounced the other powers, including Britain, for clinging on to theirs.

The Comintern emissaries, sent principally to spy out the land, had also advised the Chinese Communists on the formation of a party. But they were quick to see that it would be years before the tiny Chinese Communist Party – of which Mao Tse-tung was a founder member – would be robust enough to seize control of a country even larger than India. They would have to find more powerful allies if they wanted to bring China, like Mongolia, into their orbit.

Meanwhile, large numbers of Chinese radicals were enrolled at the University for the Toilers of the East for revolutionary training. Here they were initiated in the arts of insurrection and civil war by Bolshevik specialists. Dr Satya Sinha, one of the Indian students there at the time, recalls: 'The largest group of Comintern cadets was formed by the Chinese. When they began to pour in in still larger numbers, a separate school was reserved for them. They were put before us as ideal models . . . and we were supposed to copy them. Every now and then some Chinese guerrilla leaders who were said to have taken part in actual fighting in their country came to teach us their technique of insurrection. Huge models of Shanghai and Canton were placed before us to exhibit the proper strategy in street fighting.'

For although China had now become Moscow's first priority in Asia, the Comintern's long-term interest in India had not diminished, as Sinha makes clear. 'The idea', he writes, 'was to train us as Comintern agents and then send us back to India to play our role in the liberation of India from the British colonial yoke. Those suited to army life were to get enrolled in the Indian Army to undermine it, and the others were to function as Communist trade unionists, agitators, propagandists and insurrectionists.' Gandhi, they were told, was an agent of the British imperialists, and the Indian National Congress a reactionary, counter-revolutionary body of the bourgeoisie.

At the same time, to help speed up the revolutionary process in India and also to find out exactly what was going on within the various rival nationalist movements, the Comintern had decided to infiltrate a small number of British Communists into the country. They entered India in various guises without being detected by the authorities. One of them was a young Cambridge graduate named Philip Spratt who travelled there as a bookseller. Aged twenty-four, his mission was to report back on what he found (using invisible ink and a code based on Gray's *Elegy*), and also to help set up branches of the Workers' and Peasants' Party, behind which the Communist Party would shelter. Spratt, who later wrote an account of his undercover activities called *Blowing Up India*, was shortly to be joined by a colleague named Benjamin Bradley, ostensibly representing a firm calling itself the Crab Patent Underdrain Tile Company.

They were to work together undetected for more than two years before finally being arrested. Modern Indian historians do not credit them with achieving much, while Roy himself, who had objected to their being sent in the first place, does not so much as mention them in his memoirs. A different view, however, is taken by two American scholars. In their classic work *Communism in India*, Gene Overstreet and Marshall Windmiller write: 'Together, Bradley and Spratt became the *de facto* leaders of the Indian Communist Party.' Under them 'the Communist movement began to gather the momentum that the Indians had been unable to achieve by themselves.'

In China, meanwhile, Moscow had chosen its partner for the great task ahead – or rather he had chosen Moscow. After their overthrow, in 1911, of the corrupt Manchu monarchy, it had been the dream of Sun Yat-sen and his Kuomintang Party to transform feudal China into a modern democratic state run along Western lines. But they had proved too weak to establish any kind of central authority or rule, and China had fragmented into scores of rival kingdoms, or fiefdoms, ruled by local warlords. These had divided into two warring camps. In the north, with Peking as their capital, were those claiming to be the legitimate government of China, and accepted by the world powers as such, while in the south, with Canton as his capital, Sun Yat-sen had established a rival government with the support of southern warlords.

Intent on overthrowing the reactionary northerners and extending his enlightened policies and reforms to the whole of China, Sun himself had at first sought the help of the great powers. But his pleas had fallen on deaf ears. Democracy in the West, it was felt, was one thing, but for China's illiterate masses quite another. Moreover, under Sun's reforming zeal, the special privileges and commercial interests of the imperialist powers would be threatened. These would be far better safeguarded under the conservative warlord rulers of the north.

In despair, Sun Yat-sen had then turned to the Soviets for support. Although the southern leader was a reformer rather than a revolutionary, Moscow had been quick to respond to his overture. Here was the alliance which was needed to further Soviet aims – and which, when it had served its purpose, could be case aside. The Kuomintang, in Stalin's memorable phrase, was to be 'squeezed out like a lemon, and then thrown away'.

The man chosen for this task was Mikhail Borodin, Roy's old friend, and now the Comintern's chief trouble-shooter. While Roy had been busy plotting the overthrow of the British in India, Borodin had been on a secret mission to Britain to try to discover why the long-expected revolution had failed to materialise there. In the spring of 1921 things had looked promising when miners called for a nationwide general strike. But Moscow's hopes of a Soviet Britain had been dashed when the rest of the workforce had remained at their posts in what became known as 'the Black Friday betrayal'. In Borodin's view, the British Communists had failed the workers in their hour of need, and thus betrayed the cause of world revolution. 'In early 1922, when Borodin arrived in Britain,' recounts his American biographer, Professor Dan Jacobs, 'the British Communist party, despite Black Friday, was in disarray. It had no funds, it was losing members, and it was plagued by poor organisation.' It thus became Borodin's task to shake up and help reorganise the British party along professional lines, so that such opportunities would never be missed again.

For several months Borodin, who had somehow managed to enter the country without a passport, was able to keep one move ahead of the police and security services by means of a succession of disguises. But eventually, in the summer of that year, they received a tip that this 'most dangerous man' – as he was officially described – was touring Britain's industrial cities posing as a cloth-capped union official called George Brown. After trailing him to Glasgow, they arrested him there on August 22, more than fifty police officers taking part in the operation.

Throughout his interrogation, Borodin denied his Soviet nationality and spun his questioners a tale which Professor

Jacobs believes to have been wholly fictitious. During their search for his real identity, Scotland Yard uncovered no fewer than sixteen other aliases for Borodin. In the event, he was sentenced to six months' imprisonment, to be followed by deportation. Since he had no passport, and no known nationality, the latter presented an unusual problem. Finally, after serving his full sentence, and armed with the papers of a stateless person, Borodin was put aboard a vessel sailing for Petrograd.

A deal had been struck behind the scenes. 'Thus,' his biographer writes, 'although the British knew Borodin was a Russian, and the Russians knew the British knew, the fiction was maintained throughout that Borodin was of some other nationality.' Everyone was satisfied. The British authorities were relieved to see the back of him, while Moscow had urgent need of his services.

There were several reasons why he had been chosen to head the Comintern mission to China, although he spoke no Chinese and knew little about the country. To begin with there was his outstanding ability as a revolutionary, based on long experience in a number of countries. Added to this was a first-class brain, a persuasive tongue, and undeniable charm. Sun Yat-sen, whom Lenin regarded as a pseudo-revolutionary and certainly no Marxist, was nevertheless seen as a candidate for possible conversion. If anyone could pull this off it was Borodin, who had been responsible for evangelising Roy and others to the Marxist-Leninist gospel. Finally, although he spoke no Chinese, his English was excellent, as was Sun's. Borodin and Sun had a lot of talking to do, and communication would present no problem.

After reaching Peking by train from Moscow in the autumn of 1923, Borodin took a cargo boat down the coast to Canton, accompanied by two hundred sheep. Fearing (despite his newly grown moustache and false identity) lest British immigration officers in Hong Kong recognise him and arrest him, he had managed to find a berth on a cattle-boat which did not call on the colony. He had a narrow escape, however, when the vessel was engulfed by a typhoon off Formosa. Lucky to survive the experience (the sheep did not), Borodin finally reached Canton in October 1923.

Not everyone there was glad to see him. The right wing of the Kuomintang had been quick to suspect that Moscow was planning to use them to drive out the warlord government in the north, and then to take over the country as part of a new Bolshevik empire. But Sun chose not to heed their warnings, and Borodin and his small cadre of Soviet experts immediately set about reorganising the Kuomintang along the lines of the Soviet Communist Party, and rebuilding Sun's exhausted armies into a modern fighting force. Within nineteen days this Bolshevik T.E. Lawrence had won virtual control of Sun's armies by placing his men with all the principal units as advisers.

But Borodin and his mission had not been very long in China when they received shattering news from Moscow. Lenin, to whom they ultimately all owed their positions, had died after a series of strokes. He was only fifty-three. His death, although it was not unexpected, came as a severe blow to everyone who believed in the Revolution. To those who did not it was also to prove extremely painful. As Churchill was later to observe, the worst misfortune ever to befall the Russian people was Lenin's birth. The next worst was his death. For as Zinoviev, Trotsky and Stalin fought among themselves for the nation's leadership, darkness and fear were once more to descend over the Soviet Union. In Moscow three hundred and sixty thousand mourners shuffled past Lenin's coffin in the coldest winter of sixty years, while far away in southern China Borodin and his men wept.

The only mildly cheering news for the Bolsheviks that bitter winter was the replacement of Britain's bellicose Tory administration by the country's first-ever Labour one. Although only a minority government, and dependent on Liberal support for its survival, it might be expected to take a less hostile stance towards the Soviet Union, and certainly its election victory had led to wild rumours at home of what was in store for Britain. The abolition of the National Anthem, the Monarchy, the Boy Scouts, and even the institution of marriage was forecast. One excitable former Tory MP warned that, if defeated in Parliament, the new government would almost certainly refuse to surrender its power. If so, he declared, he would take great pleasure in 'leading the Coldstream Guards into the House of Commons'. Not everyone, however, was quite so hysterical. Anxious readers of *The Economist* were reassured that there was 'no ground for panic', and when Ramsay MacDonald, Britain's first Labour Prime Minister, announced his new Cabinet (which was anything but revolutionary) the City was reported to be 'visibly impressed'.

But the new Prime Minister was indeed anxious to improve relations with Moscow, despite strong opposition to this from many quarters, including the security services. Thus, on February 1, 1924, Britain accorded full diplomatic recognition to the Soviet Union, becoming the first major power to do so. MacDonald assured the nation that his government would 'stand no nonsense and no monkey tricks' from Moscow, and that diplomatic recognition in no way signified the least sympathy for Bolshevism. Although other governments previously hostile to the Soviet Union shortly began to follow suit, MacDonald received no gratitude from Moscow for ending its long period of isolation. Instead it condemned him as a class traitor (he was the illegitimate child of a maidservant) and certainly no kind of socialist, while Trotsky dismissed his government as essentially no different from a Tory one.

MacDonald's relations with his secret service chiefs swiftly deteriorated to the point where, it is said, he was threatening to disband them. They, in their turn, warned that if he carried out his threat they would simply go underground until he was replaced by a more patriotic Prime Minister. It was a vendetta which was to lead, in less than a year, to his defeat, and the restoration of a Tory Government. But in the meantime Moscow was busy repeating its all-too-familiar pledges that it would refrain from actions likely to harm British interests, particularly in India and China. To prevent there being any possibility of misunderstanding, Chicherin invoked the name of one of Labour's own heroes. 'Mr MacDonald', he said, 'will understand that our unbreakable friendship with the peoples of the East does not mean aggressiveness on our part. On the contrary, it means putting into practice the principles which the great Keir Hardie so magnificently advocated.'

It is unlikely that the pacifist Scot would have recognised in Borodin and his team of Red Army instructors and political advisers the embodiment of his ideals. Nonetheless, under the organising genius of Borodin, Sun Yat-sen's situation had greatly improved, both militarily and politically. But at the same time, as part of Moscow's strategy, the Kuomintang was being infiltrated by Chinese Communists who, while carefully concealing their real allegiance, were intent on seizing eventual control of the party. In addition, Borodin's agents had begun to foment Chinese anger against the foreign communities living in their midst (and especially against the British in Shanghai), by organising strikes and other forms of agitation which more often than not ended in violence.

Watching events from Moscow, the Comintern chiefs had every reason to feel pleased with the way things were going in China. Even if Europe had so far proved a disappointment, and little revolutionary progress had been made in India, in China the Marxist-Leninist precept of historical inevitability was beginning to take shape before their very eyes.

14 Skulduggery
on the Silk Road

By 1925 the British Indian authorities had become acutely aware of Borodin's activities in neighbouring China, and increasingly anxious lest the unrest he was fomenting should spill across the border into India. An intelligence summary prepared by the Political Department of the India Office in the autumn of that year warned of the dangers of what it called 'the gradual encirclement of India, on land, by Bolshevised political entities', and drew particular attention to the potential threat in Sinkiang.

It was to be expected, wrote the department's analysts, that the Soviet Government and Comintern, 'whose agents have notoriously been fomenting the present state of chaos in China . . . would make an effort to evolve out of it a means of promoting their plan of attacking British Imperial interests by making trouble in India'. The summary went on: 'There is evidence, mostly in the shape of secret but apparently reliable reports, that this anticipation is being fulfilled, and that the Bolsheviks are arranging gradually to consolidate a position in the outlying portions of the Chinese Republic which border on India, from which, presumably, they hope to maintain a constant "direct attack" in due course.'

On September 9, 1925, the British Legation in Peking had signalled to London information obtained from a Kuomintang general hostile to Moscow that the Bolsheviks were planning to infiltrate Sinkiang 'in order to attack India from the north'. To this they had added that the Soviets were certainly showing signs of increasing activity there – something which the authorities in Delhi were already well aware of.

During Colonel Etherton's long spell at Kashgar, which had lasted from 1918 until 1922, Bolshevik influence in Sinkiang had been kept at bay, at least in the region close to India's northern frontier. But since his departure, the Chinese had gradually relaxed their stance (precisely as he had forecast), allowing the Soviets to open consulates at Urumchi, Kashgar and elsewhere in Sinkiang. In exchange the Chinese had received reciprocal facilities on Soviet territory. As the Political Department's analysts put it: 'The local Chinese authorities have hitherto steadfastly refused to let Soviet representatives get a foothold. How their opposition has been overcome we do not precisely know, but the fact remains that Soviet Consular establishments do now exist at Urumchi and Kashgar. The first step has been successfully taken. The next step can only be surmised.'

Their own surmise of the Bolsheviks' next move was based on a further piece of intelligence which had just come in of a highly secret deal between the Kuomintang and Moscow. Under this, the neighbouring provinces of Sinkiang and Kansu were to be formed, with the aid of Soviet funds, into what the Political Department foresaw as a 'more or less Red Republic'. Ostensibly under the 'protection' of a Chinese warlord named Feng Yu-hsiang, so that Moscow could plead its innocence, the new Central Asian republic would point like a scimitar towards India. For it was no secret where Feng's loyalties lay. Educated by foreign missionaries, he had once been known as 'the Christian general', and was renowned for baptising his soldiers *en masse* with a hosepipe. But on discovering that the Bolshevik faith brought with it arms and gold, he had undergone a conversion and was now securely in Moscow's pocket.

From this new Red enclave, which would share frontiers with both the Soviet Union and an already Red Mongolia, the analysts feared that an infiltration of northern India would ensue. Although India was protected by 'the greatest mountain barrier in the world', this would not prevent Moscow, they considered, from sending through the passes 'parties of Soviet emissaries or single agents, loaded with propaganda and, possibly, money and small quantities of arms for seditious purposes'. And this was not the only menace which they saw the Bolsheviks posing to India's vast, ill-guarded frontiers. If, in China proper, they were able to secure 'a more or less Red south' (which Borodin appeared to be well on his way to achieving) then the infiltration of Soviet propaganda, arms, funds and secret agents would almost certainly follow from there too, together with the deliberate fomentation of disputes along the Assamese and Burmese frontiers.

This evaluation of likely Soviet strategy towards India had been ordered by Lord Winterton, the Under-Secretary for India. Passing the Political Department's conclusions to Lord Birkenhead, his chief, Winterton (who had fought with Lawrence in the Arab Revolt) observed anxiously: 'In my opinion, this is the most important Soviet move against India which has yet occurred.'

In Kashgar, meanwhile, reporting on the arrival that month of the first Bolshevik diplomats was Major George Gillan of the Indian Political Department, now British Consul-General. His Soviet opposite number – a man named Doumpiss – and a staff of six, including one woman, had moved into the building formerly occupied by the Tsarists. On October 10, at a ceremony attended by the Taoyin, or regional governor, Gillan and local Chinese and Turki dignitaries, the Red Flag was unfurled over this new Soviet outpost. 'The entire proceedings', Gillan reported, 'were singularly uncommunistic.' The Russians, festooned with decorations, appeared in morning suits which would have done credit to Savile Row. The guests, 'carefully chosen from the élite of Kashgar', were seated in accordance with local ideas of precedence, while the refreshments were on a most lavish scale. Half-way through the proceedings, the Soviet Consul-General had donned a spectacular scarlet-and-gold Turki robe, a gesture clearly aimed at winning local Muslim approval. But the newcomers' behaviour, Gillan reported to his chiefs with satisfaction, was already beginning to grate on the Chinese.

The new Consul-General wasted no time in trying to elbow his British rival into second place in the tiny diplomatic community, not to say in the eyes of the local populace. He demanded of the Taoyin that he be considered as the senior of the two, arguing that his government could not accept 'any form of superiority on the part of representatives of so backward an institution as monarchy'. Nervous of offending the Soviets, the Taoyin referred the matter to the Governor of Sinkiang, the wily but able Yang Tseng-hsin who, as it happened, had not long before been awarded an honorary knighthood by the British Indian Government. Governor Yang at once telegraphed the Taoyin instructing him to inform Mr Doumpiss that, however correct his arguments might be on Soviet territory, he must remember that he was now on Chinese territory, where different laws prevailed.

The appearance of the Bolshevik diplomats in Kashgar had filled the small White Russian community in Kashgar with foreboding. Initially, they knew, the newcomers would be in no position to harm them. But eventually, as they consolidated their position, this isolated frontier town so close to the Soviet border would no longer be safe for those who had fled there to escape Bolshevik rule. Paul Nazaroff, who had lived in exile there for four happy years, feared that in his case this would very likely mean kidnap and forcible removal to the Soviet Union, or even murder. 'My respite', he wrote sadly, 'was over.' Long before Mr Doumpiss and his comrades arrived he had left Kashgar for good, travelling alone across the Karakoram passes to India, and eventually to safety in Britain. But two of his fellow-countrymen decided to throw in their lot with the Bolsheviks. One, the former doctor to the Tsarist consulate, joined the Soviets in the same capacity, while another leading member of the White Russian community was taken on the consular payroll for duties which Gillan was unable to ascertain.

The first clash between the abrasive newcomers and the Chinese authorities came within a month of their arrival. One night a caravan of seventeen camels, laden with thirty heavy and mysterious boxes, was halted by suspicious Chinese officials as it entered the town under cover of darkness. It transpired that it had crossed illegally into China from the Soviet Union, having deliberately evaded the frontier guards. The caravan leader refused to say what the boxes contained, insisting that they were for the Soviet Consul-General and that the Chinese had no right to hold them up. He ordered the caravan forward again, but the Chinese managed to divert it somehow into the courtyard of the Taoyin's official residence.

On learning what had happened, Mr Doumpiss immediately protested to the Taoyin, angrily demanding that the caravan be released and allowed to proceed to the consulate. But the Taoyin, fortified perhaps by Governor Yang's earlier rebuff to the Soviets, refused to give way. He would only release the caravan, he said, if the Russians would disclose what was in the boxes and be prepared to open several of them in his presence. But this Mr Doumpiss refused to do. The result was an angry stalemate which lasted some two months. In the meantime, the boxes remained under close guard in the Taoyin's courtyard, the Chinese now absolutely convinced that they contained revolvers, grenades and ammunition which would eventually be used by the Bolsheviks to hatch an insurrection against them.

This confrontation between the Taoyin and the Soviets was of considerable interest to Gillan's chiefs in the Political Department. Provided it did not escalate to a point where it gave the Red Army an excuse to intervene, discord between the Soviets and their hosts was most welcome news to those responsible for the defence of India. On Gillan's latest instalment of the Doumpiss dispute someone in the Political Department wrote with undisguised satisfaction: 'The quarrel between him and the Taoyin is becoming more bitter.'

Finally, the Soviet Consul-General was forced to give way, agreeing to allow the Taoyin to inspect the contents of four boxes chosen at random. But instead of weapons, these were discovered to contain large quantities of silver, in both bullion and coin. Just what the Soviets needed this for they would not say. But in view of their reluctance to let the boxes be opened, it seemed a reasonable assumption that it was for some subversive purpose, either locally or in India.

No sooner was this row over than Mr Doumpiss was pitchforked into another confrontation with the Taoyin. This time it was over his plans to celebrate May Day by holding a public fête in Kashgar, and inviting one and all. The Taoyin had been prepared to turn a blind eye to this. But two days before it was due to take place he learned that red flags bearing revolutionary slogans were being secretly prepared in the bazaar. These, Gillan reported, urged the masses to rise up and overthrow all governments except that of the Soviet Union.

The Taoyin at once communicated this by radio to Governor Yang in Urumchi, who signalled back instructions that no government officials or Chinese citizens were to attend the fête. As a result only about thirty people turned up, mostly Russians or ex-Russian subjects. Despite this, Mr Doumpiss went ahead and delivered the address he had prepared for a far larger audience. He urged his handful of listeners to organise themselves and act, telling them they must be prepared to shed their own blood ('and presumably other people's', Gillan added tartly).

Enraged by this second defeat, Mr Doumpiss demanded an explanation from the Taoyin as to why his fête had been boycotted. The Taoyin told him that it had been to prevent the very kind of disturbances which his revolutionary slogans seemed to invite. Mr Doumpiss protested that these were totally innocuous, to which the Chinese replied that those in his possession were anything but. There the matter rested, and a month later Gillan was able to report: 'Mr Doumpiss has not yet recovered from his rebuff of May 1, and he and his staff remain quiescent.' It seems, though, that they were merely biding their time.

The following spring – on April 16, 1927 – Major Gillan reported that Mr Doumpiss had begun a whispering campaign directed against both the Chinese and the British. Word was being spread in the bazaars that 'the Soviet Republic of Kashgaria' was close at hand, and that its advent would be marked by the reward of its friends and the punishment of any who opposed it. No one, it was breathed, should pay any attention to the British Consulate-General as this would shortly be forced to close and its staff to flee the country. At the same time, anxious Muslim traders warned Gillan that Bolshevik agents were being infiltrated across the border and were planning to incite trouble.

The Taoyin, too, had heard this, and told Gillan he had ordered all travellers arriving from Soviet territory to be thoroughly searched, particularly for revolvers (evidently he feared assassination). The Bolsheviks, he had learned, were promising malcontent Kashgaris that if they succeeded in unleashing anything 'which could give the appearance of a revolt', help would be given them, though not otherwise.

Gillan pointed out to the Taoyin that if there was trouble the British Consulate-General would become a refuge for the most obvious victims of the mobs. These would include Hindu money-lenders and traders (who had British-Indian citizenship) and possibly the handful of missionaries and refugee Russians. It would thus be vulnerable to attack. The Taoyin promised him that the moment things began to look threatening he would put an armed guard around the consulate, but Gillan, knowing that the Taoyin's troops would be worse than useless in a crisis, asked him whether he would have any objection to extra men being rushed up from India. The Taoyin was quite amenable to this, even suggesting that the reinforcements be posted as orderlies rather than soldiers, and that Gillan should not seek his formal permission.

The Consul-General immediately telegraphed Delhi asking for five men to be sent as soon as possible. But there was another reason why he wanted reinforcements – or, as he put it, 'a few reliable men on the premises'. The Soviet consular staff, whose numbers had mysteriously swelled of late, had begun to spy actively on their British rivals (it is hard to believe that Gillan was not doing likewise). The Russians, he reported, were anxious to find out 'what active opposition is to be expected from us' if they took Sinkiang by force. They were also making discreet enquiries 'as to which of my staff, including menials, they can subvert, and have been discussing the feasibility of getting possession of documents from the consulate, or of seizing our mail'.

In a letter headed 'Secret', addressed to Sir Denys Bray, Foreign Secretary to the Government of India, Gillan wrote: 'They have definitely tried bribery, apparently on the assumption that I leave my secret papers lying about freely, and have tried other schemes of a comic opera nature which you will relish personally but which I will not commit to paper.' Referring to the plan to intercept his mail, Gillan went on: 'They have also discussed, but I believe abandoned as impracticable, a scheme to catch our mail on the road. They got the idea from a record in their consulate papers of a successful attempt by their Tsarist predecessors. I cannot find anything about it in our own records.'

The rules of the Great Game, it seems, had not changed – or certainly not in distant Sinkiang. But this was something at which Englishmen like Etherton and Gillan had always excelled, and it appears more than likely that the latter had his 'mole' in the Soviet Consulate-General just down the road, judging from his reports in the political and secret files of the period. In one memorandum headed 'Intelligence Agents', and addressed to his superiors in Delhi, he suggested a means of improving his existing espionage system. The ideal secret agent, he wrote, 'should come here as a trader, and should travel to sell his wares . . . No one but the Vice-Consul and myself should know who he is.' Were he to get into trouble, however, Gillan would have to disown him. 'I could not avow him as connected with the consulate, and could not give him any more assistance than would be given to any other trader.' But if such a man could be found, he told his chiefs, 'he would do very much more useful work than one who is avowedly a member of the consulate staff, and the nature of whose work is known or suspected by everyone.'

In the meantime he had to manage with two Indian Army intelligence sergeants, both posted openly to the consulate. Thus 'everyone here who is at all interested in the matter knows why they are here.' Although excellent men, he added, 'they are obvious soldiers, and it is impossible to send them out on long tours, as everyone would be on their guard against them.'

But while in Kashgar Gillan and his Russian counterpart were indulging in these shadowy pursuits, elsewhere in China there had been dramatic developments. In London, moreover, there had taken place a sensational incident which had resulted in the total severance of Britain's relations with the Soviet Union.

15 A Lady Vanishes

By the spring of 1927, relations between Moscow and London had sunk to their lowest point since the Allied Intervention, and fears were growing in the Kremlin that the capitalist powers were planning to attack the Soviet Union. The rift between Britain and Russia had begun to deepen in the winter of 1924, only months after they had established full diplomatic relations. It had followed the defeat of Britain's first Labour Government, and the triumphant return to office of the Tories.

The latter's victory had owed much to the eve-of-election publication by the *Daily Mail* of the notorious 'Zinoviev letter'. Purporting to emanate from the head of the Comintern himself, this instructed British Communists to set up secret revolutionary cells in the armed forces and to prepare for civil war. In banner headlines, the *Daily Mail* had blazoned its scoop: CIVIL WAR PLOT BY MOSCOW REDS . . . MOSCOW ORDERS TO OUR REDS . . . 'PARALYSE THE ARMY AND NAVY'. Beneath a portrait of Zinoviev, the newspaper told its readers:

> A 'Very Secret' letter of instructions from Moscow, which we publish below, discloses a great Bolshevik plot to paralyse the British Army and Navy and to plunge the country into civil war.
>
> The letter is addressed by the Bolsheviks of Moscow to the Soviet Government's servants in Great Britain, the Communist Party, who in turn are the masters of Mr Ramsay MacDonald's Government.

Whether the letter was a forgery or not is now largely academic, but its carefully timed release to the *Daily Mail* by a senior Whitehall official was clearly aimed at bringing Labour down – as indeed it did. Just who was behind this eve-of-poll thunderbolt may never be known, but high on the list of suspects must be the chiefs of Britain's security services, who were out to topple Ramsay MacDonald. Even Winston Churchill has been accused of having a hand in the affair, but it is unlikely that the whole truth will ever be known.

The hawks in the new Tory Cabinet would undoubtedly have liked to have seen the Zinoviev letter used as an excuse for severing relations with Moscow, but cooler heads had prevailed. Nonetheless, on assuming power, the Tories notified Moscow that Britain would not be ratifying two important treaties which their predecessors had negotiated, one of them general and the other commercial. Moreover, with powerful individuals like Churchill, now Chancellor of the Exchequer, fanning the flames, it could only be a matter of time before the rupture took place. The Tory press, for its part, kept up its agitation against Moscow. 'There are many dangerous Russians here at this moment', warned the *Daily Mail* on April 21, 1925, 'who never ought to have been allowed to enter, and who ought to be sent packing at the earliest moment.' The same day a leading article in the *Morning Post* declared:

> Let us make no mistake in this matter. We are again in times when Christendom is threatened by an Eastern invasion of barbarians, who are in this case assisted by secret allies and agents in our midst . . . The most notorious Bolsheviks are allowed to enter Great Britain to consult with their dupes and tools in this country, and to maintain elaborate organisations, under the guise of trade, manned by experts in all the dreadful arts of revolution.

The following year there occurred in Britain an event which seemed to confirm the suspicions of the Bolshephobes that not only was the Zinoviev letter genuine, but that his orders were being dutifully carried out by Moscow's cat's-paws within the trade union movement. This was the General Strike, in support of Britain's coal miners, which the Trades Union Congress called to start at midnight on May 3, 1926.

Despite allegations at the time, there is not a shred of evidence that Moscow was behind the strike, or in any way involved in it. The TUC was to decline an official offer of financial support from the Soviet trade unions, although more than a million pounds, ostensibly raised by levy among sympathetic Russian workers, was sent to the striking British miners. Yet, if nothing more, the Comintern had invested great hopes in the strike. In Zinoviev's words, it heralded 'a new era' for the working classes of Britain and Europe. He and the other Comintern chiefs, a historian of the period has claimed, 'hung on the telegraph wire waiting with tense impatience for every tiny item of news'. But their dreams of revolution, and of a Soviet Britain, collapsed when, after nine disappointing days, the TUC was forced to call the strike off.

The Soviet offer to fund the strike, and the contributions sent to the British miners, did little to improve relations between the two governments, and Stanley Baldwin, the Prime Minister, only refrained from breaking with Moscow for fear of endangering the peace of Europe. In China, the anti-British activities of Borodin were now becoming a cause of increasing concern in London. That summer, following the murder of several Britons at Wanhsien, on the Yangtze, Royal Navy gunboats had bombarded the town as a reprisal. Heavy civilian casualties resulted. This, in turn, had provided Borodin with invaluable propaganda against the British. Early the following year there were massive and violent anti-foreign demonstrations and strikes in Shanghai, in which the hand of Borodin could clearly be discerned. These had culminated in a Comintern-inspired uprising on February 22, which was put down with great slaughter after two days of fighting.

On February 23, Sir Austen Chamberlain, now Foreign Secretary, delivered a strong note to the Soviet Government accusing it of flagrant breaches of both its 1921 and 1923 non-interference pledges, and citing events in China and elsewhere. The note concluded: 'His Majesty's Government consider it necessary to warn the Union of Socialist Republics in the gravest terms that there are limits beyond which it is dangerous to drive public opinion.' Unless Moscow refrained forthwith from meddling in what were purely British interests, the severing of diplomatic relations and an abrogation of the trade agreement would be inevitable.

In a reply three days later, Moscow dismissed Chamberlain's threat as unlikely 'to intimidate anyone at all'. Answering his charge that Soviet leaders had made pronouncements hostile to Britain, it claimed that utterances made inside Russia did not fall within the 1921 or 1923 pledges, and that equally hostile remarks had been made by leading British statesmen about the Soviet Government. Lord Birkenhead, the Secretary of State for India, was quoted as describing the Soviet leadership as 'a band of murderers and robbers'. The Soviet reply ended, however, with an appeal for reconciliation.

But by now the Tory Cabinet had had enough, and were hell-bent on breaking with Moscow. The final rupture came on May 26, 1927. It followed an extraordinary incident which one eminent legal authority of the time was to describe as the gravest violation of international law to have taken place in Britain for two hundred years.

At 4.30 on the afternoon of May 12, some two hundred plain-clothes and uniformed police forced their way into the premises at 49 Moorgate, in the City, of the Soviet Trade Delegation and of Arcos Ltd, the official trade agency. They were armed with a search warrant not only for the offices of Arcos, which was subject to British law, but also for those of the Trade Delegation which had been granted diplomatic immunity under the 1921 trade agreement.

Convinced that the building was being used as a base for espionage and subversion – a 'nest of secret agents', *The Times* called it – the Cabinet had decided to ignore legal niceties and turn the premises upside down. They hoped, it would seem, to uncover evidence of these activities and so justify the raid.

While one group of officers ordered staff out of their offices and began to search them in the corridors, others rushed the cypher room. Struggles broke out as Soviet officials tried to protect their secret files, and several blows were exchanged. Meanwhile the telephones had been disconnected so that the Soviet Embassy could not be alerted. While experts forced open several safes in the hope of finding incriminating documents, others drilled holes in the walls, floors and ceilings in a search for hidden compartments. In all the police spent six hours combing the premises – ostensibly for a stolen secret document which was alleged to be in the possession of an Arcos employee, but which many doubted ever existed.

The results of the raid were to prove singularly disappointing. Despite the removal from the premises of secret code-books and quantities of confidential papers, no convincing evidence was found to justify Cabinet suspicions – or hopes. Nonetheless, on May 24, a Conservative-dominated House of Commons approved by 346 votes to 98 the Cabinet's decision to sever all relations with Moscow. The rupture was to last for more than two years.

Meanwhile in China too, after so promising a start, Soviet fortunes had suffered a major setback. This had begun, almost imperceptibly, with the death of Sun Yat-sen in March 1925. It was to end some two years later, with Borodin fleeing for his life across the Gobi Desert. The collapse of Moscow's strategies in China had come about in the following way.

On his deathbed Sun had dictated a last message to his followers (which some believe that Borodin himself wrote) in which he expressed the wish that they would continue to co-operate with Moscow, their 'best friend and ally', thus endorsing the role of the Comintern team. But he had named no heir, and a fierce struggle had ensued for the succession. The man who finally triumphed was his former chief-of-staff, General Chiang Kai-shek, known as the 'Red General' to the foreign communities in China. But fearful of the Communists' growing influence within the Kuomintang, and promised generous loans by bankers in Shanghai, he swung sharply to the right of the party.

At first he merely curtailed the influence of the Communists within the Kuomintang, banning them from criticising its policies, holding more than a third of the membership of any committee, or heading any department. For he still needed their co-operation in his march northwards against the warlord-held territories, and towards the ultimate goal of Peking. Although the Chinese Communists, sensing danger, now sought to break with the Kuomintang, Borodin resisted this. For it was Comintern strategy, ordained by Stalin, to go along with the Kuomintang and to seize victory from them at the last moment, from within. To abandon the Kuomintang would merely serve to strengthen the hand of the party's right wing.

In the months which followed, Chiang's revitalised forces, trained by Borodin's team of Red Army experts, won victory after victory on their historic Northern Expedition, which had for so long been the dream of Sun Yat-sen. Although unaware of the fate about to befall both the Communists and the left wing of the Kuomintang, Stalin now decided to switch Roy from the Indian front, where little progress was apparent, to give the hard-pressed Borodin a hand in China. The Russian, his once unassailable position now seriously threatened, also had personal troubles to contend with. Not only was he debilitated by malaria and dysentery, but he had just learned that his wife Fanya, herself a Comintern agent, had been captured by a northern warlord 'admiral' while sailing up the Yangtzee aboard a Soviet merchantman to join him. Intercepted by a gunboat, following a tip-off, the vessel was discovered to be carrying not only Fanya Borodin – a remarkable stroke of luck for the embattled northerners – but also three other Soviet agents, and large quantities of arms, ammunition and Communist literature.

To begin with, Fanya vehemently denied any connection with Borodin, for she was travelling under her maiden name. But then cards revealing her true identity were found in her

cabin. Also found were highly incriminating papers which, her
northern captors were to claim, proved to be top-secret plans of
their military dispositions and other intelligence. Possession of
such documents, both she and Borodin were only too aware,
meant an automatic death sentence, carried out either by strangulation or beheading. Soon rumours began to reach Borodin
that she had already been executed.

It was at this low point in Borodin's personal fortunes that a
triumphant Chiang Kai-shek chose to annihilate the Communists, to whom he owed so much but who were now no longer
needed. Stalin's 'squeezed-out lemon', declared Trotsky scath-
ingly, 'had seized power.' A massacre of Communists, real or
imagined, ensued. The slaughter began in Shanghai, which the
Communists had helped Chiang to capture only three weeks
previously, and spread to other cities now under his control.
According to Roy, some twenty-five thousand men and women
died at the hands of Chiang's terror squads during the spring of
1927.

For him and Borodin, escape was the only course left. It
would be just a matter of time before Chiang's murderous
armies came for them at Wuhan which they and the far-left of
the Kuomintang had made their base. Their mission, largely
because of Stalin's misguided trust in Chiang Kai-shek, had
ended in catastrophe, the terrible consequences of which their
Chinese comrades were now suffering. For Borodin it was a
particularly mortifying time. In Moscow, if he ever saw it again,
there would be painful inquests to be faced. Scapegoats would
clearly have to be found for this débâcle, if merely to save the
face of the infallible Stalin, and the most obvious candidates
would be himself and Roy. Their revolutionary careers, hitherto so successful, were finished, and even their lives might be in
jeopardy.

But Borodin, who now had a broken arm to add to his
ailments, had the additional worry of not knowing whether
Fanya was dead or alive. Such was his own notoriety – 'the
bogy-man of the West', the *Manchester Guardian* was to call him

– that his wife's capture had made headlines all over the world. Yet mystery continued to surround her fate or whereabouts, although *The Times* of March 10, 1927 reported from Peking that the three Comintern agents captured with her had been shot as spies.

Chiang Kai-shek was not the only one to crack down on the Communists at this time. The northern warlords had also launched a series of witch-hunts against them. On March 20, they raided schools and campuses in Peking, seizing scores of leftists. Others managed to reach the safety – or so they thought – of the Soviet Embassy. But two weeks later, with the blessing of Western diplomats, three hundred police and troops scaled the walls of the Soviet compound and began to ransack offices and buildings in which the fugitives were known to be hiding. Sixty of them were seized, together with quantities of documents and secret papers. The Dutch Minister, who watched the raid, reported seeing several Russians, their arms tied behind their backs, driven away in motor cars. They were more fortunate than some of their Chinese comrades, at least twenty of whom were executed on the spot by strangulation.

In the middle of the raid a column of smoke was suddenly spotted rising from the chimney of the Soviet military attaché's office. The legation quarter fire brigade was hurriedly summoned. It was then realised that the Russian and his staff were burning compromising papers. To prevent them from destroying any more, water was hastily pumped down the chimney while police broke into the office below. The most incriminating documents, the Dutch Minister conjectured, would have been among the first to be consigned to the flames. Nonetheless, a number which were to prove highly embarrassing to Moscow were rescued, many of them badly charred but still readable.

These included a secret directive from the Comintern in Moscow 'to organise anti-European riots', and 'to take all measures to excite the masses of the people against foreigners'. The aim of this was clearly to provoke retaliation which, in turn, would heighten Chinese xenophobia, and so on But care must be taken, the instruction added, not to provoke the Japanese, or give them an excuse for military intervention, since they were well placed to land troops in large numbers in China. The agitation should furthermore seek to exploit 'the existing antagonism between the individual foreign powers'. Great Britain, it was clear, was the principal target. The raid was denounced by the Soviet Government as 'an unheard-of violation of the most elementary rules of international law' (which it most clearly was). It also claimed that all the documents – which were later translated and published, some in facsimile – were crude forgeries.

In such an atmosphere, Fanya Borodin was fortunate not to have been quietly liquidated. She was, in fact, alive and well, held amid great secrecy in a Peking prison. But she was far from safe. Chang Tso-lin, the bloodthirsty warlord who ruled Peking, had wanted to have her judicially strangled without a trial, but had eventually been persuaded that a show-trial might make a better impression on the outside world. So, on July 12, 1927, more than three months after her arrest, Fanya was brought before a Chinese judge. The verdict, it seemed, was a foregone conclusion, for the courts were firmly under the thumb of the greatly-feared Chang.

It was with astonishment, therefore, that Peking learned that the judge had ordered her immediate release. On being told the news, an enraged Chang ordered her to be rearrested immediately, but he was too late. Within minutes of the verdict being delivered, she had vanished. And so, too, had the judge. He was already on his way to Japan, better off by $200,000 paid to him on behalf of a grateful Soviet Government by a Comintern secret agent sent specially to save Fanya from Chang's blood-lust. It was a daring and brilliantly planned operation – even if the judge did leave his wife, children and brother behind to face the music.

Believing that Fanya had fled to the Soviet Embassy, Chang demanded that she be handed over forthwith, arguing that her release was due to 'a defect in legal procedure' at the Supreme Court. This was refused. A raid ensued, but no sign was found of the missing Fanya. Vincent Sheean, an American reporter who was in Peking at the time, recounted afterwards: 'Peking was turned upside down, the trains were watched, suspected houses were raided . . . Chang Tso-lin believed, and rightly, that it would be difficult for a Russian woman with Madame Borodin's known appearance to travel far in China.'

Photographs of Fanya were circulated and posted everywhere. Vessels at Tientsin, the nearest port, were closely watched. Chang was determined not to let her slip through his fingers again. Then suddenly, ten days after her disappearance, a Japanese news-agency despatch from Vladivostok reported that she had arrived there safely after escaping from China. It quoted her in some detail on her arrest, trial and escape. Eight days later her arrival in Moscow, aboard the Trans-Siberian Express, was reported by Tass, again with graphic quotes. The story of her dramatic escape from the hands of Chang's executioners appeared in almost every newspaper in the world. Chang himself, incensed at the failure of his police, reluctantly called off the search.

But how had she done it? It was, in fact, a brilliant act of deception. All this time Fanya was still in Peking, hiding in a former Confucian temple. The problem still remained, however, of how to smuggle her safely out of China, under the noses of Chang's police, even though the hue and cry had now died down. It was at this point that Sheean, the unsuspecting American reporter, was approached by the Russian agent Kantorovich, who was playing the role of Soviet Scarlet Pimpernel, and asked for help.

'Only then', wrote the American, 'did I learn that Fanny Borodin had never left Peking at all.' The plan proposed to him was that he should escort her, posing as a sick relative of his, to Tientsin where the captain of a Soviet vessel was expecting them and would be ready to sail the moment they arrived. Sheean, who liked and admired Fanya's husband, and no doubt sensed a good story for his newspaper, readily agreed, but the plan fell through when the American woman who had agreed to lend Fanya her passport suddenly got cold feet. In the end, Fanya was smuggled safely across the frontier into neighbouring Mongolia, and made her way home from there to Moscow, which she reached early in October.

In the meantime Borodin himself, who still had no reliable news of her, and who by now had a large price on his own head, had also managed to escape. He and thirty companions had made their way more than a thousand miles across the Gobi Desert to Urga, the Mongolian capital, by then renamed Ulan Bator. They had travelled in a slow-moving convoy of ten vehicles, with petrol cans strapped to the running boards, and keeping an anxious eye out for pursuers. Much of their exhausting journey had been spent digging the heavily-laden cars and lorries out of the sand, for there were no roads to follow, only ancient caravan trails dating back a thousand years or more. Finally they had sighted in the distance the golden roofs and spires of Ulan Bator, and it was here that Borodin, weakened by months of illness and his arm still in a sling, had heard with relief of Fanya's escape. He reached Moscow not long after his wife, and they were joyfully reunited there in their small suite in the Metropol Hotel. Neither had ever expected to see the other again.

Although he and Roy were made scapegoats for events beyond their control, they were luckier than many of those who failed Stalin. After months of waiting, Borodin was summoned to give evidence before the committee of enquiry. It opened with a senior revolutionary theoretician reading a paper giving the official explanation for the catastrophe. Then came the witnesses – or rather the penitents. When Borodin was called, he knew what was expected of him. His 'evidence' corroborated in every detail Stalin's explanation for his failure in China. He confessed to his errors and accepted with suitable humility the criticisms levelled at him. He thus survived, filling various minor jobs for more than twenty years, although eventually his luck was to run out.

Roy, too, had fallen heavily from grace. Expelled from the Comintern, this one-time high-flier and favourite of Lenin's cut little ice with Stalin – who in any case had an almost pathological suspicion of foreigners. Had it not been for Borodin, who managed to arrange his swift exit from the Soviet Union, he would almost certainly have 'disappeared' like so many others. With great courage, Roy now decided to return to India and attempt, single-handed, to bring about the long-awaited revolution there.

*   *   *

Surprisingly, the hasty departure of Roy and Borodin from China had not put paid to Stalin's ambitions there. Despite one humiliating setback, he remained convinced that China could still be his. Accordingly he despatched there a new trouble-shooter, this time a fellow-Georgian named Lominadze, whose task was to organise a series of worker and peasant uprisings. These, Stalin forecast, would meet with a 'tremendous response' from the masses, and lead to the downfall of Chiang Kai-shek, the bogus revolutionary and turncoat who had made such a fool of him. For Stalin, now in the final stages of his struggle with Trotsky, had still to win absolute power in Russia, and he was in need of a spectacular victory to help him consolidate his position. He decided therefore to take a gamble. Whether by coincidence or not, the great Canton insurrection was ordered for December 11, 1927. It was the very day that Stalin planned, during the Fifteenth Party Conference in Moscow, finally to crush Trotsky.

The uprising took place at 3 a.m. At first things went well for the Communists, and by dawn most of the city was in their hands. A new revolutionary government was proclaimed. But the masses were not yet convinced. Few rallied to the Red Flag, most preferring to sit back and see what would happen next. For three heroic days the ill-armed Communists managed to hold out. But then the Kuomintang forces – forty-five thousand strong – began to advance on the city from several directions simultaneously. The assault, which was accompanied by a heavy artillery barrage, was directed from a gunboat in the Pearl River. By the afternoon of December 13, Canton's short-lived Communist rule was over.

A terrible retribution was now unleashed by the Kuomintang. A Chinese reporter from a Peking newspaper described what he saw: 'Behind the fallen brick walls, propped up against trees, lying at the street kerbs, and floating on the surface of the river – wherever you looked – were the corpses of massacred men and women. Blood seemed to be running in rivers, and the ground was strewn with brains and bowels and entrails.' The pathetic makeshift weapons of the Communists lay everywhere – stones, wooden spears and bamboo swords. From the screams and sounds in the distance, it was evident that the orgy of execution and revenge was far from over.

It is estimated that in all between six and seven thousand men and women perished in the blood-bath. Among them were five Soviet consular officials who were dragged from their offices and shot for their suspected part in the insurrection. The chief Comintern adviser (or so the Chinese survivors claimed) was one of the first to flee when he saw that the battle was lost. And yet he had been warned by the local party leaders that they were ill-prepared for an uprising, and that it could only end in catastrophe. Moscow, too, had been told this. But once Stalin had given the order there was no possible turning back.

Having crushed the uprising, Chiang Kai-shek ordered the immediate closure of all Soviet consulates and commercial agencies in areas under his control and the expulsion of their staffs. This did not include the recently opened ones in Sinkiang which was still firmly under the sway of Governor Yang. In Moscow, meanwhile, blame for this latest débâcle was being laid at the feet of everyone but Stalin. Writing in *Pravda* shortly afterwards, Chicherin, the Soviet Foreign Minister, pointed an accusing finger at Britain. 'British imperialist reaction', he declared, was to blame for the slaughter, as well as for the killing, and expulsion from China, of Soviet citizens. As in the case of the earlier failure, responsibility was also passed down the line to those on the spot (most of whom were conveniently dead). While the decision to order an uprising had beyond doubt been 'correct' and 'necessary' and 'completely in accord with the facts', those entrusted with its leadership were accused of committing 'a whole series of blunders'.

Stalin himself, although he had desperately hoped that his Canton gamble would come off, had nonetheless, with his usual cunning, covered himself against the risk of failure. Just one week before the day he had chosen for the uprising, he had told delegates to the Fifteenth Party Congress: 'The fact that the Chinese revolution has not led directly to victory over imperialism is not important. People's revolutions never succeed in the first round of the fight. They grow and consolidate in ebbs and flows. It has happened everywhere. It happened in Russia, and it will also happen in China.'

But in China, Soviet fortunes proved to be all ebb and no flow. By the end of 1928, Chiang Kai-shek was in control of most of China proper. His government had been recognised by the Great Powers, including the Soviet Union. China's Communists – largely because of Stalin's disastrous strategies – had been reduced to a hunted rabble.

To the Comintern chiefs that winter the world revolution must have seemed as far off as ever. The long-promised uprisings in Europe had failed to materialise, China had proved calamitous, while in India and elsewhere in the East they were getting nowhere at all. The post-war revolutions in Turkey and Persia, which for a while had looked promising, had turned out to be bourgeois-led, while Afghanistan had proved to be merely opportunist, as Lenin had warned Roy that it would way back in 1920. The world revolution, it had to be admitted, had got no further than Mongolia. Even Stalin is reported to have declared: 'Who are these Comintern people? In ninety years they will never make a revolution anywhere.'

But whatever Stalin's doubts might have been about the

Comintern's ability to set the world ablaze, they were not shared by the Government of India. Indeed, anxiety in Delhi had once more deepened as the result of a curious event which took place around this time at a remote spot on the Soviet-Persian frontier.

16 The Last of the Central Asian Dreamers

In the early hours of New Year's Day, 1928, the wires began to buzz frantically between Moscow and the Soviet Legation in Teheran. Two Russian officials, the Minister was informed, had vanished while on a hunting trip in southern Turkestan, and it was feared that they had crossed into Persia. One of the fugitives was privy to the innermost secrets of the Kremlin, and must therefore under no circumstances be allowed to fall into British hands. The men must be tracked down immediately and – on Stalin's personal orders – be liquidated. It did not matter how.

By now, after evading Soviet border guards, the two frightened Russians had reached a small village in northern Persia, not far from where Colonel Bailey had crossed to safety eight years earlier. Here they asked bemused officials for political asylum. One of the two defectors had particular reason to fear Stalin's vengeance. A young Kremlin official named Boris Bajanov, he had not only once served as Stalin's personal assistant, but had subsequently succeeded him as secretary to the all-powerful Politburo. He was thus in possession of Soviet secrets of incalculable importance.

British intelligence officers in Persia were quick to learn of the men's defection, and to arrange to take them under their protection. Delhi was signalled, and it was agreed that the two Russians should proceed to India for debriefing. But Soviet agents, fearful at the prospect of failing Stalin, were equally determined to stop them. A deadly game of hide-and-seek now ensued, with the Soviets endeavouring to shoot, poison or kidnap their two fellow-countrymen. Finally, after a hair-raising journey across eastern Persia by pony, car and camel caravan, the two Russians reached the safety of Simla. Here, in

the middle of April 1928, they were interrogated at length by
Frederick Isemonger, the head of the Indian Government's
Intelligence Bureau, and two colleagues from military intelli-
gence, one a fluent Russian-speaker.

It did not take them long to realise that Bajanov – described
by one British official as a man of 'considerable education and
intelligence' who would have graced the civil service of any
Western government – was an undreamed-of windfall for those
responsible for India's security. Although not a member of the
Comintern, he possessed an intimate knowledge of Soviet world
strategy. Worldwide revolution, he assured his interrogators,
was still their ultimate aim, with the East as the Kremlin's
immediate target. The British Empire was seen as the foremost
obstacle to Soviet ambitions, and war between the two powers
was regarded as ultimately inevitable. But immediate strategy
was aimed at weakening Britain and her empire from within in
order to ensure victory when war came. At present, however,
war was to be avoided at all costs, as Moscow had not the
resources to embark on one. In the meantime, Bajanov warned,
a campaign of agitation and subversion was being waged by the
Comintern, its agents being 'at the bottom of every strike' in
India. When war with Britain and her allies finally broke out,
pro-Soviet revolutions would be staged in Afghanistan and
Persia, those traditional guardians of the approaches to India.

That was the gist of what the Russian told his interrogators.
The full story of this first major Soviet defection (culled from
contemporary intelligence reports) and the attempts made to
kill him after a $5 million price was placed on his head by Stalin
is told in Gordon Brook-Shepherd's book *The Storm Petrels*, to
which I am indebted for the above, the official papers, somewhat mysteriously, being no longer available to researchers.

The accuracy of Bajanov's revelations about Soviet strategies
in Persia were, ironically enough, corroborated not long afterwards by the very man assigned by Moscow to liquidate him.
Georgi Agabekov, the agent in charge of Soviet underground
operations in Persia, himself defected eighteen months later,

after falling hopelessly in love with a British Embassy secretary in Cairo. One of his principal tasks, he said, had been to 'prepare' Kurdish and Bakhtiari tribesmen for their role in the coming war with Britain. They were to harass the British rear and to put out of action their military airfields as well as the Anglo-Persian oilfields. Agabekov claimed – before Soviet hit-men cut short his career – to have arranged, by means of bribery, the interception of all British official mail between Teheran and Delhi. He even demonstrated to his interrogators how a seal could be removed, copied, melted down and replaced, apparently intact.

The British Government was no longer prepared to take such things lying down. Nor, for that matter, was *The Times*, which shared its abhorrance of Bolshevism. On February 15, 1929, under the headline REVOLUTION IN THE EAST, it carried a long and prominently displayed warning about Moscow's ambitions in India. Drawing attention to an article in the official Soviet journal *New East*, it declared: 'A study of this magazine makes it possible to foresee which country has been selected by the Comintern for its next attack. A few years ago attention was chiefly directed to China. Now the main object of attack is India.'

The latest issue of *New East*, the writer added, carried no fewer than three articles on India, while other Soviet news-papers were constantly warning that the mistakes and failures of the Chinese revolution had to be carefully analysed so that they would not be repeated in India. The writer went on to describe the training provided in Moscow and elsewhere in the Soviet Union for revolutionaries from India and other colonial terri-tories. 'Negroes', he added, 'are paraded through the old palaces and seat themselves on the throne of the Tsars.' Institu-tions formerly used for training orientalists and diplomats were now being used to turn out professional revolutionaries trained in the art of civil war.

The timing of the article may have been more than pure chance. For it paved the way for what was shortly to ensue – a massive crackdown by the authorities on all Communists in India known to have Soviet connections, followed by a show trial. This was the outcome of months of painstaking CID work, including the surveillance of suspects, interception of mail and cracking of codes. On March 20, in a series of carefully orchestrated raids, thirty-one Communists were arrested in different parts of India, including the Englishmen Spratt and Bradley. All were charged with conspiring to deprive the King-Emperor of his sovereignty of British India – or, as the prosecutor wryly put it, to replace the Government of the King 'with that of Mr Stalin'.

The Meerut Conspiracy Trial, as it became known, was intended by the authorities to expose to the world Moscow's evil designs on India and to smash once and for all the organisation it had managed to build up there. Labour and Liberal MPs at once accused the Tories of using the 'Bolshevik bogy' as a manoeuvre for winning votes in the forthcoming general election. (If that was their intention then it was to fail miserably, for long before the trial opened they were swept out of office by a Labour administration.) One of the accused Indians even fought a seat from his Meerut prison cell, having been refused bail to travel to his constituency in Yorkshire.

The entire proceedings, beginning with the magistrate's preliminary hearing, were to take four and a half years in all. The trial itself lasted nearly three years, of which the prosecution case took thirteen months, the lengthy statements of the accused ten months, the defence two months, and legal arguments four and a half months. The judgment, totalling nearly seven hundred pages, took a further five months to prepare and deliver. In the course of their raids, and through earlier interceptions, the CID had seized mountains of documents, of which more than three thousand were produced in evidence by the prosecution. A further one and a half thousand exhibits were offered by the defence. In all some three hundred witnesses gave evidence as the case dragged monotonously on beneath the slowly-turning fans of the Meerut courtroom.

In the middle of all this, the startling news broke that Roy had been arrested in Bombay. He had been at large in India, it transpired, for seven months, keeping always one move ahead of the police. Assuming a series of disguises – a skill he had trained so many others in – he had travelled all over India, preaching revolution and making contacts. For a while he had been one 'Dr Mahmud', a disciple of Gandhi. But although his close association with Lenin and his adventures in China lent him a special glamour, his message had made little real impact. Eventually the CID had managed to trap him, though only after his betrayal, he claimed, by Indian Communists sympathetic to Moscow.

Charged, like the Meerut accused, with conspiring to deprive the King-Emperor of his sovereignty, Roy was found guilty and sentenced to twelve years' rigorous imprisonment. He appealed against his conviction, arguing in court that British India was 'an enormous tyranny', and quoting Hume and Bentham in defence of a people's right to take up arms against oppressive rule. The judge suggested drily that he would have done better if he had paid less attention to the 'attractive doctrine of political philosophers' and more to the mundane provisions of the Indian penal code. He dismissed Roy's appeal, but cut his twelve-year sentence by half.

Meanwhile, the trial at Meerut had not been without its moments of humour. To the chagrin of Philip Spratt, for example, it was to emerge that the secret code he had been given before leaving London had proved 'fairly obvious' to the CID who had solved it at a glance. Messages in invisible ink had not always remained invisible. But the conspirators had also used other codes which the CID took longer to work out. It was noticed, for instance, that a number of letters known to have come from Spratt began with the words 'Dear Brother in God'. These turned out to be (to quote a senior security service official) 'a sort of grotesque correspondence as if between clergymen'. References to the YMCA really meant the Indian Communist Party, while the Workers' and Peasants' Party became Methodists. Furthermore all the leading conspirators were given pseudonyms. Spratt became 'Desmond' and Bradley 'Fred', while certain crucial words like 'send' and 'receive' were interchanged. Other names were disguised by substituting the vowels they contained by those immediately preceding them in the alphabet (A for E, U for A, etc.).

In the short run the trial proved to be little less than disastrous for the Indian Communist movement and its Comintern sponsors. It coincided with a time of rapidly rising industrial unrest in India. Half a million workers had taken part in more than two hundred strikes during the preceding twelve months of 1928–29, and it was no secret that the Communists were heavily involved in these. Now almost the entire leadership was behind bars. It was not difficult therefore to see why the authorities had selected that moment for their crack-down, irrespective of what interpretation His Majesty's Opposition might choose to put on it. They hoped the trial would serve to shock Indian public opinion into recognising the extent of the conspiracy, its violent aims and Moscow's hand in it.

But if the Meerut trial, with its overwhelming evidence against the accused, served as a propaganda exercise for the authorities, it also provided a rare opportunity for the Communists to make their ideas known to millions whom they had hitherto failed to reach. Accused after accused stood up in court and expounded the merits of Communism at inordinate length, every word of which had to be laboriously taken down for the trial record.

Philip Spratt, who was later to desert the Communist cause, recounts in his memoir *Blowing Up India*: 'On the whole the revelation of our secret methods caused people to admire us: we had done what most young men wanted to do . . . We had our opportunity in the sessions court to make political statements, and these were widely published in the press. Several of them were long enough to make a short book, and altogether most of what can be said in favour of Communism was said.'

From the start Spratt had made no secret of his own views on the necessity for violence if British rule in India was to be overturned. At the preliminary hearing, he had told the court: 'The magistrate has quoted one of my speeches in which I said something about the brutal and violent side of our policy. I have nothing to retract from that. We admit we shall have to use violence.'

*   *   *

As the trial ground on in the sweltering heat of the plains, in distant Sinkiang Moscow's luck had at last begun to turn. Since Major Gillan had warned Delhi of trouble brewing there, and had telegraphed for reinforcements, in the ancient towns of the Silk Road there had been dramatic developments. On July 7, 1928, at a banquet held in Urumchi, a chain of events was set in motion destined shortly to plunge Sinkiang into a nightmare of bloodshed and barbarity. By the time it was over, it would have cost at least a hundred thousand lives (some put it at double this) and Sinkiang would have become a Soviet colony in everything but name.

Guest of honour at the ill-starred banquet was the grizzled Governor, Yang Tseng-hsin, the most powerful man in Sinkiang, and its autocratic ruler for seventeen years. Nominally the representative of China's central government, he was in fact Sinkiang's absolute master, merely advising Peking of his decisions. He kept the key of the radio station attached to his own belt, opening the door personally each morning and locking it again at night. He read every message himself and destroyed any of which he did not approve. Yang issued his own currency and, in return, expected no subsidy from central government. Under his firm grip the province remained so free of crime, it was said, that a wagon-load of gold bars could safely be left unguarded. Moreover he had shrewdly steered Sinkiang through both the Chinese and Bolshevik revolutions, thus sparing its populace the horrors of two civil wars.

The banquet, which followed a graduation ceremony at a law school, was attended by the Soviet Consul-General and a number of high-ranking Chinese officials. Principal of these was Yang's deputy, Fan Yao-nan. But unknown to Yang, who claimed to be able to read the truth in a man's face, Fan had long harboured a secret grudge against him, and was impatient to step into his shoes. Fan decided to have his chief assassinated. The banquet was to be the occasion.

Having no reason to suspect that anything was amiss, the Governor's bodyguards were feasting in an adjacent room where they had temporarily discarded their weapons. As the moment for the assassination approached, these were surreptitiously removed from their reach. Then, at a given signal, several young assassins disguised as graduating students drew revolvers from their sleeves and fired point-blank at the unsuspecting Governor. Although mortally wounded, he nonetheless roared out: 'Who dared do this?' They were the old man's last words. As he slumped forward, an aide dashed to his side but he also was shot dead. The rest of the guests fled, led by the Soviet Consul-General and his wife, both of whom took refuge in a lavatory.

Seeing that Yang was safely dead (some accounts say he used his own revolver to make quite sure), Fan hastily removed the keys from the Governor's belt before racing to his official residence to seize his all-important seal of office. But he found that he had been outmanoeuvred. Yang's Minister of the Interior, Chin Shu-jen, had got wind of the plot and, deciding to take advantage of it, had invented an excuse for not attending the banquet. He now sent troops to arrest Fan who, after a brief gun-battle, surrendered. Following a night of torture, it is said, Fan and ten accomplices were beheaded, and Chin took over as Governor. He was to remain there for the next five years, becoming more and more unpopular as corruption, inflation and taxation broke all records.

The flashpoint came in 1930, following the death of the hereditary Muslim ruler of the ancient oasis-town of Hami. Chin ordered that the tiny city state should now be absorbed into the Sinkiang administration, and that taxes should be greatly increased and in future paid direct to Urumchi. More-over, land was taken from Muslim families and given to newly-arrived Chinese refugees from the neighbouring province of Kansu. The deprived Muslim families were compensated, but with inferior plots of land. These were errors which the wily Yang would never have made. But what happened next could hardly have been foreseen by Chin.

Following the seduction of a local Muslim girl by the Chinese tax-collector appointed by him, the already angry population rose in uncontrolled fury. A mob gathered and lynched both the tax-collector and the girl, in what were described by one con-temporary commentator as 'circumstances of the utmost horror'. The violence spread rapidly, and among the first to be slaughtered were the unfortunate refugees who had been re-settled on Muslim land. Chin's advisers urged caution, believ-ing that a potentially very dangerous situation could still be defused. But the new Governor was determined to teach the Muslims a lesson they would never forget, and despatched a powerful force to the area led by a notoriously cruel officer. Knowing that they stood little chance against regular Chinese troops, and that fearsome reprisals lay in store for them, the ill-armed rebels took the only remaining option. They sent emissaries eastwards across the Gobi desert into Kansu to seek the backing of a formidable young Muslim warlord there called Ma Chung-yin, sometimes known as 'Big Horse'. Ma's was a name which was to be long remembered in the towns and villages of the Silk Road.

Half bandit, half soldier, he came from a family renowned for its fighting prowess. Both a brilliant horseman and crack-shot, he is said to have been a colonel at the age of seventeen (some claim fifteen). Even now he was only just out of his teens. Sent by Chiang Kai-shek to a Kuomintang military academy at Nanking, young Ma had walked out after a few months, com-plaining that there was too much theory. He had returned to Kansu and established his headquarters near the famous caves of the Thousand Buddhas at Tun-huang. From here he terrorised the surrounding countryside, his men living off the spoils of the towns he captured. Mildred Cable, one of three English missionaries living in the area at that time, describes his reign of terror in her book *The Gobi Desert*:

'The only alternative to unconditional surrender was death by the sword, and in one resisting town after another every male over fourteen years of age was slaughtered, boys under fourteen were taken over by the army to be trained as little orderlies, and the young women were left to the pleasure of the soldiers . . . At last, no city dared to answer that terrible challenge save by throwing its gates open and by placing its arsenal, food-supply, horses and all else at the disposal of young Ma Chung-yin and his brigand band.'

Unlike the Muslims of Sinkiang, who were mostly of Turkic stock, Ma and his men were Tungans, or Muslims of Chinese origin and appearance. But he had no love for the Chinese authorities who had executed his father as a reprisal for his own bloodthirsty doings. His sympathies, or at any rate his personal ambitions, lay with China's Central Asian Muslims, whether Tungans or Turkis. For he had long harboured dreams of founding a great Islamic empire in the Asian heartland. And suddenly here was his chance. He saw himself as a Central Asian Mahdi, called to deliver his fellow Muslims from infidel Chinese rule. Young Ma needed no second bidding.

*   *   *

Sinkiang now found itself plunged into a holy war which was to ebb and flow for four terrible years, bringing darkness and carnage to a previously peaceable region. It was, moreover, to give the Soviets their chance, and finally all but deliver the province into their hands. This blood-stained epoch began in 1931, in the furnace-heat of summer, with a daring march by Ma and five hundred of his men across the waterless Gobi into Sinkiang. At that time his soldiers would gladly have followed their leader, with his reckless courage, over the edge of the world had he commanded it, and hundreds of Turkis began flocking to his banner.

Ma's invasion of the province took Urumchi completely by surprise. After capturing the town of Barkul, where he was hailed as a liberator and presented with two thousand rifles, he marched on Hami. His plan was to seize the oasis-towns of the Silk Road one by one, including Urumchi and Kashgar. But the Chinese garrison in Hami held out gallantly, and Ma's ill-armed force was finally obliged to withdraw.

The various accounts of this desert war, with its advances and reverses, massacres and reprisals, conflict greatly. But according to Mildred Cable the Hami garrison was only saved from Ma's vengeance by a strange quirk of history. Just when surrender seemed inevitable, one of the defenders suddenly remembered the existence of an ancient arsenal dating from an earlier Muslim uprising the previous century. When hastily opened up it was found to contain not only swords but also large quantities of fire-arrows – terrifying weapons which were turned to deadly effect on the besiegers. Later, when Mildred Cable and her two colleagues were virtual prisoners of the rebels at the Caves of the Thousand Buddhas, they were summoned by Ma to his headquarters at Ansi to treat not only his own wounds – he had been shot through both legs – but also those of his soldiers who had been burned by these archaic but still horribly effective weapons. (Mildred recalled afterwards how this otherwise fearless tyrant had flinched at the prospect of her antiseptics.)

Although Ma's wounds kept him for the time being out of the fight, elsewhere the blood-letting continued as furiously as ever. With much of Sinkiang aflame, whole towns and villages were reduced to ashes and innocent people slaughtered by the thousand. Many who managed to survive massacre were struck down instead by typhus. Before long the epidemic reached the half-starved populace of Tun-huang. Mildred Cable describes the scene at this now-famous tourist site: 'The temple entrances were full of men and women muttering in delirium and calling on passers-by for a drink of water to slake their intolerable thirst. Dogs and wolves had a good time outside the north gate, for by ancient custom the bodies of all who died in the road-ways were wrapped in matting and buried there in shallow graves.'

It was a grim time too for the handful of other Westerners who found themselves caught up in the cruel war. One was a young German engineer called Georg Vasel, hired by the central government to construct a chain of landing strips along the route of the long-defunct Silk Road. He was to experience a series of hair-raising adventures, ending with a year in a Soviet-run secret police cell. These he describes in his book *My Russian Jailers in China*.

One night, driving between Hami and Urumchi, he came upon a village whose inhabitants had all been put to the sword only shortly before. Burned out homes, with their roofs collapsed and walls blackened, lined the streets. By the light of his torch he could see the appalling fate which had befallen those who until recently had lived in them. From their agonised postures it was obvious they had been slaughtered with fanatical cruelty.

The streets, too, were strewn with the rotting corpses of men, women and children, and the carcases of camels and horses. Vasel could see that short of driving his lorry over them it would be impossible to proceed. He asked his escort, one of Ma's officers, whether there was any other route they could take, but the man shook his head. Their White Russian driver was too shocked by the sight of this carnage to continue at the wheel, and Vasel himself had to take over. At first he tried to steer between the heaped corpses, but the heavily-laden truck nearly ended in the ditch. Vasel decided grimly that there was nothing for it but to drive straight over them. He noticed the driver crossing himself repeatedly as their wheels crunched sickeningly over skulls and limbs. But the nightmare was still not over. Beyond the village the road was strewn with hundreds more corpses belonging to Chinese soldiers butchered by Ma's troops. It was only the first such village that Vasel was to see in the coming months.

By now the insurrection was spreading westwards across the province, although its progress was slowed by the great distances between the scattered oasis-towns and villages around the desert. In February 1933, it finally reached Cherchen, on the southern arm of the old Silk Road and four hundred miles from Urumchi. Trapped there at the time was a young Swedish scientist, Dr Nils Ambolt, who was part of a scientific expedition led by the celebrated explorer Sven Hedin. He was there taking astronomic and other scientific readings when he found himself engulfed by the war. He recalled: 'This was the first time I had ever seen a revolutionary mob, wild with lust, without a trace of responsibility, fanatical, excited and terrifying, and it was not a pretty sight.'

Word had reached the town that five hundred of Ma's warriors were only two days' march away, and the Chinese *amban* was called upon by the Muslims to surrender to avoid bloodshed. He had only thirty-five soldiers of his own, all of them Turkis, who he knew would desert at the first opportunity. He decided therefore to surrender, and was forced to hand over all his arms and ammunition. To protect their lives, the Chinese now began to convert to Islam in hundreds, including the *amban* himself who took on a Muslim name. The following day Ambolt noted in his diary: 'Large crowds gathered at the mosque to enjoy the spectacle of their former ruler putting on the *sella*, or white turban, and the *meize*, the Turkish boot . . . and for the first time, in view of everyone performing his *namaz*, bowing his forehead in the dust.'

A week later the rebel forces reached Cherchen. They consisted of one captain and fifteen soldiers, one of whom was the captain's own fifteen-year-old son. However, it was too late for the *amban* to do much about it. He had already surrendered the town. At least the Chinese community had escaped massacre, even if their possessions were looted by the mob which rampaged through the town. Although Ambolt himself was unharmed, it was clear to him that it would be impossible for him to continue his scientific work. He decided to head westwards to Keriya and Khotan, and thence over the Karakoram passes to India. Things in Keriya, he found, had been far nastier. He recounts: 'On the fourth day of the revolution, thirty-five Chinese and two Hindus were murdered. The methods were mediaeval in their cruelty. Their ears were cut off, their tongues torn out, their eyes pierced in, their teeth knocked out, their hands and feet crushed . . .'

When they were finally dead their corpses were thrown to the dogs. Those whose lives were spared were forced to convert to Islam, though only after parting with all their valuables, not to say their wives and daughters too. Ambolt relates: 'Chinese women were taken from their husbands and given in marriage to Turkis. Little girls ten years old were given to men of over fifty.'

Khotan, famous for its carpets and its jade, had fared no better. Ambolt noticed freshly-dug graves everywhere, as well as putrefying corpses beside the road. In one village he passed through, a Turki officer told him how they had exterminated the Chinese garrison at Yarkand, the next town to the west. The defenders had managed to hold out for several months, but had finally agreed to surrender, bartering their weapons and all their money for their lives. Or so they had believed. But as they headed out of town with their families, Turki troops fell on them, sparing no one. Their children – Chinese 'spawn', the officer called them – were thrown on a heap, doused with paraffin, and set alight. 'We didn't want any seeds left to sprout of that race,' he told Ambolt. One need hardly add that, wherever they had the upper hand, Chin's troops were carrying out reprisals of similar barbarity against the Muslims.

In January 1934, after numerous setbacks, Ma's soldiers managed to fight their way to the gates of the walled city of Urumchi. Twice before in the previous year they had threatened the capital but had been beaten off after heavy casualties on both sides. The besieged, who included several European missionaries, had suffered appalling hardships. Aitchen Wu, a senior Chinese official who lived through those grim days, recalls: 'Dogs made wild by having eaten the flesh of corpses roamed the streets in bands.' Two of the British missionaries, whose devoted work he remembered with admiration, died of cholera while nursing the sick and wounded, and are buried in Urumchi. At one critical moment in the siege the rebels managed to seize an entire street of houses just outside one of the city gates and set up machine-guns on the rooftops. The Chinese commander, seeing the danger, immediately ordered a torch to be put to the houses, even though they were crowded with refugees. Wu, in his memoir *Turkistan Tumult*, describes the ensuing holocaust:

'As the flames swept down the long lane of wooden structures they became an inferno of horror. For the roar of the conflagration was added to the rattle of gunfire and the hideous shrieks of those who were trapped. The rebels sought safety in flight, and as they crossed the open were machine-gunned from the Red Mountain. But the fugitives had nowhere to fly to and perished to the last man, woman and child. Nevertheless, the city was saved.'

The real heroes of the siege were the five hundred recklessly brave White Russian soldiers who had stayed on in Urumchi after escaping from the Bolsheviks. But their victory had been touch and go, thanks to the paranoia of Governor Chin. Fearing that they might be planning to seize power themselves, he had deliberately kept them ill-armed and given them the worst horses. After driving back Ma's forces, the Russians decided to topple the currupt and unpopular Chin whose misrule had sparked off, and kept aflame, the Muslim insurrection. In April 1933, a coup was staged and Chin overthrown after fierce fighting between the Russians and Chin's bodyguard, under cover of which the Governor managed to escape in disguise over the wall of his residence. Chin was succeeded by the Manchurian-born garrison commander, Sheng Shi-tsai, an able though ruthless professional soldier.

Nine months later, in January 1934, Ma's troops suddenly threatened Urumchi for the third time and in greater force than ever. Carrying long scaling ladders, and led personally by Ma – now fully recovered from his wounds – they crept unseen through the hills to the west of the capital and succeeded in capturing the wireless station. But unknown to Ma, much had happened in Urumchi during those nine months. A new Soviet Consul-General had been appointed personally by Stalin, with instructions to offer Sheng the use of Red Army troops in putting down the insurrection. Normally Stalin might have been expected to back the rebels rather than the local Chinese who, officially anyway, still owed allegiance to the renegade Chiang Kai-shek. But there were good reasons why he did not relish seeing the unpredictable Ma ruling this strategically crucial region.

First there was a grave risk of this Muslim insurrection spilling over the frontier into his own Central Asian territories. The Soviets had only just succeeded, at considerable cost, in crushing the *basmachi*, and the last thing Stalin wanted was another holy war on his hands. Even more worrying were Ma's shadowy links with the hostile and aggressive Japanese. No one knows to this day what these actually amounted to, although it is certain that, in addition to a Turkish colonel, Ma had two Japanese advisers on his staff, one of whom was captured by Sheng's troops. The Japanese Foreign Office, needless to say, had immediately denied all knowledge of him.

But following Japan's occupation of Manchuria in 1931 and of Jehol in 1933, Stalin was deeply concerned about its ambitions in Asia. As one Tashkent newspaper pointed out, were a triumphant Ma to invite his Japanese friends into Sinkiang, Russia's crucial oilfields at Baku would overnight be placed within range of their bombers. Moreover Mongolia, on which the Japanese were known to have their eye, would find itself outflanked, while – worse – the Soviet Union's great new industrial centres in western Siberia would be put at risk.

Meanwhile, hard-pressed by Ma's forces, and aware that

Nanking was in no position to help him, Governor Sheng accepted Stalin's offer only too gratefully. His decision was to prove a fateful one for the people of Sinkiang.

Amid great secrecy and unknown to Ma, the first Red Army
units crossed into China during the Christmas of 1933. Not only
did they aim to take the Muslims by surprise, but the Governor
of Sinkiang had no authority to invite them onto Chinese territory. Officially, therefore, they were not there, and thus neither
troops nor vehicles bore any kind of identifying mark. To this
day, except for the Soviets themselves, no one knows for certain
just how many men there were in all, though it was probably no
more than two thousand or so.

By chance – ill chance, as it had turned out – Georg Vasel, the
young German airfield engineer, found himself at the remote
town of Chuguchak on the Sinkiang-Soviet border at the time.
It was an unhealthy place for a European just then, and it was
from a prison yard that Vasel watched 'regiment after regiment'
marching through the snow towards Urumchi, followed by
'greyish-green monsters – armoured cars with machine-guns
mounted on their steel turrets'. He recounts:

'They had brand-new rifles of the latest make, with bayonets
fixed, and they were in semi-civilian garb. I knew instinctively,
however, that they belonged to the regular Soviet army. The
people stared at the invaders in dumb dismay, but neither by
look nor word did they dare voice their feelings.'

Shortly afterwards he heard the sound of aircraft approaching. Looking up, he saw a squadron of bombers, obviously
Soviet but bearing no markings. 'They were flying eastwards,
fairly low and very slowly,' he wrote. 'They had come from the
west, from the Soviet frontier, and were making for Urumchi,
the town which was beleaguered by General Ma.'

A message smuggled into the prison claimed that the first
Soviet troops to encounter Ma's forces had been routed some

thirty miles from Urumchi, abandoning weapons and equipment, including their armoured cars. But the truth had been very different. Ma's Tungans, fanatically brave but ill-trained and poorly armed, had encountered the full force of the Soviets. Shelled, machine-gunned and bombed (gassed, some claim), they had finally been driven back in disorder. Even now little is known about the battle, beyond its outcome. Some two thousand Tungans are said to have perished. Hotly pursued by avenging Red Airforce bombers, the rest – including Ma himself – fled westwards along the northern arm of the old Silk Road, plundering and terrorising towns and villages as they went, and losing the sympathy they had once enjoyed among the Turkic population.

Ma, whose followers had been driven back from Urumchi twice before, appears this time to have considered the possibility of defeat, even if he was unaware of an impending Soviet intervention. For he had ordered his troops to detain, at the oasis-village of Korla, members of Sven Hedin's scientific expedition together with their four Ford trucks. Hedin, aware that Ma had his eye on the vehicles, had tried to give him the slip. But he had been pursued by Tungan cavalry and, following a brief shoot-out, brought back with the vehicles to Korla, Ma's temporary headquarters. There – after surviving a bombing raid by Soviet pilots who evidently mistook them for Tungans – Hedin found himself forced to hand over his four trucks and their drivers so that Ma could use them for his own escape along the Silk Road.

The Swedish explorer, himself a formidable and ruthless man who in his earlier years had more than once shot it out successfully with Central Asian bandits, had little choice but to accede. But such was the reputation of Ma that he feared that he would never see his drivers – two Swedes and two Mongols – or the lorries again. It seemed likely that Ma, when he had finished with the drivers' services, would simply shoot them lest they carry back to his pursuers news of his whereabouts or immediate plans.

On safely reaching the oasis of Kucha, half way to Kashgar, Ma decided he was now out of range of the Soviet bombers which had struck such terror in the hearts of his troops, and therefore no longer needed the Swedish trucks. Although the drivers, by careful flattery, had got on extremely well with this would-be Napoleon of Central Asia, this was obviously an anxious moment for them. But instead of silencing them with a bullet, as they had feared, Ma thanked them warmly and apologised for having had to commandeer their trucks. He not only paid them (admittedly in notes issued by himself, and now worthless), but he also gave them a personally signed pass to see them safely through Tungan lines.

Their troubles, however, were not yet over, for they shortly ran into the advance-guard of Sheng's pursuit force. Composed largely of Cossacks, it was commanded by a Russian general riding beside the driver in a truck, who regarded them with the utmost suspicion. He found it difficult to believe that Ma would ever have allowed them or their valuable trucks to fall into the hands of his pursuers. To him there was only one possible explanation. They must be working for Ma, or at least be in sympathy with him. Nonetheless they were allowed to rejoin a greatly relieved Hedin at Korla where they all found themselves under arrest for having helped Ma to escape.

Finally reason prevailed. Not only was Hedin an explorer of world renown, with powerful allies in many countries, but he had been sent to Sinkiang by the recognised Government of China to survey the region scientifically for the benefits of its impoverished populace. On the whole he was best left alone. It was thus agreed that he and his men had been the victims of circumstances, and they were allowed to go free and continue with their work.

Meanwhile Ma, after his head start in the Swedish trucks, had reached the safety of Kashgar, which his Tungan supporters had managed to wrest from the Turkis, with whom they were now in open conflict. He had told Hedin's drivers that he intended to use Kashgar as the springboard for his conquest of

Central Asia. Indeed, within a few days of arriving there he had made himself so much at home that he was observed playing tennis at the Swedish mission station.

Then came the bombshell. All of a sudden, and without any warning or explanation, he handed over command of the Tungan forces to his half-brother. The next day he left Sinkiang for ever, riding westwards into Russia aboard a Soviet truck, never to be seen again. Just why he went remains a total mystery to this day. No one knows what promises or pressures were used by the Russians to induce him to abandon his dream of delivering his fellow Muslims from infidel rule, and accept exile in the Soviet Union. All that is known is that he paid more than one visit to the Soviet Consulate-General before disappearing.

Not long after his mysterious departure from the scene, the Tungan forces occupying Kashgar were driven out by Sheng's Soviet-aided troops, and forced to withdraw through Yarkand to the major oasis of Khotan in the south. Through its puppet Sheng, Moscow's hand now stretched from Hami in the east to Kashgar and Yarkand in the west. And Yarkand, as every amateur strategist knew, controlled the crucial passes into northern India.

The Soviets, it seemed clear to the defence chiefs in India, had at last stolen a march on them in Central Asia. Their worst fears, foreshadowed in so many intelligence reports of the past, now looked like coming true. For the first time in history, an Indian Government intelligence handbook published in 1935 pointed out, 'the Russian border will march with that of India'. It was of small comfort to Delhi that the Tungans who controlled the oases of the south (though not the passes leading into India) were fanatically anti-Bolshevik, or that Moscow had by now withdrawn its troops from Sinkiang. For the Soviets had left behind them more than enough 'advisers' to ensure that the greatly indebted Sheng remained firmly in their pocket.

Having no representative in Urumchi, the British Indian authorities had considerable difficulty in discovering what was happening beyond the immediate confines of Kashgar. It soon became clear, however, that Moscow was intent on eradicating what British influence remained in the province. One victim was India's ancient trade with Sinkiang through the Himalayan passes. Soviet officials, according to reports from Kashgar, had taken over the Chinese customs post at Yarkand, thus strangling the principal caravan route between the two territories – one, moreover, which dated back more than a thousand years to the era of the Silk Road. By 1935 India's trade with Sinkiang had shrunk to about one-twentieth of what it had been before the Russian Revolution. But what Sinkiang lost in imports from India was more than replaced by Soviet-made goods, including cheap imitations of popular British products.

Life now became increasingly difficult for the British Consulate-General in Kashgar, as the handful of travellers who managed to get there at this time confirmed. One of these was Peter Fleming, the writer and traveller, who was sent by *The Times* to try to discover what exactly was going on in China's mysterious back-of-beyond. Wisely avoiding Urumchi – and the likelihood of ending up in prison like the unfortunate Vasel – he and his Swiss travelling companion, Ella Maillart, decided instead to try their luck with the Tungans, taking the southern arm of the old Silk Road. Fleming's conclusions are too long to go into here, but he dismissed current fears in Delhi and Whitehall that the Soviet Union was planning to expropriate Sinkiang by armed invasion. Such a move, he argued, would provoke Japan beyond endurance – the last thing that Stalin wished to do. And anyway it was quite unnecessary. Moscow, he reported, 'can do, and does, almost as she likes in Sinkiang', although he found few signs 'that the ground is being broken for Sovietization'.

But he poured scorn on any fears of a military threat to northern India. The 'bottle-neck' Himalayan passes, he wrote after crossing them himself, 'could be held by a handful of men', while even the infiltration of Bolshevik agents would not be difficult to prevent. Others, however, were less sure. Among them was Colonel Reginald Schomberg, a veteran traveller in

Chinese Central Asia, described by Sven Hedin as 'a famous power in the secret service of India'. After a long tour through the region, the colonel had warned in a twelve-page report to his superiors:

'It is apparently not realised in India or England what a real menace the Soviet is in Central Asia. East of a line running north and south through Peshawar there is no system of intelligence at all, and yet the territories that border on India are the arena of active anti-British propaganda . . . It requires no great effort of imagination to realise the danger of unchecked Red intrigue in India, Tibet and the border states of Chitral, Punial, etc.'

In the event, Peter Fleming's assessment was to prove the more accurate. For the truth was that Stalin's strategic priorities were changing. More and more were the Japanese beginning to replace the British as the bogy-men of the East. While the British continued to lose sleep over Moscow's designs on India, Stalin was becoming increasingly aware of the rise of this new fascist power. Better by far that India should remain, for the time being anyway, in British hands than become part of the Mikado's expanding empire.

For during the mid-1930s, the world witnessed not only Hitler's spectacular rise to power in Europe, but also the remorseless advance into China of the imperial Japanese armies. In Stalin's mind there now arose the spectre of the Soviet Union having to fight, on two fronts thousands of miles apart, and alone, both Germany and Japan.

In desperation he called for a worldwide crusade against fascism in which communists, socialists and nationalists would join hands in the defence of democracy (the prefix 'bourgeois' was discreetly dropped). Almost everything else now took second place, as the task of rallying world opinion to the Popular Front Against Fascism was made the Comintern's first priority. In India, nationalists like Nehru, hitherto denounced as pseudo-revolutionaries and imperialist lackeys, all of a sudden found themselves embraced as comrades. Olive branches were held out, too, to governments previously regarded as hostile, including Britain. For in the short term Stalin needed all the allies he could find. When Anthony Eden visited the Kremlin in 1935, Stalin ordered 'God Save the King' to be played. The Comintern, meanwhile, was told to tone down its anti-imperialist propaganda, and Russia even joined the League of Nations, which Lenin had nicknamed 'the robbers' den'. It was by no means the last such somersault which Stalin would perform during the next few years.

*   *   *

Among those who were to find themselves the innocent victims of the anti-fascist crusade was the unfortunate German, Vasel, then still languishing in an Urumchi jail. Originally arrested because of suspected sympathies for Ma, he now found himself accused – if merely because of his nationality – of being a fascist spy. He was to spend a year in a Soviet-run prison, awaiting trial. At first he had been kept in solitary confinement (part of which had been spent in a futile hunger-strike), but then he had been moved into a cell already occupied by a lice-ridden Chinese forger, who was kept permanently shackled, and who had been denounced to the authorities by his wife during a domestic quarrel. By the middle of the second month the cell had filled up considerably – with both lice and fellow prisoners. His companions included White Russian officers, a Chinese general and assorted aliens. All were accused of being Japanese spies, a crime punishable by torture and execution.

During Vasel's interrogation, his OGPU inquisitor had screamed at him: 'You Germans are a nation of spies. You work in collusion with Japan. You fascist dogs!' Eventually, after months of hunger and hardship, and perpetual fear of execution, Vasel was sentenced by an 'anti-imperialist' court to four years' imprisonment. Some days later, however, he and a giant fellow-German named Willy Dorn, who had been kept shackled for months and had managed to survive typhus, found themselves unexpectedly freed and expelled. On their way to Peking they passed through the oasis of Hami where they tried to discover what had become of a fellow-countryman who had disappeared there two years earlier without trace. But people were reluctant to talk and they left none the wiser. For months afterwards, Vasel was to have nightmares about firing-squads, and driving his truck over heaps of human skulls. All the same, he had escaped with his life, unlike thousands of other innocent people, including one German, who were rounded up during Sheng's anti-fascist purge and shot.

But the terror unleashed in Sinkiang could not compare in scale or sheer horror with that which was beginning to get under way in the Soviet Union. Between 1934 and 1938 Stalin was to decimate the ranks of the Party hierarchy, the armed forces, the civil service and the country's scientific and intellectual élite. What had begun as a purge of suspected Trotskyists now turned into a full-scale witch-hunt for German, Japanese and other foreign spies. With so many foreigners in its ranks and on its staff, the Comintern was an obvious target for Stalin's paranoia. 'Life', wrote Arno Tuominen, a Finnish member of the Comintern's Presidium, 'was a gamble from one day to the next . . . We lived as though in a nightmare . . . and each remaining member gambled from day to day that he would not be the one for whom the bells of the Kremlin would toll next.' No one was safe, and even Zinoviev himself had been among the earliest to be arrested, and eventually tried, on charges of murder and treason.

*   *   *

News of the Moscow trials and executions was greeted at first with disbelief, and then dismay, by socialists and Soviet sympathisers everywhere, and nowhere more than in India. It seemed hardly credible that those who had given birth to the Revolution – men like Trotsky and Zinoviev – had all along been plotting in secret to destroy it. Yet this was what accused after accused had confessed to, and paid the inevitable price for.

In India, particularly, admirers of the Soviet experiment could hardly fail to compare the fate of these old revolutionary heroes, and thousands of lesser fry, with that of their own revolutionaries who had been convicted of treason at Meerut. No one had been sentenced to death, and nor had the prosecution suggested that anyone should be. Five of those convicted, including Philip Spratt, had been jailed for twelve years (later greatly reduced on appeal), while Bradley and two others had been given ten years (also greatly reduced). Following the appeal, and protests from the Archbishop of York, Albert Einstein and H.G. Wells, nine of the convicted were immediately set free, while in the end Spratt and Bradley, who had been in custody throughout the lengthy trial, served only two years and one year of their respective sentences. All this was in benign contrast to the blood-letting and terror taking place in Moscow.

And that was merely the first of a number of ideological shocks which were to emanate from the Kremlin during the coming months, and which loyal Communists and their sympathisers everywhere would be expected to take in their stride. Stalin's somersaults, however, were not entirely the result of free choice, but were forced upon him by events. For by 1937, his anti-fascist crusade having failed, he had lost all hope of inducing Britain, France or anyone else to join him in preparing any effective resistance to Hitler. It was now clear to him that in Spain the Soviet-backed Republic would in the end be defeated by General Franco, which would leave Hitler free to turn his full attention towards the Soviet Union, for which he had a particular loathing. There was, Stalin could see, only one solution. Without allies, he would have to try to come to some kind of an accommodation with Nazi Germany.

On August 23, 1939, to the dismay of Communists and non-Communists alike, a non-aggression pact was signed in Moscow between these two diametrically opposed ideologies. Thus, at a stroke of his pen, Stalin had revoked his widely-trumpeted anti-fascist drive, merely to buy himself a breathing-space. For the rest of Europe it was to prove catastrophic, freeing Hitler's hands for his immediate invasion of Poland. But by opting out of the war which followed, Stalin hoped also to enjoy the spectacle of the European powers locked in a suicidal struggle.

For European Communists in particular, the Nazi-Soviet pact was to cause intense embarrassment, since it carried with it the obligation of refusing to resist Hitler. Indian Communists, on the other hand, faced no such test of conscience. With Britain engaged in a life-and-death contest with Germany, their hopes of throwing off the imperial yoke were obviously greatly heightened. Nor was this confined to the Communists: many Congress members too saw the European conflict as an imperialists' war which had nothing to do with India, but which they should take every advantage of.

But Gandhi, among others, found himself in a quandary. While opposed on pacifist grounds to any participation in the war, he saw it as a struggle between democracy and fascism, and had no wish to stab Britain in the back by deliberately sabotaging her war effort, as many Indians were demanding. At the same time, he was convinced that the British would lose the war. Any promises they might make of giving Indians independence after the war in return for the co-operation of Congress – as Nehru was demanding – he regarded as worthless. It was like 'a post-dated cheque on a failing bank', he declared. The British Indian Government, in the meantime, had not gone out of its way to win sympathy for its cause. Without consulting Indian opinion, on September 3, 1939 the Viceroy had declared India to be at war with Germany.

India now once again found itself threatened from the north, as plans for a grandiose adventure began to take shape in the minds of Hitler's strategists. Their immediate aim was to tie up in India as many British troops as possible, by using Afghanistan as a forward base for a joint Soviet-German threat to the sub-continent. This offered, by way of an inducement to Moscow, the post-war prospect of warm-water ports on the Indian Ocean. It also required the co-operation of the Afghans, who were offered the restoration of their ancient boundaries – which included Baluchistan, Sind, Kashmir and the western

Punjab – in exchange for this. At a time when an end to British rule in India seemed a real possibility, the offer must have represented a considerable temptation. But the Afghans, for so long the sworn foes of the British, turned it down. 'It was a fine gesture at one of the darkest moments in British history,' wrote Sir William Fraser-Tytler, British Minister to Kabul at the time.

Overnight it was all to become academic anyway. On June 22, 1941, without any warning, Hitler's panzers swept into the Soviet Union, catching Stalin completely off his guard. It was, in the words of Molotov, the Soviet Foreign Minister, 'an unparalleled act of perfidy . . . by fascist brigands covered with blood'.

Once again everything had to be thrown into reverse, just as foreign Communists had adjusted themselves to the Comintern's comradely line on fascism. Moscow suddenly found itself allied to its former arch-foe Britain, after years of trying to foment revolution there and in India. The situation was to call not only for major rethinking, but also for a new vocabulary. Within a matter of hours, 'the Imperialist War' was to become 'the People's War' and, finally, 'the Great Patriotic War'. Indian Communists were now ordered by the Comintern to back Russia's new ally, Britain. Everything, they were told, had to be subordinated to the survival of the motherland of the Revolution. Long-term dreams like national liberation would have to wait until the war was over.

The command came as a severe blow to Indian Communists. Obedience to Stalin's call would mean sacrificing all the gains they had managed to make in the Indian body politic since the release of the Meerut prisoners. For the rest of the Indian liberation movement, subject to no one's orders, was still strongly opposed to any participation in the war. Yet the Communists were now preparing to abandon the liberation struggle, and thus bring comfort to the beleaguered British – simply to serve the interests of the Soviet Union. This turn-about was to do irreparable harm to Moscow's prospects in India, leaving the

Communists isolated from the mainstream of the freedom movement when the countdown to independence began after the war.

But with things going from bad to worse for both the Soviet Union and the Allies, Mahatma Gandhi was not the only one to be convinced of an eventual Axis victory. In the winter of 1942, as Hitler's panzers drove deeper and deeper into Soviet territory, in distant Sinkiang Stalin's puppet Governor Sheng was beginning to have doubts about the future. So much so that on October 5, 1942 he presented Moscow with an ultimatum to remove its advisers within three months. For Sheng, ever an opportunist, had no wish to end up on the losing side.

18 The East Fails to Ignite

Sheng claims in his memoirs to have discovered a plot by Stalin to assassinate him and take Sinkiang over completely. He learned of it, he says, from a Miss Liu Yun, 'one of the Kremlin's most trusted agents, who had become personally enamoured of me'. As a result he was able to scotch the plot whose purpose, he tells us, was to deliver all of Sinkiang's oil and other resources into Soviet hands. Whether this was simply invented afterwards to justify his expulsion of the apparently beaten Russians, or merely the paranoia of a despot – or even possibly true – will never be known. But Sheng delivered his ultimatum at a time when Soviet fortunes were at an all-time low, and when he knew that they would be in no position to contest it. Protesting angrily, they withdrew their advisers from Sinkiang after capping twenty-five oil-wells and removing all their plant and equipment. Once again, after a most promising start, Stalin had lost out in Asia.

Not content with merely getting rid of the Russians, Sheng now unleashed an anti-Communist witch-hunt which, in sheer terror and scale, totally eclipsed his earlier persecution of suspected fascists. Barbaric methods of torture were used to extract confessions. 'By 1944,' according to Owen Lattimore, the distinguished Central Asian scholar and traveller, 'about 80,000 people had been imprisoned.' A reporter from the now-defunct *New York Herald Tribune* told of one suspect 'whom General Sheng's experts began to skin alive', but who wisely signed a confession after they had removed the first square inch of his skin.

Just how many innocent people were liquidated during Sinkiang's latest round of blood-letting will never be known, but both Mao Tse-tung's brother and Sheng's own sister-in-law were among his victims. Meanwhile, once more in need of a benefactor and, if necessary, a protector, Sheng switched allegiance to Chiang Kai-shek. But not for very long. As the Red Army gradually began to force back Hitler's armies, Sheng realised that he had blundered badly. Once again he set about changing horses. In April 1944, after claiming to have uncovered a plot by Chiang Kai-shek to overthrow him, he began to round up Kuomintang officials unfortunate enough to have been posted to Sinkiang. He went so far even as to approach Stalin – clutching an olive branch in hands still stained with Communist blood – and invite him back into Sinkiang, which he suggested might be absorbed permanently into Soviet Central Asia. Stalin, clearly having had enough of Sheng's treachery, did not even answer, intending presumably to settle the score in his own time.

Chiang Kai-shek, too, was determined to remove the two-faced Sheng, but was anxious to avert further bloodshed. He therefore offered him a specially-created ministerial post in the central government, carrying a salary but no duties or responsibilities. Sheng decided to accept and to leave Urumchi while the going was good. So it was that in September 1944 his ten years of tyrannical rule came to an end. Not long afterwards he moved on with his ill-gotten wealth to Formosa, and there, unmourned by anyone, he died.

For the first time in years, relative peace was restored to the ancient oasis towns and villages of the Silk Road, although the final struggle between the Kuomintang and the Communists for possession of Sinkiang was still to come. Following the Communist victory in 1949, Soviet experts were to return for a while, contributing greatly to the region's development. But this time they were to remain firmly under Peking's control, until the celebrated ideological rift opened up between the two neighbours and once again the Russians packed their bags and left for home.

British interest in Sinkiang, or in India for that matter, had by that time long ceased. The spectre of the Comintern no longer haunted them. No more did they have to worry about what might be brewing on the far side of the Pamirs. To the initial disbelief of Moscow, they had given away the greatest of their imperial prizes after defending it so strenuously for so many generations.

There is little more to tell. Lenin's great dream of an empire in Asia, like those of Sternberg, Enver and Ma, had ended in failure. For thirty years the East had stubbornly refused to ignite to the Bolshevik torch. Somehow, somewhere, it had all gone wrong. The Comintern's shadowy operations in Asia, just as in Europe, had largely been a waste of money and effort. Moscow's one permanent gain had been Mongolia.

But what of the long-forgotten individuals who fought on either side in this undeclared war on the frontiers of empire for the hearts and minds of Asia's millions?

The fates of Enver Pasha and Ungern-Sternberg, 'the Mad Baron', we already know. That of Ma, the would-be Mahdi of Central Asia, is still shrouded in mystery, although it seems likely that he was liquidated in the late 1930s on the orders of his host, Joseph Stalin, who found no further use for him.

Mikhail Borodin, the one-time revolutionary hero and scape-goat for Stalin, was to fare no better. On May 29, 1951, at the age of sixty-seven, this former bugbear of the Western intelligence services died in one of Stalin's most infamous labour camps, far away from his beloved wife Fanya. Thirteen years too late, in 1964, he was officially rehabilitated, and Fanya was allowed to publish a short memoir of him. Between them they had given everything to the cause and to their country, including their eldest son, who was killed in action as a colonel in the Red Army in the early days of the Great Patriotic War.

Borodin's old friend Roy, with whom he had once dreamed of world revolution, was to withdraw from active Indian politics, a disappointed man, and devote the rest of his life to a philosophy he termed 'radical humanism'. This one-time firebrand who had failed so totally to strike a chord in the Indian masses died in 1954 at Dehra Dun in northern India, also at the age of sixty-seven.

The fate of Grigori Zinoviev, whom Lenin had put in charge of the world revolution, and who was a rival to Stalin for Lenin's crown, was perhaps the grimmest of all. Arraigned on trumped-up murder and treason charges, this once electrifying demagogue became a victim of the very system he had helped to create. After a humiliating trial at which he confessed to everything he was charged with, he was sentenced to be shot.

Some of the other old-guard Bolsheviks liquidated in the purges are said to have gone to their deaths most bravely, defiantly cursing Stalin. Not so this man whose very name had once filled British officials with dread. Throwing himself on the floor on the way to his execution, and weeping for mercy, he was put out of his misery by an NKVD officer with one shot from a revolver.

What became of Georg Vasel after his release from jail in Urumchi I have been unable to discover. But Paul Nazaroff, ever in fear of pursuit, was eventually to make his way to South Africa to escape Stalin's hit-men, finally dying there in 1942. A few years ago, in a copy of Nazaroff's memoir *Hunted Through Central Asia* which had once belonged to Colonel Bailey, I came upon a poignant footnote to both men's escapes from the Bolsheviks. It was a letter from Nazaroff to Bailey, written from Kashgar in November 1920, congratulating his English friend on his 'narrow escape'. Describing how he himself had managed to evade the Bolsheviks for so many months, he mentions that he has lost everything, including his home and land, mines, precious collections of minerals and ores, his library, horses and dogs – all of which had been seized by the Bolsheviks. What happened to his wife he does not say, but so far as I can discover he was never to see her again.

Bailey himself, who has been described as the last player in the Great Game, was to serve the British Indian Government for another eighteen years, first as a political officer in Sikkim, later as Resident in Srinagar, and finally as Minister Plenipotentiary to the Royal Court of Nepal. In 1938 he and his wife sailed for home and retirement. When war broke out he immediately volunteered for active service, but was told that at fifty-seven he was too old. Instead he joined the Home Guard. He died at his home in Norfolk in April 1967, at the age of eighty-five. His long obituary in *The Times* was headed: COLONEL F.M. BAILEY – EXPLORER AND SECRET AGENT. It recounted, for a new generation of readers, the story of his extraordinary adventures beyond India's frontiers, nearly half a century before. With his passing, the last survivor of those stirring days in Asia's back and beyond was gone.

For the British, at least, the Great Game was well and truly over.

Bibliography of Principal Sources

The following list of titles, although far from exhaustive, includes all those I found especially valuable when researching this book. Except where otherwise indicated, all were published in London, though many are long out of print. Obituaries and articles in contemporary journals have largely been excluded, although these are usually clearly identified in the text. Nor have I listed the numbers of the individual files I used in the political and secret series in the India Office archives since this would not interest the majority of readers. I would be happy, however, to pass these on to others researching in this field.

Alioshin, Dmitri. *Asian Odyssey*. 1941.

Ambolt, Nils. *Karavan. Travels in Eastern Turkestan*. 1939.

Anon. 'The Basmachis. The Central Asian Resistance Movement, 1918–1924'. *Central Asian Review*, Vol. VII, No. 3. 1959.

Aydemir, Sevket. *Makedonya'dan Ortaasya'ya: Enver Pasha*. Vol. III: 1914–1922. Istanbul, 1978.

Bailey, Col. F.M. 'A Visit to Bokhara in 1919'. *Geographical Journal*. February, 1921.

— *Mission to Tashkent*. 1946.

Barmine, Alexander. *One Who Survived*. New York, 1945.

Bawden, C.R. *The Modern History of Mongolia*. 1968.

Becker, Seymour. *Russia's Protectorates in Central Asia: Bukhara and Khiva, 1865-1924*. Cambridge, USA, 1968.

Blacker, L.V.S. *On Secret Patrol in High Asia*. 1922.

— *Pathans, Planes and Petards*. Privately printed. n.d.

Bose, Arun Coomer. *Indian Revolutionaries Abroad, 1905–1922*. Patna, India, 1971.

Brandt, Conrad. *Stalin's Failure in China, 1924–1927*. Cambridge, USA, 1958.

Brook-Shepherd, Gordon. *The Storm Petrels*. 1977.

Brown, Anthony Cave and MacDonald, Charles B. *On a Field of Red. The Communist International and the Coming of World War II*. New York, 1981.

Brun, Capt. A.H. *Troublous Times*. 1931.

Cable, Mildred and French, Francesca. *The Gobi Desert*. 1942.

Caroe, Olaf. *Soviet Empire. The Turks of Central Asia and Stalinism*. 1953.

Carr, E.H. *The Bolshevik Revolution, 1917–1923*. Volume III. 1953.

Clubb, O. Edmund. *China and Russia*. New York, 1971.

Congress of the Peoples of the East. Baku, September 1920. Translated from Russian. 1977.

Davidson, Basil. *Turkestan Alive*. 1957.

Donaldson, Robert H. *Soviet Policy toward India: Ideology and Strategy.* Cambridge, USA, 1974.

Ellis, C.H. *The Transcaspian Episode, 1918–1919.* 1963.

Etherton, Lt.-Col. P.T. *In the Heart of Asia.* Boston, 1926.

Eudin, Xenia Joukoff and North, Robert C. *Soviet Russia and the East, 1920–1927.* Stanford, USA, 1957.

Fischer, Louis. *The Soviets in World Affairs.* 2 vols. 1930.

Fleming, Peter. *News from Tartary.* 1936.

Fraser-Tytler, W.K. *Afghanistan.* 1950.

Friters, Gerard M. *Outer Mongolia.* 1951.

Haithcox, John Patrick. *Communism and Nationalism in India.* Princeton, USA, 1971.

Hedin, Sven. *Big Horse's Flight. The Trail of War in Central Asia.* 1936.

Hodges, Major Phelps. *Britmis. A Great Adventure of the War.* 1931.

Intelligence Bureau, Home Department, Government of India. *Communism in India. 1924–1927.* Calcutta, 1927.

— *India and Communism.* Simla, 1935.

Isaacs, Harold R. *The Tragedy of the Chinese Revolution.* Stanford, USA, 1951.

Jacobs, Dan. N. *Borodin.* Cambridge, USA, 1981.

Kapur, Harish. *Soviet Russia and Asia, 1917–1927.* Geneva, 1966.

Krist, Gustav. *Prisoner in the Forbidden Land.* 1938.

Krivitsky, W.G. *I Was Stalin's Agent.* 1939.

Lattimore, Owen. *Pivot of Asia.* Boston, 1950.

Laushey, David. *Bengal Terrorism and the Marxist Left.* Calcutta, 1975.

Ma Ho-t'ien. *Chinese Agent in Mongolia.* Baltimore, USA, 1949.

Macartney, Sir George. 'Bolshevism as I saw it at Tashkent in 1918'. *Journal of the Royal Central Asian Society,* Vol VII. 1920.

Maclean, Fitzroy. *A Person from England and Other Travellers.* 1958.

— *To the Back of Beyond. An Illustrated Companion to Central Asia and Mongolia.* 1974.

Maillart, Ella K. *Forbidden Journey. From Peking to Kashmir.* 1937.

Malleson, Gen. Sir W. 'The British Military Mission to Turkestan'. *Journal of the Royal Central Asian Society,* Vol. IX. 1922.

Marriott, Sir J.A.R. *Anglo-Russian Relations, 1689–1943.* 1944.

Nazaroff, Paul. *Hunted through Central Asia.* 1932.

— *Moved On! From Kashgar to Kashmir.* 1935.

— *Kapchigai Defile.* 1980.

North, Robert C. and Eudin, Xenia J. *M.N. Roy's Mission to China.* Berkeley, USA, 1963.

Northedge, F.S. and Wells, Audrey. *Britain and Soviet Communism.* 1982.

Nyman, Lars-Erik. *Great Britain and Chinese, Russian and Japanese Interests in Sinkiang, 1918–1934.* Lund Studies in International History. Malmo, Sweden, 1977.

O'Dwyer, Sir Michael. *India as I Knew it.* 1925.

Ossendowski, Ferdinand. *Beasts, Men and Gods.* New York, 1922.

Overstreet, Gene D. and Windmiller, Marshall. *Communism in India.* Berkeley, USA, 1959.

Park, Alexander G. *Bolshevism in Turkestan, 1917–1927.* New York, 1957.

Pozner, Vladimir. *Bloody Baron. The Story of Ungern-Sternberg.* New York, 1938.

Roy, M.N. *Revolution and Counter-Revolution in China.* Calcutta, 1946.

— *Memoirs.* Bombay, 1964.

Rywkin, Michael. *Russia in Central Asia.* New York, 1963.

Samra, Chattar Singh. *India and Anglo-Soviet Relations (1917–1947).* 1959.

Sayers, Michael and Kahn, Albert E. *The Great Conspiracy against Russia.* New York, 1946.

Sheean, Vincent. *In Search of History.* 1935.

Sinha, Satya. *The Chinese Aggression.* Delhi, 1961.

Spratt, Philip. *Blowing Up India.* Calcutta, 1955.

Stewart, George. *The White Armies of Russia.* New York, 1933.

Strasser, Roland. *The Mongolian Horde.* 1930.

Swinson, Arthur. *Beyond the Frontiers. The Biography of Colonel F.M. Bailey.* 1971.

Teichman, Sir Eric. *Journey to Turkistan.* 1937.

Tuominen, Arvo. *The Bells of the Kremlin.* Hanover, USA, 1983.

Vasel, Georg. *My Russian Jailers in China.* 1937.

Wheeler, Geoffrey. *The Modern History of Soviet Central Asia.* 1964.

— 'Encounters with Communism in Asia'. *Asian Affairs.* October, 1977.

White, Stephen. *Britain and the Bolshevik Revolution.* 1979.

Whiting, Allen S. and General Sheng Shih-ts'ai. *Sinkiang: Pawn or Pivot?* Michigan, 1958.

Wu, Aitchen K. *Turkistan Tumult.* 1940.

Index

Peter Hopkirk's other titles are also
available in John Murray paperback

FOREIGN DEVILS ON THE SILK ROAD
The Search for the Lost Treasures of Central Asia

The Silk Road, which linked imperial Rome and distant China, was once the greatest thoroughfare on earth. Many centuries later legends grew up of lost cities filled with treasures and guarded by demons. Foreign explorers began to investigate these legends, and very soon an international race began for the art treasures of the Silk Road. Peter Hopkirk tells the story of the intrepid men who led these long-range archaeological raids.

ISBN 0 7195 6448 4

£9.99

TRESPASSERS ON THE ROOF OF THE WORLD
The Race for Lhasa

In this remarkable and ultimately tragic narrative, Peter Hopkirk recounts the forcible opening up of Tibet by inquisitive Western travellers during the nineteenth and twentieth centuries, and the race to reach Lhasa, the sacred capital of this medieval Buddhist kingdom.

ISBN 0 7195 6449 2

£9.99

THE GREAT GAME
On Secret Service in High Asia

For nearly a century the two most powerful nations on earth – Victorian Britain and Tsarist Russia – fought a secret war in the lonely passes and deserts of Central Asia. Those engaged in this shadowy struggle called it 'The Great Game', a phrase immortalized in Kipling's *Kim*.

ISBN 0 7195 6447 6

£9.99

ON SECRET SERVICE EAST OF CONSTANTINOPLE
The Plot to Bring Down the British Empire

Under the banner of a Holy War, masterminded in Berlin and unleashed from Constantinople, the Germans and the Turks set out in 1914 to foment violent revolutionary uprisings against the British in India and the Russians in Central Asia. It was a new and more sinister version of the old Great Game, with world domination as its ultimate aim.

ISBN 0 7195 6451 4

£9.99

QUEST FOR KIM
In Search of Kipling's Great Game

This book is for all those who love *Kim*, that masterpiece of Indian life in which Kipling immortalized the Great Game. Fascinated since childhood by this strange tale of an orphan boy's recruitment into the Indian secret service, Peter Hopkirk here retraces Kim's footsteps across Kipling's India to see how much of it remains.

ISBN 0 7195 6452 2

£9.99

Order your copies now by calling Bookpoint on
01235 827720 or visit your local bookshop

Read more . . .

William Blacker

ALONG THE ENCHANTED WAY

A spellbinding memoir set in rural Romania

When William Blacker first crossed the snowbound passes of
northern Romania, he stumbled upon an almost medieval world.
There, for many years, he lived side by side with the country people,
a life ruled by the slow cycle of the seasons, far away from the frantic
rush of the modern world.

But Blacker was also intrigued by the Gypsies, those dark, footloose
strangers of spellbinding allure who he saw passing through the
village.

'Enchantment is the key word – one wonders whether this might be
the book of a lifetime, with all its youthful vigour . . . Five stars'
Daily Telegraph

'A tour de force' John Julius Norwich

*Order your copy now by calling Bookpoint on 01235 827716 or
visit your local bookshop quoting ISBN 978-0-7195-9800-5
www.johnmurray.co.uk*

Read more ...

Alice Albinia

EMPIRES OF THE INDUS: THE STORY OF A RIVER

A mesmerising history of the Indus River's civilizations, emperors and explorers

The Indus rises in Tibet, flows west across India, and south through Pakistan. For millennia it has been worshipped as a god; for centuries used as a tool of imperial expansion. Following the river upstream and back in time, *Empires of the Indus* takes the reader on a voyage through two thousand miles of geography and more than five thousand years of history.

'A magnificent book, a triumphant melding of travel and history into a compelling story of adventure and discovery' *Financial Times*

'Impressive and original' *Daily Telegraph*

'As history, it is spellbinding. As the first book of a young writer, it's an impressive achievement' *New Statesman*

Order your copy now by calling Bookpoint on 01235 827716 or visit your local bookshop quoting ISBN 978-0-7195-6005-7 www.johnmurray.co.uk

From Byron, Austen and Darwin
to some of the most acclaimed and original
contemporary writing, John Murray takes pride in
bringing you powerful, prizewinning, absorbing
and provocative books that will entertain you
today and become the classics of tomorrow.

We put a lot of time and passion into what we
publish and how we publish it, and we'd like to
hear what you think.

Be part of John Murray – share your views with us at:

www.johnmurray.co.uk
johnmurraybooks
@johnmurrays
johnmurraybooks